2308

WL 830

book
st

PAIN

Management and Control in Physiotherapy

PAIN

Management and Control in Physiotherapy

Edited by

PETER E. WELLS
BA, MCSP, DipTP, SRP

Superintendent Physiotherapist, St Stephen's Hospital, London.

VICTORIA FRAMPTON
MCSP, SRP

Superintendent Physiotherapist, Thanet District General Hospital, Margate.

DAVID BOWSHER
MA, MD, PhD, MRCP(Ed), MRCPath

Reader (Clinical), Department of Neurological Sciences, University of Liverpool. Director of Research, Pain Relief Foundation. Honorary Consultant in Pain Relief, Centre for Pain Relief, Walton Hospital, Liverpool.

BUTTERWORTH
HEINEMANN

Butterworth-Heinemann Ltd
Linacre House, Jordan Hill, Oxford OX2 8DP

 PART OF REED INTERNATIONAL BOOKS

OXFORD   LONDON   BOSTON
MUNICH   NEW DELHI   SINGAPORE   SYDNEY
TOKYO   TORONTO   WELLINGTON

First published 1988
Reprinted 1988, 1991

© Peter E. Wells, Victoria Frampton, David Bowsher 1988

British Library Cataloguing in Publication Data
Pain: management and control in physiotherapy
    1. Pain − treatment   2. Physical therapy
    I. Wells, Peter E.   II. Frampton, Victoria
    III. Bowsher, David
    616'.0472   RB127

ISBN 0 7506 0473 5

Printed and bound in Great Britain by
Butler & Tanner Ltd, Frome and London

Contents

Section I

Anatomy, Neurophysiology and Pharmacology

Section II

Physiotherapy Modalities in the Management of Pain

Section III

Special Areas of Intervention

Preface

Pain is a problem for the majority of patients managed by physiotherapists, and in many cases acute or chronic pain from a variety of sources can be relieved altogether by appropriate physiotherapy intervention. This book highlights the unique contribution of the physiotherapist in the management and control of pain, bringing together information on pain control using a wide range of modalities and special techniques, with critical discussion of the part each can play in the overall treatment of pain.

Physiotherapy must increasingly be seen as a first option. Frequently, patients referred for assessment and treatment have already received courses of analgesics or anti-inflammatory drugs, or have undergone surgery, yet report only partial relief, if any, from their pain. Such patients are often depressed, apprehensive and sceptical and it says much for the skills of the physiotherapist that success in pain control is frequently achieved in spite of such formidable physical and psychological odds.

The effective relief of pain not only improves the wellbeing of the individual patient, but may also have major financial implications for that person's family or dependants, and for the national economy. For example, in the United Kingdom in 1982, the total cost of low back pain to the National Health Service was estimated at over £150 million (1982 figures) and is calculated to have cost a further £1000 million in lost production.

It will be clear to readers of this book that physiotherapy, using relatively low-cost techniques, has a major part to play in both clinical and economic terms in the management of pain. The movement of more physiotherapists into primary health care signals still greater involvement of the profession in prevention, advice and early treatment and this too leads to greater cost-effectiveness in the management of many common pain problems.

Our aim in this book is to provide the physiotherapist, whether in training or in practice, with an up-to-date review of the anatomical and physiological basis of pain, some knowledge of the pharmacology of pain control, and an understanding of the contribution of various physiotherapy modalities to the overall treatment of pain. We conclude by reviewing a number of special areas where physiotherapy intervention has proved particularly effective.

It is our hope that both students and qualified physiotherapists, together with the medical practitioners who refer patients for their care, will find within these pages the information necessary to encourage good practice, provoke thought, and stimulate further investigation.

In order not to encumber the text with alternative pronouns, the editors have made all physiotherapists female and all patients male throughout the book. This accords with reality only in that it gives a 50:50 distribution between the sexes.

Finally, the editors would like to express their thanks to Caroline Creed of Heinemann Medical Books for all her dedicated hard work during the various stages of book development.

Peter E. Wells
Victoria Frampton
David Bowsher

List of Contributors

Robert Baxter FFARCS
Consultant in Anaesthesia and Pain Relief, Greenwich District and Blackheath Hospitals and St Joseph's Hospice, London.

David Bowsher MA, MD, PhD, MRCP(Ed), MRCPath
Reader (Clinical), Department of Neurological Sciences, University of Liverpool. Director of Research, Pain Relief Foundation. Honorary Consultant in Pain Relief, Centre for Pain Relief, Walton Hospital, Liverpool.

Elizabeth S. Chaney MCSP, SRP
Senior Physiotherapist (Respiratory Care), University Hospital, Queen's Medical Centre, Nottingham.

Victoria Frampton MCSP, SRP
Superintendent Physiotherapist, Thanet District General Hospital, Margate, Kent.

Jean Gifford MCSP, DipTP, SRP
Private Practitioner, Falmouth, Cornwall.

Louis Gifford BSc, PGCE, MCSP, Grad Dip Adv Manip Ther
Private Practitioner, North Adelaide, South Australia. Part-time Tutor in Advanced Manipulative Therapy, School of Physiotherapy, South Australia Institute of Technology.

A. J. Guymer MCSP, DipTP
Clinical Tutor in Physiotherapy, Westminster Hospital, London.

David A. Jackson MCSP, LicAc, SRP
Superintendent Physiotherapist, St John of God Hospital, Richmond, North Yorkshire.

J. L. Low BA, MCSP, DipTP, SRP
Senior Teacher of Physiotherapy, School of Physiotherapy, Guy's Hospital, London.

Betty O'Gorman MCSP, SRP
Superintendent Physiotherapist, St Christopher's Hospice, Sydenham, London.

Nigel P. Palastanga BA, MCSP, DMS, DipTP
Assistant Principal, School of Physiotherapy, Addenbrooke's Hospital, Cambridge.

Margaret Polden MCSP, SRP
Superintendent of Obstetric Physiotherapy, Hammersmith Hospital, London.

Alison T. Skinner BA, MCSP, HT, DipTP, SRP
Senior Teacher, The School of Physiotherapy, Middlesex Hospital, London.

Ann M. Thomson BA, MCSP, DipTP, SRP
Assistant Principal, School of Physiotherapy, Middlesex Hospital, London.

Peter E. Wells BA, MCSP, DipTP, SRP
Superintendent Physiotherapist, St Stephen's Hospital, London.

Introduction

PETER E. WELLS

The public do not generally associate physiotherapists with the management and relief of pain. Ask anyone, even a doctor or nurse, what they understand a physiotherapist's role to be in the medical team and their answers will almost certainly revolve around concepts such as 'getting people going after illness or accident', 'mobilising patients who have had a fracture', 'teaching people to walk again' and so on. In turn, what is done in these situations will be related to strengthening, mobilising and coordinating certain functions and activities. While not incorrect, this stereotyped and narrow view of the role of physiotherapy omits, for example, the great part played by physiotherapists in the management and control of pain. Part of the reason for this may well stem from the fact that the physiotherapy model of examination, assessment and treatment is related primarily to malfunction and disability and not to the medical model of disease processes and pathology.

Even when a patient's complaint includes a degree of pain, or is largely one of pain, he will often regard the pain relief gained as a result of specific physiotherapy procedures as a spin-off from something else, which it may be. Consider, for example, the patient with an acutely painful neck and grossly restricted movement. During the initial treatment, let us say by various manipulative procedures, the movement of his neck dramatically improves. He may well remark with surprise at this improvement in function ('I wasn't able to look behind me an hour ago!'), and then secondarily he will notice that the level of pain has dropped. His conclusion, and it will be at least in part correct, is that the physiotherapist was intent upon *mobilising* his neck, getting him *moving*. On the other hand, it is likely that the physiotherapist was intent upon *directly altering the behaviour of the pain*, as a result of which movement has improved. Perhaps, within examples like this, lies the root of the lack of appreciation of a specific physiotherapeutic role in the management of pain. Hence the various physical methods for pain relief employed by physiotherapists are often seen as peripheral and apart from the drugs, surgical procedures and counselling offered by doctors. They are, of course, not much different; after all pain relief is pain relief. Where acupuncture or manipulation or corrective exercise and advice has produced the relief of chronic, intermittent low back pain (which a variety of drugs have not been effective in relieving), then the worth and suitability of the approach in this case is clear.

Is all this important? The answer, for a number of reasons, must most definitely be yes! One example, the management of chronic headache, deserves a mention. This condition, frequently a distressing and disabling one, is among the most common if not *the* most common with which patients consult their general practitioners. A large proportion of such patients are women.

A great many of these headaches arise from mechanical disturbances in the cervical joints, often perpetuated by poor postural alignment of the head–neck and neck–trunk and long-standing muscle imbalance. These very commonly occurring problems, which may include disturbing symptoms affecting the eyes and ears and facial pain, are generally very responsive to judicious manual treatment of the offending joints, postural and muscle re-education and detailed advice about avoiding further episodes. How many of these problems are referred to physiotherapists for treatment? Very few, unless, of course, those in a position to refer them are made aware of what can be done by *physical agencies* and how complete and lasting such relief can be.

It is a prime example of a situation where a lack of understanding of the alternatives to drugs, surgery and 'learning to live with it', condemns the sufferers to years of chronic pain.

The potential for effective pain relief which physiotherapy offers across a wide spectrum of medical care is only slowly becoming generally recognised. The reluctance of many people to take drugs for pain, unless these are highly effective and short-term, is increasingly evident and is an important factor motivating such sufferers to seek alternatives. Physiotherapists must inform the public of their important role in this field and educate medical practitioners, including those in primary health care, of the many safe, effective and inexpensive procedures available for the management of pain problems by physiotherapy.

Section I

Anatomy, Neurophysiology and Pharmacology

Chapter 1

Clinical Aspects of Pain

PETER E. WELLS

INTRODUCTION: THE SELECTION OF TREATMENT

The contents of this book reflect the diverse situations in which physiothera-pists, as part of their daily round, are called upon to assist those in pain. The response to their management will largely depend upon the cause of the symptoms and the matching of suitable modalities to the cause. Broadly speaking, it is those pains which have a mechanical origin (e.g. most low back pain, many degenerative joint conditions and certain types of headache) which are most likely to respond to mechanically based treatment, such as the manipulative procedures, corrective exercise and postural realignment. Conversely, those caused by the inflammatory response of certain 'disease' processes or trauma (e.g. acute tenosynovitis, pelvic inflammatory disease, sinusitis, recent haematomas and certain types of osteoarthritis) are more likely to respond to physical modalities which may alter aspects of this process, such as ultrasonics and pulsed or unpulsed shortwave diathermy. Many pain problems, of course, arise from a mixed cause, i.e. both mechanical and inflammatory (e.g. osteoarthritis, sprained ankle and surgical wounds) and may require a two-pronged approach. The specialised sensory techniques of transcutaneous electrical nerve stimulation (TENS) and acu-puncture have a wide application across a spectrum of acute and chronic pain problems.

The balance between the mechanical and inflammatory causes of pain in a given situation are often impossible to decide, e.g. severe retropatellar pain in a young patient diagnosed as having chondromalacia patellae. It is only a retrospective assessment of the response to different modalities which may give some idea of which contributed more to the patient's symptoms. The response to anti-inflammatory drugs would be of great interest in such a case.

Frequently, as is made clear in a number of chapters throughout this book, the complex nature of the cause of many patients' symptoms demands a high degree of expertise from the physiotherapist in order to identify effective procedures which will bring benefit to the patient, e.g. as with brachial plexus lesions or in a case such as a painful hemiplegic shoulder (Davies, 1985). Similarly, as in some instances of terminal disease, in situations where physical modalities may not be able to alleviate pain to any appreciable extent at least it should not be made worse by anything the physiotherapist does. In such situations, the physiotherapist has an invaluable role in monitoring the response to activities which she is attempting to maintain and will gather essential information in order to help make the administration of drugs maximally effective (*see* Chapter 17, p. 281).

As with many other methods regularly in use for pain control, the selection of physiotherapy procedures entails a degree of empiricism. The difference between an informed and critical empirical approach and an unthinking, blunderbuss one is frequently the difference between success and failure. The informed and critical approach begins with a thorough recording of the patient's symptoms and the behaviour of those symptoms.

Recording the Subjective Findings

It is necessary to follow a clear and systematic line of questioning in order to elicit a very accurate and thorough picture of the patient's pain and other symptoms.

The format for such an examination and its recording recommended by Maitland (1986) is as good as any and better than most. It is particularly intended for the examination of musculoskeletal complaints, but the headings followed are suitable for helping define and assess the symptoms likely to fall within the sphere of management of any of the specialised areas of physiotherapy.

The more the physiotherapist knows of the many facets of the patient's pain (or other symptoms), the better position she is in to manage it effectively.

The main aim must be to gain control of the pain and in so doing to alter it, reduce it, and where possible obliterate it. This depends upon the ability of the physiotherapist to assess accurately the many factors relating to the condition and its response throughout treatment. Assessment is discussed in more detail later (p. 9).

THE SUBJECTIVE EXAMINATION

The following points must be clarified before any treatment is undertaken:

1. *What, at the time of examination, is the patient's main problem in his own opinion?* Is it pain or is it weakness, stiffness or something else?
2. *Where precisely does he feel the pain (and other symptoms, such as numbness, pins and needles)?* The patient, with the relevant areas uncovered, should demarcate clearly with his hand each area and whether these areas run

together or are separate and clear-cut with their own boundaries. These areas *must* be entered on to a body chart, with heavier shading for the more intense symptoms (Fig. 1.1). Each area should be given a number 1, 2, 3, etc., and the relevant areas clear of symptoms ticked.

3. *Is the pain (each area separately) superficial (on the skin) or deep (below the skin) or deeper still (e.g. deep inside a joint or deep in the chest or pelvis)?*

4. *What type or kind of pain is it?* That is, how would they describe its *quality*, e.g. throbbing, burning, shooting, etc.? Any other words of description, in addition, should be recorded, e.g. 'sickening', 'dreadful', 'punishing', 'frightening' (*see* Chapter 2, p. 14). It is not uncommon to have different kinds of pain with one disorder.

5. *Is the pain (area by area) constant or intermittent? If constant, is it varying?*

6. *What is the characteristic behaviour of each area of pain?* In other words, what makes the pain worse and what makes it better? Both activities and postures must be explored, e.g. the activities which may make a specific pain worse might be walking, running, going up or down stairs/steps, coughing, deep breathing, lifting, turning suddenly, typing, etc. Postures causing or aggravating pain might include: sitting, kneeling, lying on the affected area, keeping the part in one position, etc. A note should also be recorded if the patient reports the pain is worse when they are stressed or at the time of menstruation, etc.

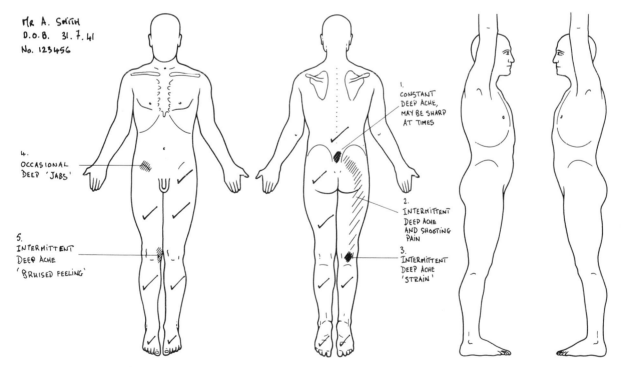

Fig. 1.1 Clear and concise recording on the body chart is essential to provide a quick and accurate check of the symptoms. New symptoms which appear after the recorded date must be added to the body chart and dated.

It is important, in addition, to know how much of the aggravating activity can be undertaken or for how long a posture can be maintained before the pains complained of are brought on or made worse. Furthermore, what must the patient then do? Must he move to another position, e.g. lie flat, stand up, or stop the activity because of the pain? When this is so, how quickly does the pain go or take to return to its previous level?

Finally, the physiotherapist must have clearly in her mind the daily, weekly and even monthly pattern of behaviour of the pain. A typical 24 h cycle of behaviour should have been elicited to answer the following questions:

(a) *Does pain interfere with sleeping?* If so is it worse at night than in the daytime? Is it transient at night allowing the patient to go back to sleep quickly? Is it so bad that the patient must get up, walk around, take drugs, etc at night? (Severe, intractable night pain may indicate serious pathology for which the patient will require a rapid referral back to his doctor.) How many times is the patient woken by pain?

(b) *Is pain present on waking or does it start when rising or once the patient is up?* When is it first felt and what position or activity precedes it?

(c) *In general, does the pain steadily worsen or improve as the day progresses?*

(d) *Is the pain activity-dependent?*

7. *What was the precise history of onset of this episode and have there been similar episodes in the past?* If similar pain has occurred in the past, did it require treatment? What treatment was received? What effect did it have? If any previous treatment did help, was the pain completely relieved?

It is possible to make some important deductions if all this information has been elicited. These conclusions do not primarily relate to an attempt to diagnose the problem, but are firstly related to the choice of a suitable initial treatment approach and secondly to the precise assessment of the effect of that treatment upon the patient's symptoms.

Analysing the Information from the Subjective Examination

The information gathered needs to be assessed critically before any form of objective examination ('looking, testing, feeling') is begun. Accepting that 'the vitally important physiotherapist's examination is less of a diagnostic sorting procedure than an "indications" examination' (Grieve, 1975), what are the 'indications' which may be gleaned from it so far?

The following should be decided:

1. *Which structures should be tested as possibly contributing to the symptoms?* This question will naturally be relevant only in cases where the musculo-skeletal structures are thought to be contributing to the symptoms or where spinal nerve root irritation, compression or tension are involved. The major concern is whether the symptoms to be treated have a local

cause or are referred, or, as occasionally happens, there is a dual origin. While the medical diagnosis frequently localises the source of the symptoms, it does not always, and much time and effort is often wasted if the physiotherapist fails to follow up the medical diagnosis with specific localising tests, e.g. 'inversion sprain of right ankle' does not include the fact that such an injury frequently involves the calcaneocuboid joint. If the physiotherapist does not realise this and test for it but treats the lateral ligament only, then part of the patient's symptoms are likely to persist, even when he has regained good inversion and ankle stability. Likewise a patient with 'backache and sciatica' may be found to require treatment principally directed to the mobility of the pain-sensitive structures in the spinal and intervertebral canal, as opposed to the vertebral joint structures themselves.

The diagnosis, as stated before, will not necessarily direct the physio-therapist to the most suitable and effective treatment in such a case, but aspects of their own examination will.

2. *Is the pain (area by area) severe or not severe?* Severity may be assessed by marking a linear scale (*see* Chapter 2, p. 15) or by assessing the degree to which activities are curtailed by the pain (e.g. the patient must stop walking because of the pain, cannot concentrate when it is bad, wakes up at night with the pain and then has difficulty sleeping because of it, etc.).

3. *Is the condition, and are the symptoms, irritable?* Since mechanically based pain and that associated with inflammation can be aggravated by certain movements, activities or postures depending on how much is undertaken (including time), an assessment can be made of the way the symptoms have reacted to a given amount (vigour and time) of those provoking actions or postures. Irritable symptoms are those which can be easily provoked (i.e. a small amount of the provoking activity), have a high intensity or severity and do not settle immediately after the activity is stopped but continue for a time. This assessment of irritability is most commonly used with regard to musculoskeletal symptoms (Maitland, 1986), but is well worth trying to apply in other situations as a further degree of insight into the patient's problems may be gained.

4. *What is the nature of the problem?* Some insight is needed into the mechanisms which are giving rise to the patient's symptoms. One example, already discussed, is the degree to which mechanical, inflamma-tory or other factors are responsible for the pain. While the underlying causes of some symptoms are not always easily determined with certainty, some hypothesis should be made which seems to explain a group of findings. The hypothesis will be supported if the patient reacts in the predicted way to a certain line of management and treatment.

Another example in terms of the nature of a patient's pain is that met when treating brachial plexus lesions (*see* Chapter 10, pp. 92, 108). Clearly, the physiotherapist will not be in the strongest position to select the most appropriate measures unless she has a good understanding of how and why the pathological process involved is manifesting itself in the particularly intense pain so characteristically complained of in these cases.

The effort taken to decide the degree of severity and irritability of the patient's condition as well as the attempt to fathom the nature of the patient's problem is well rewarded by the rational guidelines which can then be drawn to indicate how the objective examination should be carried out, i.e. will it need to be searching, extended and even vigorous or kept to a minimum, and carried out with a few selected tests and palpation?

The objective examination

In a book such as this, which deals with a variety of types of pain arising from different causes, it is not appropriate to recommend a detailed specific format for the objective part of the physiotherapist's examination. Commonly, but by no means exclusively, where pain is a prime concern, it is a part of the musculoskeletal system which is at fault and requires a detailed objective examination. Aspects of this examination are discussed in Chapter 13 (p. 207).

Whatever form the objective examination takes, it must always start with a detailed *observation* of the patient. In particular, with regard to pain, protective or antalgic postures, willingness to move, facial expressions and the position in which the patient prefers to be in an attempt to gain relief must all be carefully noted. Next, a comprehensive and systematic *testing* of appropriate movements and structures should seek to identify abnormalities, particularly with regard to the precise behaviour of the symptoms complained of in relation to particular active and passive movements or actions. The most succinct graphical recording and discussion of these relationships is that of the so-called 'movement diagrams' (Maitland, 1986). These movement diagrams demonstrate, by a clear and simple method, the way in which the three factors being explored—pain (local and referred), muscle spasm and inert tissue resistance—are interrelated in any given movement examined passively.

The final section of the objective examination, *palpation*, seeks to identify various tissue abnormalities, such as undue tissue tenderness, soft tissue thickening, bony abnormalities and generalised or discrete muscle spasm, as well as attempting to reproduce the patient's symptoms. In this last instance, the reproduction of the patient's pain or other symptoms is only attempted *if the severity, irritability and nature* allows. In most instances it does and the information gathered from skilful palpation is invaluable forming, in many cases, the most informative part of the whole examination.

Where the examination of a painful joint condition is being carried out, an assessment of the characteristics of the various accessory movements of that joint forms a very significant part of the palpation section.

RESPONSE TO TREATMENT

During a course of treatment for a painful condition it is firstly more relevant to ask the patient *'How have you been?'* than to enquire *'How are you?'* The response of the patient's symptoms to the treatment and alterations in their signs shown on testing are the factors by which progress is assessed and upon which the next treatment is planned. While there is frequently a degree of immediate response, and this may be great or small, it is the behaviour of the symptoms between treatments which is the main factor we seek to influence. The physiotherapist needs to ask the patient three things at the start of reassessment:

'How were you in the few hours following treatment?'
'How have your symptoms been since the treatment and up to now?'
'How are your symptoms now?'

Treatment may result in the patient being:

'better'
'the same'
'worse'.

It is essential, of course, before further procedures are carried out that this is clarified for all the patient's symptoms. In other words, if the response to the question *'How have you been?'* is *'better'* then what precisely has been better, all the symptoms or just some of them? Better than when or what?
In what way are the symptoms better? Are they:

less severe?
less irritable (i.e. taking more to provoke, and settling more quickly)?
less widespread?
less disturbing at night?
starting later in the day?
lasting a shorter period?
enabling the patient to do more?
requiring fewer analgesics?
occurring less often over a period of 1 week (e.g. headache)?

In addition, the patient's *attitude* to his pain may change for the better. For example, he may be no longer terrified that the pain referred from his thoracic spine into his chest is from his heart (assuming that the patient was sent for a referred chest pain, which has mimicked a visceral problem, the latter having been excluded by his doctor).

If the patient reports that his symptoms are the *same*, then the main aspects of his subjective complaints must be repeated to refresh the memory and determine that his symptoms really *are* unchanged. Often small aspects of the patient's condition change (for better or worse) without him really being aware of it and with careful, though not laborious, questioning he will realise that something has in fact altered. If unchanged, then time should not be wasted repeating ineffectual treatment, but clearly the dosage and particular technique of administering a certain modality must be explored before it is changed entirely for something else.

A report by the patient that the symptoms have been *worse* since the last treatment must be explored carefully; they may be worse for a number of reasons. Assuming that the treatment chosen and the way it was carried out were suitable, two possibilities need to be considered:

1. The patient felt much better and so did something he should not have done and aggravated his condition.
2. The condition happens to be worse because its nature is such that there are good days and bad days and this happens to be a bad day (hence one reason to carefully clarify the behaviour of the symptoms over 24 h immediately after treatment).

The reason, whatever it is, can only be ascertained by careful questioning. It is in clarifying with the patient what aggravates and what eases his pain, and in explaining why that *prophylaxis* begins.

During the ongoing process of careful questioning, and response to the patient's questions, a subtle process of education is under way in which the patient comes to understand his symptoms more clearly. He responds by observing the behaviour of his symptoms and in doing so he is able to be more objective about them. This in turn is used by the physiotherapist who is all the while attempting to make the patient's observations of his symptoms more objective.

If the patient reports that the symptoms are worse since last time, then the current treatment session will aim to bring the symptoms and signs back to the situation existing at the start of the last treatment session. If the treatment itself seems to have aggravated the symptoms in some way, the situation can usually be rectified by altering the 'dosage' of treatment or modifying or changing the technique.

It is easy to see from the whole process briefly described here how the important role of the physiotherapist in education and prevention flows logically from their skills as communicators.

REFERENCES

Davies P.M. (1985). *Steps to Follow*, section 12.2 the painful shoulder. Berlin: Springer-Verlag.

Grieve G.P. (1975). Manipulation. *Physiotherapy;* **61(1)**: 11–18.

Maitland G.D. (1986). *Vertebral Manipulation*. London: Butterworths.

Chapter 2

Acute and Chronic Pain and Assessment

DAVID BOWSHER

INTRODUCTION

Touch, hearing and sight are *sensations* because we have sense organs specifically activated by mechanical, sound and light energy respectively. Pain is also a specific sensation brought about by damage or threat of damage (see below, p. 12), although, of course, there is no outside form of energy called 'pain'. Other forms of energy, such as (harmless) magnetism or (harmful) ionising radiation do not produce any sensations because we have no sense organs specifically activated by them. There are nerve endings in muscle (muscle spindles) which are activated by lengthening, and yet we are not consciously aware of their excitation, because the central connections of the spindles in the spinal cord and brain do not bring their activity to consciousness.

These self-evident considerations immediately illustrate two things about *all* sensations: (1) there must be a form of energy which specifically activates a sense organ (receptor); and (2) the connections within the spinal cord and brain which convey the impulses coming from the receptor must be so arranged that their activity becomes conscious.

A receptor may in general terms be defined as a structure, usually a nerve ending, which converts some specific form of energy into nervous impulses. Specific receptors for pain will be described on p. 18ff.

A third factor, *modulation*, should also be considered. Modulation means that information from a receptor can be changed, enhanced, diminished, or even suppressed, either in the periphery or in the brain. For example, we cease to be aware of the contact of our clothes, although they excite touch receptors, because the receptors themselves cease to respond; this is a form of peripheral modulation called *adaptation*. When concentrating on a television programme, our auditory receptors may fail to inform us that the telephone is ringing; this is a form of central modulation whereby auditory information is suppressed within the brain so that we can concentrate on the audiovisual content of the programme which occupies our attention.

ACUTE AND CHRONIC PAIN

Pain has been defined by the International Association for the Study of Pain (IASP) as 'an unpleasant sensory and emotional experience associated with actual or potential tissue damage, or described in terms of such damage'. A damaging stimulus is a *noxious* (noxa = harm, damage) stimulus, and may produce pain in a normal conscious subject; but an anaesthetised patient, for example, does not feel pain inflicted by the surgeon's knife, though the stimulus remains noxious. Only the highest (conscious) centres of the nervous system have been functionally inactivated by the anaesthetic, so the functionally intact peripheral nerves are still carrying messages engendered by noxious stimulation—these are *nociceptive* (i.e. pain-receiving) messages—even though pain is not consciously felt. Because pain is a private and subjective experience, we can only know that animals other than man have *nociceptors*, i.e. receptors responding specifically to noxious stimuli; but we may deduce from their behaviour that they probably feel pain as well.

Like all other sensations, pain has a threshold; that is to say, noxious stimulation must reach a certain intensity before pain is felt. This is the *pain perception threshold*, strictly defined as the *least* intensity of noxious stimulation at which a subject consciously perceives pain. Large numbers of psychophysical experiments carried out on normal healthy subjects with artificial (but measurable) stimuli, such as electric shock, radiant heat, or mechanical pressure show that the pain perception threshold, like other sensory thresholds, is fairly constant from person to person. Using radiant heat applied to the skin, for example, pain is perceived at about 45°C.

We cannot be certain that experimentally inflicted pain in normal subjects can be equated with pathological pain in ill patients; but so far as the pain perception threshold is concerned, it is probably so. One very obvious reason why this is uncertain is because people do not seek therapeutic help at the very moment of feeling the first mild twinge of pain.

From the clinical point of view, a far more important threshold is the *pain tolerance level*, defined as the *greatest* intensity of noxious stimulation an individual can bear; it might have been better to have called it the pain *intolerance* level. This varies widely from person to person, and in the same person under different conditions. Factors, such as cultural background, motivation and emotional significance of pain can alter tolerance level. For instance, someone may experience little or no pain while rescuing a child from a burning house, while the same individual might understandably regard having a lighted match applied to the skin for no reason whatsoever as intolerably painful. The important fact to bear in mind from the clinical point of view is that patients do not seek help until their pain has gone *beyond* tolerance level.

Patients describe pain in very different terms if left to their own devices. This makes interpretation very difficult at times. It must, however, be regarded as axiomatic in clinical practice that any pain feels as bad to the sufferer as he says it does. The practical problem posed by such considerations is how to assess a patient's pain as objectively as possible.

PAIN ASSESSMENT

Of the many methods devised, three are in fairly widespread use, and are described below:

The McGill Pain Questionnaire

In order to overcome the differing values attributable to different patients' own descriptions, Melzack (1975) devised a list of words arranged in 20 groups (Fig. 2.1). The patient is asked to underline or circle not more than one word in any group (or every group, if he wishes) which applies to or describes his pain. This is believed to be more objective because the patient is forced to use words defined or at least chosen by the physiotherapist, not by the patient. Groups 1 to 10 are *somatic* words defining the physiological characteristics of the pain; groups 11 to 15 are *affective* words defining its subjective characteristics; group 16 is *evaluative* describing intensity; and groups 17 to 20 are miscellaneous.

Scoring is relatively simple, and is done both for all 20 word groups taken together, and separately for the groups in each of the four categories described above. The first parameter is the *total number of words chosen* (maximum 20). An *intensity score* is calculated by assigning the value 1 to the first word in any group, 2 to the second, and so on; the intensity score is the sum of all these values. It only takes a patient about 10 min to fill in the McGill pain questionnaire. Many workers find that it is a useful diagnostic aid if administered at a patient's first visit. Whether the progress of therapy can be satisfactorily assessed by subsequently administering the questionnaire at regular intervals is a matter of debate; some physiotherapists are enthusiastic, others sceptical.

The Submaximal Effort Tourniquet Test

This is a remarkable way of 'matching' a patient's pain (Smith *et al.*, 1966). A sphygmomanometer cuff is inflated on the patient's elevated arm to above systolic arterial pressure. The patient then clenches and unclenches the fist rhythmically. In order to standardise this procedure, a grip dynamometer must be used to ensure constant force, and a metronome to ensure constant rate. As the muscles contract in the ischaemic arm, a cramp-like pain develops. The patient is instructed to stop when this is judged to be of the same intensity as the pathological pain complained of. The time from start to

13

Look carefully at the twenty groups of words. If any word in any group applies to *your* pain, please circle that word — but do not circle more than *one word in any one group* — so you must choose the *most suitable word* in that group.

In groups that do not apply to your pain, there is no need to circle *any* word — just leave them as they are.

Group 1	Group 2	Group 3	Group 4	Group 5
Flickering	Jumping	Pricking	Sharp	Pinching
Quivering	Flashing	Boring	Gritting	Pressing
Pulsing	Shooting	Drilling	Lacerating	Gnawing
Throbbing		Stabbing		Cramping
Beating		Lancinating		Crushing
Pounding				

Group 6	Group 7	Group 8	Group 9	Group 10
Tugging	Hot	Tingling	Dull	Tender
Pulling	Burning	Itching	Sore	Taut
Wrenching	Scalding	Smarting	Hurting	Rasping
	Searing	Stinging	Aching	Splitting
			Heavy	

Group 11	Group 12	Group 13	Group 14	Group 15
Tiring	Sickening	Fearful	Punishing	Wretched
Exhausting	Suffocating	Frightful	Gruelling	Blinding
		Terrifying	Cruel	
			Vicious	
			Killing	

Group 16	Group 17	Group 18	Group 19	Group 20
Annoying	Spreading	Tight	Cool	Nagging
Troublesome	Radiating	Numb	Cold	Nauseating
Miserable	Penetrating	Drawing	Freezing	Agonising
Intense	Piercing	Squeezing		Dreadful
Unbearable		Tearing		Torturing

Fig. 2.1 The McGill pain questionnaire. Patients are asked to underline not more than one word from any or all of the 20 groups which best describe their pain. The simplest scoring methods involve: (1) total number of words underlined; (2) intensity, measured by allotting score 1 to the first word in any group, 2 to the second, and so on. The first 10 groups of words are somatic (describing what the pain feels like), 11–15 are affective, 16 is evaluative, and 17–20 miscellaneous.

finish measures the intensity of the pain at that moment. The remarkable feature of this test, according to its proponents, is that virtually all patients, even though their pathological pain may not be in the least cramp-like, can nevertheless 'match' it. Again, the test can be repeated at every session in order to evaluate progress.

The Visual Analogue Scale

Because of the ease and simplicity of its administration, this is by now the most widely used method of measuring pain (Bond and Pilowsky, 1966). The patient is presented with a strip of paper on which is a line 10 cm long (Fig. 2.2). At one end is written 'no pain' and at the other 'the worst pain I ever felt', and the patient is asked to mark the line at the point corresponding to the intensity of pain at that very moment. The remarkable thing about the visual analogue scale (VAS) is its constancy; even though a patient only sees

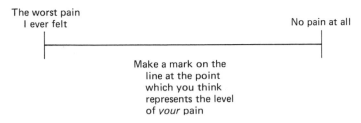

Fig. 2.2 The visual analogue scale used to determine the severity of the pain experienced by the patient. This is all there is to it! Simple, but very useful.

the scale for as long as it takes to mark it, if the pain intensity is the same, it will be marked in exactly the same place the next day. The VAS is thus an extremely useful, and of course very rapid, method of evaluating the effects of treatment. Its disadvantage is that it cannot be used for comparing one patient with another, since two individuals with apparently the same intensity of pain will mark the line in different places. However, its value in tracing the progress of a single patient is immense.

In 1894 Goldscheider noted that when a painful stimulus is applied to a hand or foot, most (but not all) people experience a double pain sensation—at first, sharp, well-localised pain which ceases as soon as the transient stimulus (e.g. a pin or heat spot) is removed, followed by a dull, poorly localised ache which continues for some time after withdrawal of the stimulus. These phenomena have been called *first* or *rapid* and *second* or *slow* pain respectively. Like other sensory modalities, they can be dissociated by ischaemia. If an arm is made ischaemic by a sphygmomanometer cuff inflated to above systolic pressure, sensation disappears in inverse proportion to the size (and therefore the oxygen/metabolic requirement) of the afferent nerve fibres concerned. Thus, low-threshold mechanical sensations (touch, vibration, joint position sense, etc.) carried by large A-beta nerve fibres are the first to disappear; pricking or first pain sensations disappear a little later when small myelinated or A-delta nerve fibres are inactivated; tissue-damage or second pain, associated with unmyelinated or C peripheral afferent nerve fibres, is the last to disappear. It may be noted that when ischaemia is reversed (e.g. by removal of an intervertebral disc which has been pressing on a nerve root), sensations return in the reverse order. More recently, direct proof of these correlations has been provided by the technique of *microneurography*, whereby needle electrodes are inserted through the skin directly into peripheral nerve bundles, and are able to record from single nerve fibres in response to appropriate distal stimulation. In 1972, two pairs of workers (van Hees and Gybels, 1972; Torebjörk and Hallin, 1972) succeeded in recording human A-delta and C fibres; their work has been confirmed and

15

extended many times since, and more recently they have been able to stimulate single nociceptive fibres in man (see p. 19).

The critical, and unanswered, question is: to what extent can experimental or induced first and second pain be equated with acute and chronic clinical pain? Acute clinical pain is accompanied by a number of phenomena, such as increased heart rate, raised blood pressure, and pupillary constriction—all signs of sympathetic activity—while chronic pain does not have such an accompaniment. Experimental first and second pain, perhaps because they are too evanescent, are unaccompanied by autonomic activity, except when the subject is apprehensive. However, apart from this, first and second pain have features which are not only very similar to acute and chronic pain, but of considerable significance for the understanding of their characteristics (Bowsher, 1982). These are shown in Table 2.1.

Whether or not first and second pain can be equated with acute and chronic pain, it is certainly the case that all these types of sensation are produced by the activation of receptors (nociceptors) which generate nervous impulses in their associated nerve fibres; receptor and fibre together constitute a sensory unit. The same sensory units are certainly concerned in the production of experimental and clinical pains, though it is possible that in the latter case additional sensory units may also be involved (see p. 28).

Clinically, there is a third type of pain which is completely different from all others. This is *neurogenic pain*, which is not caused by activation of peripheral receptors, but by damage to the peripheral or central nervous system (excluding acute compression, such as may occur in prolapsed

Table 2.1   The Characteristics of First and Second Pain

Function	First, Rapid (or ?Acute) Pain	Second, Slow (or ?Chronic) Pain
Adequate stimulus	Pinprick, heat	Tissue damage
Nerve fibres	A-delta (small myelinated)	C (unmyelinated)
Conduction velocity	5–15 m/s (11·0–33·5 mph)	0·5–2·0 m/s (1·0–4·5 mph)
Distribution	Body surface (including mouth and anus)	All tissues except brain and spinal cord
Reflex response	Withdrawal (flexion), phasic muscle contraction	Spasm, rigidity, tonic muscle contraction*
Biological value	Causes organism to avoid possible tissue damage	Brings about enforced rest of damaged part, so promoting natural healing
Effect of morphine	Very little	Suppression of pain sensation, abolition of spasm

*Note that this reflex reaction involves both agonists and antagonists, which is part of the definition of spasm or rigidity; it is a pathological rather than a physiological reaction.

intervertebral disc). Neurogenic pain is usually of a burning and/or shooting nature; it is virtually unresponsive to opioid (narcotic) analgesics; it is accompanied in most cases by autonomic disturbances, and despite its severity does not usually interfere seriously with sleep (Bowsher, 1987). Examples of neurogenic pain are post-herpetic neuralgia, causalgia, trigeminal neuralgia, and thalamic syndrome. There is no muscle spasm in neurogenic pain.

REFERENCES

Bond M.R., Pilowsky I. (1966). The subjective assessment of pain and its relationship to the administration of analgesics in patients with advanced cancer. *J. Psychosomat. Res*; **10**: 203.

Bowsher D. (1982). A note on the distinction between first and second pain. In *Anatomical, Physiological, and Pharmacological Aspects of Trigeminal Pain* (Matthews B., Hill R.G., eds) pp. 3–6. Amsterdam: Excerpta Medica.

Bowsher D. (1987). Neurogenic pain. In *Textbook of Neurology* (Swash M., Oxbury J., eds) in press.

Melzack R. (1975). The McGill pain questionnaire: major properties and scoring methods. *Pain*; **1**: 277–99.

Smith G. M., Egbert L. D., Markowitz R. A., Mosteller R., Beecher H. K. (1966). An experimental pain method sensitive to morphine in man: the submaximum effort tourniquet technique. *Pharmacol. Exp. Therap*; **154**: 324–32.

Torebjörk H.E., Hallin R.G. (1972). Activity in C fibres correlated to perception in man. In *Cervical Pain* (Hirsch C., Zotterman Y., eds) pp. 171–8. Oxford: Pergamon Press.

van Hees J., Gybels J. M. (1972). Pain related to single afferent C fibers from human skin. *Brain Res*; **48**: 397–400.

Chapter 3

Nociceptors and Peripheral Nerve Fibres

DAVID BOWSHER

INTRODUCTION

It has already been stated that pain receptors (nociceptors) are associated with small myelinated and unmyelinated nerve fibres in the periphery. It is of some importance to consider more closely the mechanisms and connections of these sensory units.

A-DELTA NOCICEPTORS

A-delta nociceptors are mostly distributed fairly superficially on the body surface (skin), including its infoldings into the mouth and anus at either end of the alimentary canal; but they have also been described in small numbers in joints and muscle. Organised non-neural receptors associated with A-delta nerve terminals have been described in the skin of experimental animals (Kruger and Rodin, 1983). These receptors, which transduce high-intensity stimuli into nerve impulses, are distributed as a series of sensitive spots within the receptive field separated by insensitive areas. The majority of these nociceptors are sensitive only to high-intensity mechanical stimuli; a small number are also sensitive to noxious temperature changes (above 45°C). A-delta fibres carry these messages to the spinal cord or brainstem at an average speed of 15 m/s (just under 35 mph or 55 km/h). It is not yet known with certainty what the transmitter substance in these sensory units is.

C POLYMODAL NOCICEPTORS

Nociceptors with unmyelinated fibres have been very intensively investigated both in man and experimental animals. They are found in the deeper part of the skin and in virtually every other tissue except the nervous system itself. These nociceptors, which account for over 90% of primary afferent C fibres in primates, have fairly small but homogenous receptive fields. They are frequently sensitive to mechanical, thermal, and chemical noxious stimuli, and so have come to be called *polymodal nociceptors*. They are not really separately sensitive to different forms of energy, but to a factor common to damaged tissue, however the damage is caused. The nature of the actual chemical substance which excites the nerve endings is unknown, but pain-producing chemicals such as bradykinin are active in extraordinary low concentrations.

C polymodal nociceptors are the well-known 'free nerve endings' in which the nerve terminals themselves are the receptors. The sensory units are commonly silent unless activated by noxious stimulation. The unmyelinated nerve fibres conduct the nociceptive messages towards the central nervous system at an average velocity of about 1 m/s (2.25 mph = 3.5 km/h). These fibres contain a characteristic peptide, substance P, which is probably their transmitter substance.

NOCICEPTORS AND PAIN SENSATION

Torebjörk and Ochoa (1980) have been able to stimulate single A-delta and C nociceptors in cutaneous nerves in the human arm. When A-delta fibres are activated, sharp pricking or stinging sensations are referred to small punctiform areas of skin, while C fibre stimulation produces dull aching pain in larger skin patches 5–10 mm in diameter. The production of burning pain requires the coactivation of C polymodal nociceptors and heat receptors, which form another group of sensory units with unmyelinated fibres.

When polymodal nociceptors are stimulated repeatedly, or the tissue which they innervate is damaged, they show sensitisation; that is to say they either respond at lower intensities of stimulation and/or respond at higher rates than before to a given stimulus. A-delta nociceptors also sometimes show sensitisation, but to a lesser degree. These phenomena may partly explain the hypersensitivity of injured tissue. However, it is believed that chemical substances travelling along afferent nerve fibres coming from damaged/inflamed tissues may also sensitise wide dynamic range central cells in the spinal cord (*see* Chapter 4, p. 28) so that they respond to almost any peripheral stimulus with a 'pain-type' discharge pattern. This must not be confused with peripheral (denervation) supersensitivity, when partly or relatively denervated muscle becomes hyperexcitable due to pathology of the efferent (motor) neurons. But there is also frequently concomitant disorder of the afferent (sensory) fibres, so that afferent sensitisation may be added to effector (i.e. muscle) supersensitivity, producing a very marked motor and sensory effect when trigger spots are stimulated.

Both A-delta and C nociceptors have their cell bodies, of course, in the spinal dorsal root or trigeminal nerve ganglia. The proximal parts of all the A-delta axons and 70% of the C polymodal axons enter the central nervous

19

system through the dorsal (or sensory trigeminal) roots, as classically described. But 30% of C polymodal proximal axons double back to the mixed nerve and enter the spinal cord or brainstem through the ventral (motor) root (Coggeshall *et al.*, 1975). This provides at least part of the explanation for the failure of dorsal rhizotomy (cutting of dorsal root) to abolish pain, though, of course, all other sensory fibres are cut. The C fibres which have entered through the ventral root ascend within the substance of the spinal cord or brainstem and terminate in the same manner as those fibres which have entered through the dorsal (sensory) root. Details of spinal cord circuitry will be described in Chapter 4 (Fig. 4.2*a*, p. 24); but here it is necessary to describe those features which are responsible for referred pain in the periphery.

Referred Pain

Two mechanisms are known which may account for the phenomenon of referred pain, whereby tissue damage in one location is felt as pain in another. The simpler, but more recently discovered basis is the existence of *bifurcated axons* in peripheral sensory nerves (Taylor *et al.*, 1984). They and other workers have demonstrated, both anatomically and physiologically, sensory units which have one branch supplying skin and another branch coming from muscle or some other subcutaneous structure. Such branched sensory units have a single cell body in a dorsal root ganglion and a single proximal axon travelling to the spinal cord from the ganglion cell (Fig. 3.1).

The second mechanism consists of the *convergence* of separate peripheral sensory units onto the same cell in the spinal cord (Fig. 3.2). This phenomenon has recently been extensively reinvestigated and found to be

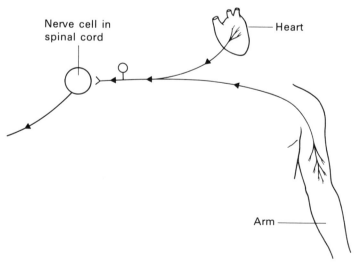

Nerve cell in
spinal cord

Heart

Arm

Fig. 3.1 Referred pain due to branched sensory neurons. The primary afferent shown has branches supplying both heart and arm.

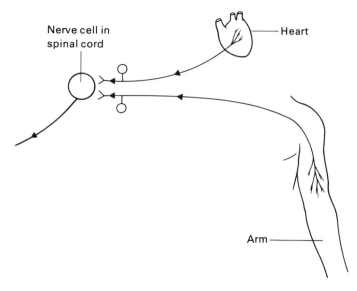

Fig. 3.2 Referred pain due to convergence. The nerve cell in the spinal cord receives input from two different peripheral neurons, one supplying the arm, the other the heart. Since the central cell is more 'used' to getting input from the arm, input from the heart may be interpreted as coming from the arm.

very widespread. Thus, nociceptors coming from viscera and travelling to the spinal cord in sympathetic or splanchnic nerves contact the same dorsal horn cells as do nociceptors coming from skin and travelling in somatic nerves. Many of the classical referred pains, such as heart to left upper limb and gall-bladder to shoulder have been shown to be due to somatovisceral convergence.

REFERENCES

Coggeshall R.E., Applebaum M.L., Fazan M., Stubbs T.B., Sykes M.T. (1975). Unmyelinated axons in human ventral roots; a possible explanation of the failure of dorsal rhizotomy to relieve pain. *Brain;* **98**: 157–66.

Kruger L., Rodin B.E. (1983). Peripheral mechanisms involved in pain. In *Animal Pain* (Kitchell R.L., Erickson H.E., eds) pp. 1–26. Maryland, USA: American Physiological Society.

Taylor D.C.M., Pierau Fr-K., Mizutani M. (1984). Possible bases for referred pain. In *The Neurobiology of Pain* (Holden A.V., Winlow W., eds) pp. 143–56. Manchester: Manchester University Press.

Torebjörk H.E., Ochoa J.L. (1980). Specific sensations evoked by activity in single identified sensory units in man. *Acta Physiol. Scand;* **110**: 445–7.

Chapter 4

Central Pain Mechanisms

DAVID BOWSHER

INTRODUCTION: PAIN PATHWAYS

The main pathways responsible for relaying information about noxious stimulation to higher centres have been known for some time, though contemporary research continues to refine the details. Most recent experimental investigations have been concentrated on trying to understand what goes on at the immediate point of entry of nociceptive afferents into the spinal cord or brainstem.

The Dorsal Horn of the Spinal Cord

The grey matter of the spinal cord can be seen, particularly in thick stained sections, to be divided into nine *laminae* or layers; or ten counting the grey matter surrounding the central canal (Fig. 4.1). In addition to the connections to be described, two general principles of spinal grey lamination should be borne in mind:

1. Each lamina contains several, or indeed in some cases many, morphologically and functionally different types of cell; so that the input–output characteristics of any given lamina are not homogeneous. When, below, it is stated that 'neurons' in lamina ... receive afferents from ... and send their axons to ...', this does not mean *all* neurons in the lamina behave in this way, but merely that there is a group which does.
2. Wherever else they send axons (and most axons are branched, sometimes very extensively), cells of each lamina send axon branches to laminae deeper in the grey matter.

Cells bordering the tip of the dorsal horn constitute the narrow *marginal zone* or lamina I; deep to it is the *substantia gelatinosa* (SG) or lamina II. The rest of the dorsal horn is made up of laminae III, IV, V and VI, which collectively used to be known as the *nucleus proprius* of the dorsal horn. All six laminae of the dorsal horn receive primary afferent fibres from the periphery, whereas

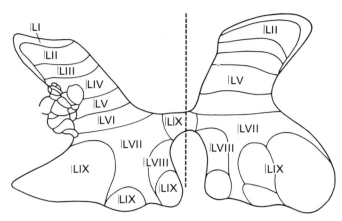

Fig. 4.1 Laminae (LI–X) in the grey matter of the dorsal horn of the adult human spinal cord—in the cervical region on the left and in the lumbar region on the right.

the *intermediate grey matter* made up of laminae VII and VIII consists of interneurons which neither receive from nor project to structures outside the central nervous system; their input comes from more superficial laminae or from axons descending from higher brain centres. The *ventral (anterior) horn* contains the motor neurons of lamina IX, whose axons, of course, leave the spinal cord to innervate muscles in the periphery.

Unmyelinated (C) peripheral afferent axons, and therefore polymodal nocicepters, end in lamina II (Fig. 4.2*a*). Indeed, it is the lack of myelin in lamina II which gives it its gelatinous appearance and hence the name of substantia gelatinosa. Small myelinated (A-delta) high-threshold mechanical or mechanothermal nociceptors terminate in lamina I (as do a minority of unmyelinated polymodal nociceptors) and in the lateral part of lamina V, in the 'neck' of the dorsal horn. Other, non-nociceptive, myelinated primary afferents end in lamina V as well as in other dorsal horn laminae (except laminae I and II).

Because cells in lamina I mostly receive their input only from nociceptors, they respond only to noxious stimuli and so are said to be nocispecific. Many cells in lamina V and deeper, on the other hand, show convergence of (often indirect) input from both nociceptive and non-nociceptive primary afferents. They respond therefore to both noxious and non-noxious input, though with a different pattern of impulses; they are known as *wide dynamic range* (WDR) cells. A third category of spinal neurons is made up of those cells which respond only to non-noxious (or *innocuous*) peripheral stimuli; but these are not dealt with here.

Ascending Pathways (see Fig. 4.4)

For pain to become conscious, the nervous activity engendered in the spinal grey matter by nociceptive afferent excitation must travel up to the brain. Since it has been known for three-quarters of a century that surgical section

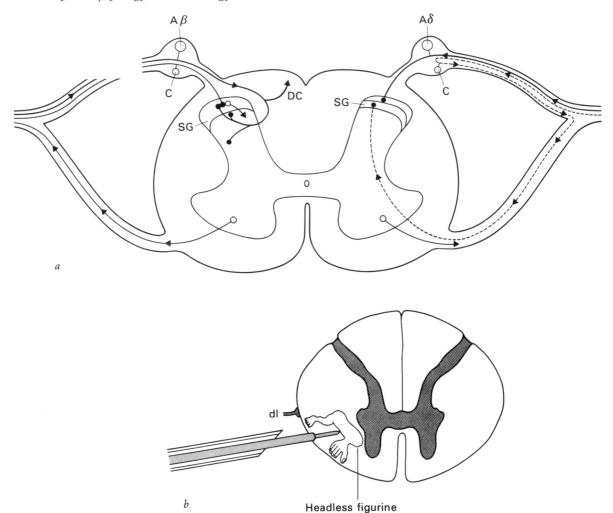

Fig. 4.2a and **b**   A diagrammatic representation of the human spinal cord at the second cervical segment is shown in *a*. DC = dorsal column; SG = substantia gelatinosa. Fig. 4.2*b* (after Lahuerta, 1985, personal communication) can be compared to a headless figurine, and shows how the body below the head is represented in the anterolateral funiculus of the white matter. The surgeon, guided by the dentate ligament (dl), can insert an electrode as shown, and coagulate (i.e. destroy) the 'pain fibres' of the mixed spinothalamic and spinoreticulodiencephalic pathways (see text).

of the anterolateral quadrant of the spinal white matter (Fig. 4.2*b*) abolishes pain on the opposite side of the body below the level of operation (Spiller and Martin, 1912), a practical way to explore pain pathways is to consider the origins and destinations of ascending fibres in the anterolateral funiculus (bundle of white matter). This whole subject has recently ben reviewed by Vierck *et al.* (1985).

Terminations in the Brain

Destinations were investigated earlier than origins using the various methods available at different times for tracing fibres which degenerate following anterolateral cordotomy (see e.g. Bowsher, 1957; Boivie, 1979), or the forward (anterograde) transport of tracer substances from the level of section (see e.g. Mantyh, 1983). Essentially fibres in the anterolateral funiculus terminate in three main supraspinal destinations (Fig. 4.3):

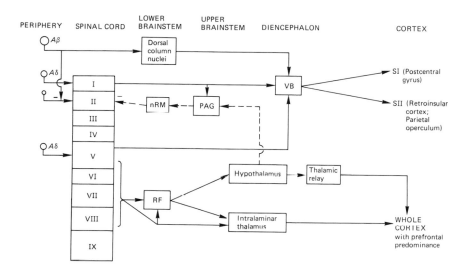

Fig. 4.3 Block diagram to show connections responsible for pain sensation (input from A-delta and C peripheral nociceptors), and also low-threshold mechanoreceptive pathway (peripheral A-beta fibres); other innocuous pathways are not shown. RF = reticular formation; nRM = nucleus Raphe magnus; PAG = periaqueductal grey matter; VB = ventrobasal nuclear complex of thalamus; SI and SII are the first and second somatosensory areas of the cerebral cortex, the locations of which are shown in brackets on the diagram. Dashed lines represent descending pathways, the ultimate effect of which is inhibitory in lamina II of the spinal cord, as indicated by the minus sign next to the arrow head. Collaterals from primary A-beta fibres also inhibit C fibre terminals; this is also shown by a minus sign.

1. The *medial reticular formation* of the lower brainstem.
2. Some of the *intralaminar nuclei* of the thalamus.
3. The *ventrobasal nuclear complex* of the thalamus.

To these should be added a fourth minor, but important, target:

4. The *periaqueductal grey matter* (PAG) of the upper brainstem.

Since these terminal areas are all below the cortex, further relays (which will be discussed later in this chapter) must carry noxiously generated impulses to the cerebral cortex, and thus to consciousness. Before considering this aspect, however, it seems reasonable first to look at the origins of the four pathways contained in the spinal anterolateral funiculus. This has become possible because of the fairly recent discovery that the enzyme horseradish peroxidase, which when injected into the region of axon terminals, is transported back along the fibres to the cells of origin, where it can be rendered visible by a histochemical process. Of course this technique cannot be employed in man, but Willis and his colleagues have employed it extensively in the monkey—in which the pathways, together with their origins and terminations, are believed to be identical to those in man.

The results of such experiments have been recently reviewed by Willis (1985). To take them in the same order as the destinations which have been summarised above, cells marked by horseradish peroxidase injected into:

1. the medial brainstem reticular formation are mainly in laminae VII and VIII of the spinal grey matter, and to a lesser extent in lamina V;
2. the intralaminar thalamic nuclei are also chiefly in laminae VII and VIII, with small quantities in laminae V and I;
3. the ventrobasal nuclear complex of the thalamus are mostly in laminae I and V;
4. the periaqueductal grey are principally in lamina I, and to a slighter extent in lamina V.

It will be noted that cells in lamina V project to all destinations. They are not necessarily the same cells, since human lamina V contains at least eight different neuron types (Abdel-Maguid and Bowsher, 1985). However, physiological experiments in various animal species have shown that some axons branch to the intralaminar and ventrobasal thalamus, and others to the reticular formation and intralaminar thalamus, and yet others to the periaqueductal grey matter and ventrobasal thalamus. The input–output relationships of the spinal grey matter are illustrated diagrammatically in Fig. 4.3 which also shows some other important connections:

1. The brainstem reticular formation projects on to the intralaminar thalamus, and also the hypothalamus.
2. The ventrobasal thalamus actually receives its major input from low-threshold non-nociceptive mechanical receptors in the periphery (A-beta fibres), which relay through the dorsal column (gracile and cuneate) nuclei in the lower brainstem.

Therefore, when we see that the ventrobasal thalamus projects mainly to the principal somatosensory area (SI) in the postcentral gyrus, it is perhaps not surprising to learn that lesions in this part of the brain abolish almost every kind of somatic sensation *except* tissue damage pain (but including pinprick sensation).

Mechanisms of Pain Sensation

Nociceptors activated by tissue damage send their impulses mainly through the reticular formation and intralaminar thalamus to the whole cerebral

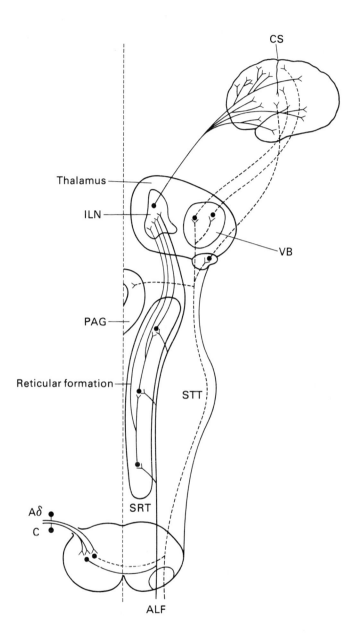

Fig. 4.4 Diagram of central 'pain pathways'. Input from both A-delta and C nociceptors is relayed to the opposite anterolateral funiculus (ALF) of the spinal white matter. The mainly A-delta-driven spinothalamic pathway (STT) is shown as a broken line, giving off collateral branches to the periaqueductal grey matter (PAG) on its way to the ventrobasal thalamus (VB), whence it relays to the postcentral gyrus behind the central sulcus (CS). The spinoreticulodiencephalic pathway is shown as a solid line (SRT) projecting to the reticular formation and thence to the intralaminar nuclei (ILN) of the thalamus. These relay to virtually the whole cortex, but with prefrontal predominance. Note how the two pathways, inextricably mixed in the spinal cord, 'come apart' above it — which is why destructive operations for pain relief cannot be satisfactorily performed above spinal cord level.

cortex (Fig. 4.4), though predominantly to prefrontal regions. This is too big an area for a natural or surgical lesion to abolish pain. Note also that a parallel projection from the reticular formation to the hypothalamus also reaches the prefrontal cortex. This may explain why there are autonomic concomitants to acute tissue damage type pain.

Lastly, it should be noted that although peripheral C fibre input is principally to spinal grey lamina II, output to the tissue–damage–pain pathway is chiefly from WDR cells in laminae VII and VIII. This means that convergent intraspinal circuitry must exist between input and output, and several synapses are known to be involved. This may help to explain why pain elicted by activation of C polymodal nociceptors is less well-localised than pinprick sensation (which excites A-delta nociceptors).

The mechanisms so far described may be adequate to explain how messages from externally applied noxious stimuli are processed, but they certainly do not explain chronic pain. For instance, inflamed joints or broken bones are exquisitely painful if they are simply handled in a gentle manner, activating only low-threshold mechanoreceptors which certainly do not normally give rise to painful sensations.

Guilbaud and her collaborators have examined virtually all fibres, pathways and relays concerned with pain in the peripheral and central nervous system of rats with allergic polyarthritis. In the periphery they found that primary afferent nociceptors, normally silent except when stimulated, are continuously active, and that low-threshold (non-nociceptive) mechanoreceptors from joints discharge at very high rates (Guilbaud *et al.*, 1985). More significantly perhaps, WDR cells in the dorsal horn discharge with a 'nociceptive pattern' when activated via these non-noxious peripheral afferents (Iggo *et al.*, 1984).

Why do WDR cells change their firing pattern? Circumstantial evidence has led Morley (1985) to speculate that primary nociceptive afferents in damaged areas may be chemically altered, and that some chemical modulator substance (perhaps present normally, but now in higher concentration) released from central terminals within the spinal cord or brainstem is able, directly or indirectly, to 'sensitise' WDR cells in the cord so that they respond abnormally to input from normally innocuous primary afferent messages. Such a mechanism may be implicit in the demonstration by Mense (1982) that aspirin raises the peripheral threshold of primary nociceptive afferents.

REFERENCES

Abdel-Maguid T.E., Bowsher D. (1985). The grey matter of the dorsal horn of the adult human spinal cord, including comparisons with general somatic and visceral afferent cranial nerve nuclei. *J. Anat*; **142**: 33–58.

Boivie J. (1979). An anatomical reinvestigation of the termination of the spinothalamic tract in the monkey. *J. Comp. Neurol*; **186**: 343–69.

Bowsher D. (1957). Termination of the central pain pathway in man: the conscious appreciation of pain. *Brain;* **80**: 606–22.

Guilbaud G., Iggo A., Tegner R. (1985). Sensory receptors in ankle joint capsules of normal and arthritic rats. *Exp. Brain Res;* **58**: 29–40.

Iggo A., Guilbaud G., Tegner R. (1984). Sensory mechanisms in arthritic rat joints. In *Advances in Pain Research and Therapy*, Vol. 6 (Kruger L., Kiebeskind J., eds) pp. 83–93. New York: Raven Press.

Mantyh P.W. (1983). The spinothalamic tract in the primate: a re-examination using wheatgerm agglutinin conjugated to horseradish peroxidase. *Neuroscience;* **9**: 847–62.

Mense S. (1982). Reduction of the bradykinin-induced activation of feline group III and IV muscle receptors by acetylsalicylic acid. *J. Physiol;* **326**: 269–84.

Morley J.S. (1985). Peptides in nociceptive pathways. In *Persistent Pain: Modern Methods of Treatment*, Vol. 5 (Lipton S., Miles J.B., eds) pp. 65–91. London: Academic Press.

Spiller W.G., Martin E. (1912). The treatment of persistent pain of organic origin in the lower part of the body by division of the anterolateral column of the spinal cord. *J. Amer. Med. Assoc;* **58**: 1489–90.

Vierck C.J., Greenspan J.D., Ritz L.A., Yeomans D.C. (1985). The spinal pathway contributing to the ascending conduction and the descending modulation of pain sensations and reactions. In *Spinal Afferent Processing* (Yaksh T.L., ed) pp. 275–330. New York: Plenum Press.

Willis W.D. (1985). Nociceptive pathways: anatomy and physiology of nociceptive ascending pathways. *Phil. Trans. Roy. Soc. Lond;* **B308**: 253–86.

Chapter 5

Modulation of Nociceptive Input

DAVID BOWSHER

INTRODUCTION

The phenomenon cited at the end of the preceding chapter, namely that aspirin raises the threshold of peripheral nociceptors, is an example of *peripheral modulation* (see Chapter 4, p. 28); indeed it is the only known example of peripheral modulation of pain, since adaptation only occurs to a very slight extent. All other forms of pain modulation take place within the central nervous system (CNS).

PAIN MODULATION

The Gate Control Theory

This theory of pain modulation was put forward by Melzack and Wall in 1965. Although the details are still much disputed by research workers, the theory has proved enormously fruitful not only in our understanding of pain mechanisms and their modulation, but also in enabling us to devise methods of controlling pain on a rational basis. At its simplest, the theory postulates that within the spinal cord there are mechanisms which may 'open the gate' to impulses generated by noxious stimulation, so that we become abnormally aware of them (e.g. banging an inflamed joint), and others which tend to 'close the gate' so that we are less aware of noxious input.

A simple, obvious and well-known example of the latter is the everyday phenomenon of 'rubbing a pain better'. This obviously works (to a greater or lesser extent), otherwise the whole human race would not do it instinctively! It appears that low-threshold cutaneous mechanoreceptors (A-beta fibres), the main central axons of which pass up the dorsal columns without synapse until they reach the gracile and cuneate nuclei, give off segmental collaterals on entering the spinal cord (Fig. 5.1). These axon collaterals terminate *on* the terminals of A-delta and C nociceptor fibres in the outer laminae of the spinal grey matter. When low-threshold mechanoreceptors are activated by rubbing, their collateral endings partially excite the nociceptor terminals, so

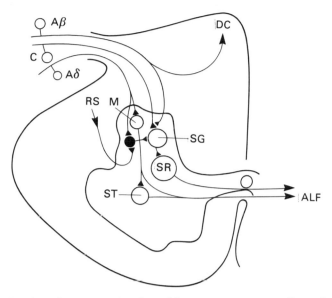

Fig. 5.1 Spinal cord circuitry. C polymodal nociceptors excite cells in the substantia gelatinosa (SG), which converges onto spinoreticular cells (SR) in deeper layers. Acting on the C terminals are terminals of collateral axons of A-beta fibres, whose main fibres pass up the dorsal columns (DC). Thus TENS stimulation applied to peripheral A-beta fibres or antidromic stimulation of DC fibres in the spinal cord will presynaptically inhibit C terminals. A-delta fibres end on marginal layer (M) cells in lamina I, as well as on deeper (lamina V) spinothalamic (ST) cells; but they also have collaterals reaching inhibitory enkephalinergic interneurons (solid black) in the substantia gelatinosa, which inhibit relay cells (SG) in the substantia gelatinosa. Since the inhibitory interneurons are driven by A-delta primary afferents, the effective stimulus will be pinprick (i.e. acupuncture); fibres descending from the brainstem (RS) also reach these inhibitory interneurons; since they are enkephalinergic, their action is reversible by naloxone. ALF = anterolateral funiculus.

that when impulses come along the nociceptor fibres, they find the terminals in a refractory state, i.e. in a state of reduced excitability, so that the quantity of transmitter substance released from the nociceptor terminals in response to impulses coming along their own fibres is reduced or even abolished. This way of 'closing the gate' is an example of the physiological mechanism of *presynaptic inhibition.*

Transcutaneous Electrical Nerve Stimulation (TENS)

It will be seen immediately that this mechanism is the basis of pain relief by transcutaneous electrical nerve stimulation, and indeed TENS was the first (and very successful) deliberate application of the gate control theory (Wall and Sweet, 1967). TENS is *high-frequency low-intensity* stimulation—low intensity because it only activates the largest low-threshold cutaneous nerve fibres; and high-frequency because not only are these large fibres capable of carrying impulses at higher rates than smaller fibres, but because TENS is in fact most effective at relatively high stimulation rates. The anatomical arrangement of these A-beta fibres (see Fig. 5.1) means that the segmental collaterals can also be activated by excitation travelling backwards (*antidromically*) down the dorsal column fibres; so that *dorsal column stimulation* (DCS) also works, at least in part, by the same mechanism.

Vibration

Electricity is not the only way of exciting peripheral A-beta fibres; they can be selectively activated by vibration. Vibration has long been used in physiotherapy, but has recently been reinvestigated by Lundeberg (1983) with particular reference to pain, and found to be a very useful alternative to TENS.

It is now realised that there are several different 'gate mechanisms' within the spinal cord, and indeed at higher levels of the nervous system as well. The following paragraphs will examine some of them.

Pharmacological Pain Modulation (Opioids)

Looking at pain modulation from another aspect, it has been known for centuries that morphine abolishes tissue damage type pain—but not pinprick sensation or neurogenic pain. In the early 1970s, several research groups discovered that certain neurons have morphine *receptors* or *binding sites*. These pharmacological receptors must not be confused with physiological peripheral receptors, which transduce external energy into nerve impulses. Pharmacological receptors are in fact sites on the membrane of the nerve cell or its processes (dendrites) at which a particular substance (in this case morphine) acts either to excite or to inhibit the neuron. In this sense, all transmitter substances in presynaptic nerve terminals act at specific receptors, which are in fact postsynaptic sites on target neurons. Morphine, of course, is not a naturally occurring transmitter substance; but it imitates naturally occurring transmitters, the first of which, the *enkephalins*, were discovered in 1975. Other subsequently discovered natural *opioid* substances include beta-endorphin and dynorphin.

Morphine binding sites are not only found in *some* (but not all) neurons in pain pathways, but also in some neurons in the respiratory and vomiting centres, which is why respiration is depressed and nausea elicited by morphine. This is a useful example of the general, and important, axiom that no transmitter and no type of receptor or binding site is specific to a single functional system, such as the 'pain system'.

Based on the facts given in earlier chapters, it is easy to predict that morphine binding sites will be found on neurons in the spinoreticulodiencephalic pathway chiefly responsible for the perception of tissue damage type pain, but *not* to any great extent in the direct spinothalamic pathway mainly responsible for the perception of sharp pricking pain.

In fact, a heavy concentration of opiate receptors is found in the substantia gelatinosa (lamina II) near the tip of the dorsal horn of the spinal grey matter. Since this is close to the surface of the spinal cord, opiates introduced into the spinal subarachnoid space by intrathecal (or even epidural) injection or infusion easily seep into the substantia gelatinosa and produce analgesia, hopefully without producing less desirable effects by action at higher levels of the CNS.

It is, of course, implicit that the naturally occurring transmitters imitated by morphine, and therefore morphine itself (and other narcotic analgesics) *inhibit* the neurons upon which they act. It is now known that within the substantia gelatinosa there are short-axoned *enkephalinergic interneurons*, the terminals of which make contact with other neurons in laminae I and II which they thus inhibit. It is therefore of interest to enquire how these inhibitory enkephalinergic interneurons are activated.

Acupuncture

It transpires that A-delta primary afferent nociceptors make synaptic contact with the interneurons; such contacts may be collateral branches of axons terminating in laminae I and/or V. Peripherally, A-delta nociceptors are activated by pinprick stimuli; within the spinal cord, their synaptic action is most effective at a stimulation rate of 2 or 3/s (2–3 Hz). Pinprick stimulation at 2 or 3 Hz is commonly known as acupuncture; it is more accurate and helpful to consider it (in contrast to TENS) as *high-intensity low-frequency*

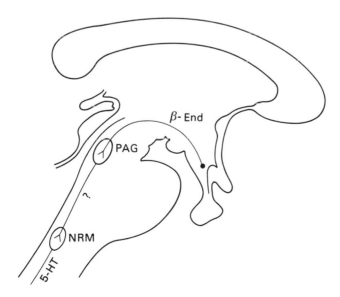

Fig. 5.2 Descending inhibitory pathways. Beta-endorphinergic (β-End) cells in the hypothalamus project to the periaqueductal grey matter (PAG); thence fibres with an unknown transmitter (?) pass to the lower brainstem (NRM), from which a final serotoninergic relay (5-HT) passes down the dorsolateral white funiculus of the spinal cord to excite the enkephalinergic interneurons shown in Fig. 5.1.

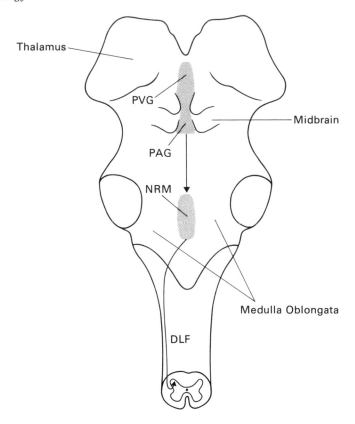

Fig. 5.3 Dorsal view of descending inhibitory pathways from periventricular (PVG) and periaqueductal (PAG) grey matter to relay (NRM) in the medulla oblongata, whence serotoninergic fibres pass in the dorsolateral funiculus (DLF) down the spinal cord to enkephalinergic interneurons in the substantia gelatinosa (see Fig. 5.1).

stimulation. Acupuncture points appear to be where small bundles of A-delta afferents (accompanied by sympathetic efferents) pierce the deep fascia. They can of course be stimulated electrically; unfortunately this is sometimes called 'acupuncture-like TENS', which is confusing as TENS and acupuncture are almost opposites. Since acupuncture is enkephalinergic, its effects can be reversed by the opioid antagonist drug naloxone (Sjölund and Eriksson, 1979).

This explanation, however, is only true for acupuncture applied within the same segment as the pain (segmental acupuncture); the mechanism of remote acupuncture must be different (Figs 5.2 and 5.3).

The other known input to enkephalinergic interneurons in the substantia gelatinosa is from fibres descending from the brainstem. One group of such fibres uses 5-hydroxytryptamine (serotonin) as its transmitter. These brainstem serotoninergic neurons appear to be driven from the periaqueductal grey matter (PAG) in the midbrain. It will be recalled that the PAG obtains an input, probably a collateral input, from the direct spinothalamic pathway—particularly that part arising from cells in lamina I of the dorsal horn, in which A-delta primary afferent nociceptors terminate. Thus a pinprick-stimulus-generated loop from the marginal layer (lamina I) to the PAG and back again, relaying through the lower brainstem to the substantia gelatinosa (lamina II) may explain remote (non-segmental) acupuncture (see also Chapter 4).

Neurochemical Pain Modulation

Two interesting biochemical features of this circuit should be noted. The first is that removal of serotonin is counteracted by tricyclic antidepressant drugs, thus leaving more of the transmitter at its site of action and so facilitating the activity of the inhibitory enkephalinergic neurons. Tricyclic drugs, in relatively low dosage, are therefore accessory analgesics.

It may be mentioned parenthetically that another group of fibres descending from neurons in the brainstem to the dorsal horn are noradrenergic, i.e. their transmitter is noradrenaline. They too have an analgesic action, but it is by direct inhibition of dorsal horn nociceptive neurons, not via an enkephalinergic interneuron. Tricyclic drugs also reduce noradrenaline removal, so they promote this kind of non-opioid analgesia as well. Perhaps this is why the tricyclics are one of the few drugs which are useful in neurogenic pain, which is resistant to narcotic (opioid) analgesics.

When considering the lamina I→PAG→brainstem→lamina II circuit, the second interesting neurochemical feature is that a microinjection of morphine into the PAG produces a very profound analgesia (Tsou and Jang, 1964). It is now known that there is a pathway from the hypothalamus (to which the prefrontal cortex projects) to the PAG; and that the transmitter substance in this pathway is beta-endorphin. Since opioids, including beta-endorphin, are universally inhibitory, it has been supposed that inhibitory PAG interneurons are inhibited by the hypothalamus, thus disinhibiting (i.e. exciting) the projection neurons from the PAG to the lower brainstem. Neurosurgeons have succeeded in suppressing pain by implanting stimulating electrodes in the PAG.

In this chapter, a number of ways in which pain can be modulated have been briefly reviewed. We have seen that nociceptive circuitry can be interfered with by several manoeuvres—by high-frequency low-intensity stimulation (vibration or TENS), low-frequency high-intensity stimulation (mechanical or electrical acupuncture), or by chemical manipulation. All of these change pain tolerance level, not the pain perception threshold; the latter is modulated only by aspirin, acting peripherally at the receptor (physiological transducer).

It must not be imagined that these methods must all be used independently of one another. For instance, electrical stimulators are often used at variable parameters so as to attempt to produce analgesia almost simultaneously by TENS and by electroacupuncture. More interestingly, chemical modulation by the administration of tryptophan, a serotonin precursor, is sometimes used in association with TENS.

The time factor remains to be mentioned. If all the modulatory mechanisms worked only in the ways described in this chapter, their duration of analgesic action should only exceed the duration of the eliciting stimulus by quite a short time. Yet, in fact, analgesia often lasts a remarkably long time after stimulation has ceased. This can only be explained by a mechanism akin to that described in Chapter 4 (p. 28), but this time probably within the CNS. Just as neuromodulatory chemicals, probably peptides, may be responsible for long-lasting pain, so long-term chemical changes within the neurons must presumably be responsible for long-lasting pain relief, by changing the responsiveness of the neurons themselves. The nervous system does not live by electricity alone!

REFERENCES

Lundeberg T.C.M. (1983). Vibratory stimulation for the alleviation of chronic pain. *Acta Physiol. Scand;* **suppl. 523**: 1–51.

Melzack R., Wall P.D. (1965). Pain mechanisms: a new theory. *Science;* **150**: 971–9.

Sjölund B.H., Ericksson M.B.E. (1979). The influence of naloxone on analgesia produced by peripheral conditioning stimulation. *Brain Res;* **173**: 295–302.

Tsou K., Jang C.S. (1964). Studies on the site of analgesic action of morphine by intracerebral microinjection. *Sci. Sinica;* **13**: 1099–1109.

Wall P.D., Sweet W.H. (1967). Temporary abolition of pain in man. *Science;* **155**: 108–9.

Chapter 6

Neuropharmacology of the Pain Pathway

ROBERT BAXTER

INTRODUCTION

Until recent times, the traditional pharmacological approach to pain was, after instituting therapy for the basic cause, to prescribe one of a variety of analgesic drugs. The more potent agents were reserved for acute pain or advanced cancer and were often given in inadequate dosage with too long an interval between doses. The idea that the patient had to earn relief through a period of suffering was seldom consciously voiced, but was the principle underlying the regime. An over-reaction to the fear of addiction, combined with a false religious idea that suffering ennobled the spirit, led particularly to excessive caution in the administration of opiates.

This uncritical approach to pain relief is still seen, but developments in the understanding of pain mechanisms have allowed a more rational approach to the selection and administration of drugs for the control of pain. Drugs can be used to affect pain at a wide range of sites along the nociceptive pathways, ranging from action against the pathological process producing pain to modulation of the cerebral response at the emotional level.

The physiological pathways have been reviewed in Chapters 3 to 5 (pp. 18–36). A summary of the normal nociceptive pathway with specific reference to sites of potential pharmacological modulation may be helpful at this stage.

PERIPHERAL NOCICEPTORS

As explained in Chapters 3 to 5 (pp. 18–36), direct stimulation of high-threshold mechanoreceptors (HTMR) or polymodal receptors (PMR) produces an afferent neuronal discharge which is perceived as pain. However, the nociceptors can be sensitised by a wide range of tissue chemicals. Some of these chemicals are the mediators of inflammation, whereas others are released when cells are disrupted. In regenerating damaged nerves, neurochemicals released as part of normal autonomic autoregulation can produce pathological responses. This will be discussed in more detail later (see p. 40).

The initial work was largely carried out on HTMR endings, and it is still not clear if the same chemicals operate in the same way on both HTMRs and PMRs. Deep tissue nociceptor sensitisation may have a different chemical pattern to skin, and is poorly understood. It is not even clear what chemical pattern is responsible for pain in ischaemic muscle. It seems at least possible that simultaneous activity of multiple chemicals are responsible for sensitisation of receptors, whether by a synergistic action or by one chemical sensitising the receptor to the activity of another. Prostaglandin E_2 infusion has been shown to sensitise nociceptors so that a subsequent application of bradykinin (a chemical released from damaged cells) produces more pain than usual, and serotonin (5-hydroxytryptamine) enhances nociceptor responses to both acetylcholine and bradykinin. Much remains to be elucidated in this field.

There is considerable evidence that a proportion of C fibres are continuously sampling the chemical make-up of the tissues in which they arise, and thereby leading to altered sensitivity of the dorsal horn and the WDR cells in the cord by chemical changes at the cord end of the C fibre. It may be that this mechanism plays a major role in the persistence of chronic pain, and especially in the sometimes bizarre sensory changes that can occur in the areas surrounding a site of pathology (Wall, 1984).

The principles underlying pharmacological treatment of pain at the peripheral nociceptors are:

1. the reduction of nociceptor sensitising chemicals;
2. the reduction of pressure on nociceptors;
3. the inhibition of nerve conduction at receptor level;
4. the prevention of C fibre uptake and transport of damaged chemicals.

NERVE FIBRES

In the absence of nociceptive transmission along nerves, it is assumed that pain would disappear. Unfortunately, the activation of WDR cells, and other changes occurring more centrally than the dorsal horn, may lead to persisting pain despite interruption of peripheral afferent fibres. It appears, therefore, that neural blockade may have its greatest significance in cases of acute pain, e.g. cancer pain.

Nerve transmission is easily blocked by local anaesthetic agents at any level between the receptors and the spinal nerve roots. Local anaesthetics stabilise the cell membranes to prevent the free passage of ions across the membrane. This effectively prevents the passage of impulses. Truly long-acting local anaesthetics do not, at present, exist for therapeutic purposes, although it may be possible to synthesise a slowly metabolised, locally active agent from certain species of sea-snakes whose venom is a potent and very prolonged inhibitor of ionic passage across cell membranes.

Neurolytic agents cause disruption of the axonal sheaths by Schwann cell and basement membrane damage. Regeneration (see p. 40) may be responsible for the return of pain and abnormal sensation, which may be of a different character from the original pain. In such cases it has been suggested that a cross-connection of afferent fibres and receptors of differing sensory modalities could be responsible for the altered character of the pain on its return. The ideal neurolytic would produce only an axonal destruction, leaving the Schwann cells intact. This would allow for the possibility of normal recovery, provided that the cell body in the dorsal root ganglion remained intact, and could easily be repeated if the pain recurred.

THE SPINAL CORD

The potential analgesic effects of modification of spinal cord serotonin and noradrenaline levels were discussed in Chapter 5 (p. 35), as was the site of action of opiate administered at spinal cord level. The pharmacological options at this level will be discussed below.

Opiate activity at spinal cord (and cerebral) level is determined by the affinity of the drug used for the various receptors of endogenous opioids found within the central nervous system. To date, five separate opioid receptors have been identified, although only one has been found in the vas deferens of the rat. The other four have been demonstrated in man, and have been shown to respond to different analgesics and to be responsible for different patterns of analgesia and side-effects.

Painful peripheral muscle spasm may be modulated by certain agents which act on the fine neuronal networks in the spinal cord. In many cases the mode of action is only postulated, but interference with the central noradrenergic fibres which affect the activity of the motor reflex pathway seems to be the most likely mode of action for the majority of these agents.

THE CEREBRAL LEVEL

A rich concentration of opioid receptors giving a site of action for the opiate analgesic agents is found in the human brain. Mild analgesics at this level are either weak opioids, or, like paracetamol, appear to act on the cerebral prostaglandin synthesis mechanisms to produce analgesia in ways that are poorly understood.

Antidepressant drugs of the tricyclic and monoamine oxidase inhibitor groups alter the cerebral as well as spinal levels of serotonin and noradrenaline. They have mood-altering as well as analgesic properties and therefore have a useful dual role in the patient suffering from chronic pain. The neurochemistry of mood and psychological response is immensely complex and is still very poorly understood, but many of these agents can favourably

39

modulate pain perception and response and affect adrenergic and serotoninergic levels in the brain.

NERVE INJURY

Close examination of the mechanisms of pain following nerve injury gives clues to the pathology underlying sympathetic dystrophy and neuromatous pain.

When a peripheral nerve is damaged, a series of physiological changes occurs. Initially, there is a barrage of afferent signals from the proximal end at the site of the crushing or cutting injury. This barrage is an intense, repetitive burst of impulses lasting only a matter of seconds and is followed by a quiescent period which lasts approximately 24 h until the ends of the nerves begin to seal over.

As the sealing process completes sprouting begins to develop from the proximal end of the damaged nerve. As many as 50 sprouts may develop from a single axon to 'explore' the volume around the site of injury. In the case of a crushed nerve, where the axons are damaged but the basement membranes are intact, the sprouts are able to locate the proximal Schwann cell tubes and a high degree of recovery with minimal sequelae may be anticipated. When the Schwann tubes have been disrupted, however, sprouts enter the surrounding tissue. Some will locate the distal ends of the Schwann cell tubes, but the remainder will either curl back proximally along the intact neuron, or form a neuromatous mass at the severed end. If the end has been ligated, as in surgical amputations, virtually all the sprouts form a neuroma although a few will always escape into the tissues.

Even when the cutting of the nerve has been performed with a meticulous surgical technique (and resuturing has been equally meticulous) at least 25% of fibres will not be able to send a sprout into a distal Schwann cell, and will form a neuroma at the site of repair.

Neural sprouts differ markedly in their properties from normal nerve fibres or receptors (Wall and Gutnick, 1974), and their differences are discussed below:

1. *Spontaneous activity.* Sprouting nerve endings produce a spontaneous electrical discharge. In a crushed nerve, with all the sprouts remaining contained within the Schwann cells, this activity peaks after 1 week and then falls away completely. In the severed nerve, however, spontaneous activity in the developing neuroma rises over a 2 week period and then declines progressively to reach a low but indefinitely sustained level by the end of 1 month after injury.
2. *Mechanical sensitivity.* Normal neurons will only respond, except at their receptors, to a very strong mechanical impulse. Sprouts, however, are sensitive to very slight mechanical stimuli once they have become spontaneously active. This is shown by Tinel's sign produced by gentle

tapping over a regenerating nerve end producing sensations referred into the area of skin formerly served by the nerve. This effect explains the hyperaesthesia in a healing wound.

3. *Adrenaline sensitivity*. The sprouts are extremely sensitive to the adrenergic actions of adrenaline and its analogues. They are therefore markedly stimulated by the potent agonist noradrenaline, which is the effector agent released by sympathetic nerve endings in the tissues.

The application of noradrenaline to these sprouts produces a powerful afferent barrage, after a latent period of several seconds. This may imply some intermediate process, but the latent period is still something of a mystery. The afferent barrage induces a reflex increase in sympathetic activity, thus releasing more noradrenaline and thereby worsening the pain. This action gives a sound basis for many of the phenomena seen in sympathetic dystrophies and gives a rationale for the use of a sympathetic blocking agent in this condition.

A number of other ideas are being explored concerning the physiology of pain. Chapter 5 (p. 35) mentioned the roles of serotonin and noradrenaline in the spinal cord, and it is possible that there are other transmitter mechanisms to be identified with yet more scope for modulation techniques in the future.

REFERENCES

Wall P.D. (1984). In *Textbook of Pain* (Wall P.D., Melzack R., eds) pp. 12–13. Edinburgh: Churchill Livingstone.

Wall P.D., Gutnick M. (1974). Ongoing activity in peripheral nerves: 2. The physiology and pharmacology of impulses originating in a neuroma. *Exp. Neurol*; **43**: 580–93.

Chapter 7

Drug Control of Pain

ROBERT BAXTER

INTRODUCTION

Many patients receiving physiotherapy are also being managed on a drug regime. The physiotherapist needs to understand the rationale for the use of the various drugs, as well as their effects, to assess the possible implications for the choice of physiotherapy techniques and approaches. In addition, the drugs may modify the patient's mood or perception of pain sufficiently to be significant in assessing the outcome of physiotherapy.

In Chapter 6 the physiological pathway for an outline of possible sites for pharmacological intervention was examined. This pathway is re-explored below and the most useful drugs at each site identified.

PERIPHERAL MODULATION

Non-steroidal Anti-inflammatory Drugs (NSAIDs)

There is a remarkable variety of these agents available (23 different agents in seven chemical classes are listed in the current British National Formulary), and all have certain features in common. All have actions inhibiting the synthesis and/or release of various prostaglandins. When given in single doses they have primarily an analgesic action, which is usually apparent within 24 h, but when given in a repeated dosage they also result in an anti-inflammatory response. Thermographic studies show a reduction in skin temperature which progresses over 3 weeks, but is not accompanied by further reduction in pain. They are a pharmacologically confusing group, with poor correlation between their plasma levels and analgesic efficacy. Regrettably, there is no consistent relationship between the chemical class of the drug and its clinical actions. This makes it difficult to predict which agents will be of use in any given condition in a specific patient.

The choice of agent is best determined by the symptom pattern. If pain is constant, then a relatively long-acting agent like diclofenac, naproxen, azapropazone or piroxicam gives a convenient dosage regime (although the long elimination period of piroxicam may produce a problem of cumulation in the elderly patient with declining renal function). When morning stiffness is the major complaint, indomethacin at bed time is a useful option, with flurbiprofen as an alternative. For intermittent pains, fenoprofen has been recommended as a fairly rapidly acting drug.

Side-effects are common to all these drugs, although the incidence varies. The most common by far is gastrointestinal disturbance, ranging from mild indigestion, which can be overcome by taking the medication with food, to serious haemorrhage. A previous history of gastroduodenal ulceration is a relative contraindication to the use of these agents, but if they are clearly required in a patient with a history of gastroduodenal ulceration, agents with the lowest known incidence should be tried first, e.g. fenbufen. The suppository route of administration does seem to reduce the incidence of gastrointestinal effects considerably. In all such cases, the patient should be warned to discontinue therapy and seek medical advice should symptoms of gastric disturbance develop. If the suppository route is chosen, it is prudent to ensure that the patient is aware of the correct use. The patient who, when instructed to place the suppositories in the back passage, places them in the back corridor of his house instead of the terminal orifice of the alimentary tract, is not entirely legendary, although failure to insert the suppositories deeply enough so that they are rejected instead of absorbed is more common!

Other side-effects are much rarer. Blood dyscrasias have been reported with phenylbutazone (aplastic anaemia), and the use of this drug is now reserved for the patient with ankylosing spondylitis who fails to obtain relief with other anti-inflammatory drugs. Skin rashes have rarely been reported with existing agents, and in a few patients these drugs may precipitate rhinitis, asthma or angioneurotic oedema.

An excellent review of the role of these drugs can be found in Huskisson (1984).

Other Anti-inflammatory Preparations

Gold salts inhibit prostaglandin synthesis and also bind some elements of the immune system. This gives them a valuable role in the patient suffering from severe rheumatoid arthritis, although 25% of patients report significant side-effects, and a further 25% minor side-effects.

Penicillamine and chloroquine are thought to stabilise the membranes surrounding the lysozymes in the cells. The enzymes contained in the lysozymes are potent mediators of tissue pain when released.

Azathioprine is an immunosuppressant drug, and probably acts in soft tissue disease by reducing the immune reactions which can induce swelling. This property is used in severe rheumatoid arthritis.

Steroids

Steroids are potent inhibitors of tissue swelling. They probably act by reducing the leakage of fluid from cells into the interstitial space. Their indirect analgesic action is by reducing swelling, and therefore pressure, in the tissues. This effect is particularly valuable in cancer pain, when it is the therapy of choice in pain from distended encapsulated organs, and in cases of malignant compression or infiltration of nerves. They have proven value in control of severe headache from intracranial tumours, presumably operating by producing a reduction in intracranial pressure.

Steroids are of unquestioned value in such conditions as polymyalgia rheumatica, but their use in the past for rheumatoid arthritis has created many problems. They relieve the symptoms without arresting the disease process, and their side-effects of adrenal suppression, osteoporosis and immunosuppression produce considerable morbidity.

The most commonly used steroid is dexamethasone, which is especially indicated for central nervous system pain. Both prednisone and prednisolone are also popular. Depomedrone is widely used epidurally for nerve root pain.

Drugs Altering Metabolism

A number of options exist to lessen pain by altering the metabolism in painful tissue. It is not possible to list all of these agents, but a number of examples may be given to illustrate the wide range of indirect methods used to alleviate pain.

Some vasodilator agents have been used in acute ischaemic episodes to try and improve blood flow and oxygenation of the tissues. The classical example of this is the use of nitroglycerine for angina, but naftidrofuryl oxalate (Praxilene) has been used for peripheral blood flow with patchy results.

Calcium antagonists are of value in myocardial pain as they depress contractility and therefore reduce oxygen demand. Calcium metabolism may also be altered with calcitonin in bone pain from Paget's disease or cancer secondaries.

Colchicine is used in acute gout, where its role appears to be to limit the migration of leucocytes into the painful joint in response to the urate crystal deposition.

There are many other examples of drugs altering the metabolism in painful tissue, but these will suffice.

Other drugs such as antibiotics, by destroying the bacteria producing infection, reduce the inflammatory response around the infected area. This is a useful technique in the control of pain from infected superficial malignant secondaries.

ACTION ON PERIPHERAL NERVES

Nerve Conduction

Local anaesthetics

The most widely used agents for the inhibition of nerve conduction are the local anaesthetic agents. These drugs inhibit the passage of ions across the cell membrane stabilising the membrane and preventing conduction of impulses along the nerve. A variety of agents are available of varying potency, speed of onset and duration of action. The potential side-effects of these drugs are related to the membrane stabilising effect, and are, in serious forms, those of myocardial depression or convulsion. If placed in excessive volume into the cerebrospinal fluid, sympathetic blockade can produce a massive drop in blood pressure which can be fatal if untreated, as it can spread to the respiratory nerve roots.

Local anaesthetics may be applied at many sites. Topical injection of myofascial trigger points or irrigation of surgical wounds with local anaesthetics have both been used with success in the periphery. Intravenous injection into the limb isolated by a tourniquet is a useful method in minor and short surgical procedures on the limb, with the major limiting factor being tourniquet pain. Direct blockade of peripheral nerves is an easy procedure to the experienced anaesthetist, and much peripheral surgery can be undertaken under neural blockade, with a useful period of complete postoperative analgesia being a valuable bonus to the technique. There is no doubt that the requirement for major analgesic drugs is markedly reduced by local anaesthetic techniques when compared to the same procedures under general anaesthesia without any local block.

The disadvantage of local anaesthetics is that all modalities are blocked, with both myelinated and unmyelinated fibres being affected. This severely limits the usefulness of the agents, as motor loss is disabling. In the short-term, such as the postoperative case, this is not a disadvantage, but in longer term analgesia motor loss is seldom acceptable. In any event, the duration of action of the available local anaesthetics is measured in hours, so prolonged effects require either repeated procedures or the placement of an indwelling catheter to allow further increments of drug without further needle punctures.

When used in conditions associated with excessive firing of neurons, including neuromas and spastic muscles, there is considerable anecdotal evidence to suggest that the duration of benefit may far exceed the pharmacological duration of the agent used. The author has produced 5 days relief of spastic spasms in the abductor hallucis longus muscle with 1 ml of local anaesthetic applied to the motor nerve supply, and has observed up to 4 days of complete, plus a further 7 days partial, relief of pain in an amputation stump neuroma by a small volume of local anaesthetic applied 5 cm proximal to the pain site. The mechanism of these prolonged actions remains unclear, and one can only welcome them when they provide unexpectedly prolonged relief.

The most commonly used local anaesthetic agents are lignocaine, bupivacaine and prilocaine. The latter is gaining popularity because of its low toxicity, and is particularly valuable for high volume plexus blocks. Bupivacaine has a prolonged duration which is a valuable property for postoperative analgesia, but does mean that a toxic reaction to a high or inadvertent intravenous dose may also be prolonged.

Neurolytic agents

The earliest recorded attempts to produce a permanent nerve block were at the start of the 20th century, some 30 years after the first experiments with local anaesthetics. Ethanol (ethyl alcohol) was the first agent used, and still retains its popularity for some procedures, especially coeliac plexus ablation for the pain of upper abdominal tumours. Ethanol has a relatively low systemic toxicity, but is a local tissue irritant, causing pain on injection. There is a significant incidence of neuritic pain after an alcohol nerve block, with some series reporting over 50% of patients developing neuritis after a peripheral nerve block.

Phenol is widely used for neurolysis. It may be prepared in aqueous solution, or dissolved in glycerine. In the latter form, it is a hyperbaric solution which sinks in cerebrospinal fluid, and is the agent of choice for intrathecal nerve root injections. Phenol in glycerine is also used as an alternative to aqueous phenol for peripheral injection; being a relatively viscous solution, it is thought to be less likely to spread away from the injection site. The drug has a local anaesthetic action, and a warm tingling sensation is reported by the patient almost immediately after injection. It has a shorter duration than alcohol, but is associated with a lower incidence of motor or bladder paresis when used intrathecally.

Chlorocresol has been used for many years as a preservative in drug ampoules, and it is a known neurotoxic agent. It has been used deliberately in a hyperbaric solution for intrathecal nerve block, and although it seems to carry a higher success rate than phenol, it is also associated with more side-effects. Its use has never become widespread.

Ammonium sulphate in 10% solution has a fairly selective action against the C fibres, and is said to produce very little (if any) motor loss or sensory deficit. Its one disadvantage is that the drug produces local pain for about 30 min after injection. It has never achieved great favour, but perhaps a further evaluation is due in view of the recent advances in the knowledge of the role of the C fibre.

Neurolytic blockade is an attractive prospect when faced with a patient with persisting pain. However, apart from ammonium sulphate perhaps, all the agents produce major sensory and motor deficits, which are commonly unacceptable to the patients. In addition, there is a recovery of function which may in itself cause problems. Because of the destruction of the Schwann cells and basement membranes, axon sprouting from the damage site leaves many sprouts unable to enter Schwann tubes. This may lead to locally derived neurogenic pain from the site of injection, with a positive Tinel's sign often present.

Adrenaline blocking agents

The realisation that sympathetic dystrophies may be due to peripheral release of noradrenaline from sympathetic nerve terminals onto adrenaline-sensitive sprouts led to attempts to find a suitable agent to block the noradrenaline effects. In 1974, Hannington-Kiff reported the successful use of guanethidine for this. Guanethidine acts by causing a release of noradrenaline from the sympathetic terminals and then blocking its reuptake. The synthesis of noradrenaline in the nerve terminals is very slow, and the reuptake is the major mechanism by which the nerve terminals maintain their levels of this transmitter. A dramatic improvement in all the symptoms and signs of sympathetic dystrophy is commonly seen, although in some patients repeated blocks at intervals of 2–3 days may be needed to achieve real benefit.

In the presence of a clear-cut sympathetic dystrophy, persistence may be needed. The author has seen patients who did not begin to respond until 10 blocks had been performed, and one case (in which sympathetic dystrophy was of 32 years duration) 35 procedures were required before a result lasting more than a few hours was achieved. The drug is diluted in 30–100 ml of saline and injected via an indwelling intravenous needle into the isolated limb after exsanguination by the elevation and application of a tourniquet. An initial exacerbation of the burning element of the dysaesthesia occurs, but this resolves within 2–3 min. It may be minimised by the addition of a small volume of lignocaine to the mixture, but the resulting slight impairment of motor and sensory function reduces the range of mobilisation and sensory re-education that can be achieved in the physiotherapy department immediately after the procedure. As a result of this, many clinics are reverting to the pure guanethidine and saline mixture.

Similar results have been reported recently from some centres with ketanserin, an agent which blocks the action of serotonin. This has been reported to be effective when used both with and without a tourniquet, and some workers claim success with oral as well as intravenous administration. Not all units have been impressed with the results, and further evaluation is needed.

Anticonvulsants

Carbamazepine has a long history as a useful drug for the control of trigeminal neuralgia. However, a common reason for its failure is inadequate dosage. If the patients who have not benefited by the drug have not been given a dose just below the level at which they experience side-effects, then there has not been an adequate therapeutic trial. Some patients are unable to tolerate a reasonable dose, but may be enabled to do so by giving small doses of syrup rather than tablets, and thus the daily dose can slowly be increased in much smaller increments than a tablet regime would allow.

Carbamazepine has also been used in post-herpetic neuralgia, when there is a distinct stabbing element to the pain, but the effects are much less consistent in this condition, and many clinics find sodium valproate to be a better alternative with fewer side-effects. Despite the massive scarring and degeneration of myelinated fibres in the post-herpetic nerve, the use of anticonvulsants to stop spontaneous discharge is often disappointing. Post-herpetic neuralgia is a mixed picture of peripheral and central pain, and therapy for both components is usually required.

Some limited success has been reported in neuromatous peripheral pain with the use of anticonvulsants. A test technique of giving progressive intravenous increments of lignocaine under ECG control is used to see if the patient obtains relief of pain at less than toxic doses. If benefit is obtained, it is useful to try a trial course of an anticonvulsant such as phenytoin. Care is needed to avoid a toxic dose, and monitoring of blood levels is recommended to establish whether the patient is having a therapeutically adequate dose or not. The majority of patients are unable to tolerate a sufficient dose, but for those who can, the method is valuable.

SPINAL CORD AND CEREBRAL LEVEL

The prospects for producing analgesia at spinal cord level are becoming exciting. Apart from the techniques which induce the patient's own enkephalin release by A-beta stimulation (e.g. TENS, acupuncture, ultrasound, massage, vibration, etc), there are now pharmacological options for analgesia at this level.

Psychotropic Agents

The endogenous enkephalins are released from fine enkephalinergic neurons in the dorsal horn of grey matter in the spinal cord. It is known that the A-beta fibres release enkephalins from these, with serotonin being the likely transmitter for this purpose. I addition, there is evidence that descending fibres from nuclei in the brainstem release enkephalin by means of an adrenergic transmitter. Antidepressant drugs of two groups have been shown to have an analgesic effect, with raised CSF levels of the transmitters in response to drug administration. With the tricyclic antidepressants, e.g. amitriptyline, it has been shown that after 1 year of treatment between 50 and 70% of patients obtain useful relief from a tricyclic antidepressant in a diverse range of peripheral pain conditions. A small percentage of patients

(3–20% in differing series) experience side-effects ranging from a dry mouth and drowsiness to delirium, but most patients with significant side-effects are taking a combination of drugs and the side-effects cannot be attributed to the tricyclic antidepressants alone. In overdose, tricyclic antidepressants may cause serious defects in myocardial conduction, but overdose of these drugs in pain patients is exceedingly rare.

The other major group of antidepressant drugs is the monoamine oxidase inhibitor group (MAOI). Relatively few studies have been undertaken with these drugs, which lost popularity because of the risk of interactions. The MAOIs inhibit the metabolism of adrenaline-like chemicals in the body, which is consequently unable to cope with the ingestion of such agents in food. Certain foods, especially cheese, beef extracts and certain red wines are rich in monoamines, and may cause severe adrenergic crisis in the patient taking MAOIs. Some opioid analgesics may also cause a crisis, with pethidine being the most commonly implicated.

It is possible that the antidepressants have analgesic action at both cerebral and spinal level, but it is apparent that they do have an analgesic as well as an antidepressant action, and the analgesia may well be produced at dosage levels below those associated with the antidepressant action.

Neuroleptic drugs have long had their main place in the therapy of schizophrenia, with anxiety control in terminal care and a dissociative action in anaesthesia being their other roles. Some studies have been undertaken on these drugs in chronic pain, and there does appear to be a useful role in the control of central nervous system pain, especially after stroke. Uncontrolled studies suggest that a combination of tricyclic antidepressants and neuroleptics may be more useful than either agent used alone. The phenothiazine drugs are the agents of choice, with one in particular (methotrimeprazine) having been shown to be a good analgesic, although producing considerable drowsiness in some patients.

Sedatives and tranquillisers have been used widely in chronic pain patients. They have some value in allaying anxiety or aiding sleep, but their role is very dubious at present in view of growing evidence that the duration of pharmacological benefit is limited and there are potential addiction hazards. Benzodiazepines, especially diazepam, do have useful muscle relaxant properties operating on fine interneurons at spinal cord level, but the dose required commonly causes drowsiness, and better relaxants at this site are available.

The use of psychotropic drugs in pain control is reviewed by Monks (1981).

Muscle Relaxants

The use of benzodiazepines was discussed above. Several other drugs have useful muscle relaxant properties, although the site of action varies. Methocarbamol acts like benzodiazepines on fine interneurons at spinal cord level, and it seems likely that baclofen also acts at this level. Orciprenaline probably acts on adrenergic fibres descending into the dorsal horn, while dantrolene acts directly on muscle fibres, inducing weakness as well as an antispasmodic effect.

Analgesics

Non-steroidal analgesics were considered earlier in this chapter. The other analgesics may be classified into simple and narcotic groups.

Simple analgesics

Apart from the non-steroidal anti-inflammatory agents, the only peripherally acting simple analgesic is paracetamol. This drug is thought to act on non-inflammatory aspects of prostaglandin metabolism, and some workers have postulated an action on cerebral prostaglandins as well. In therapeutic dosage it is a safe, simple and efficient agent, but as little as 10 g (20 tablets) has caused fatal hepatic necrosis when taken as a single dose.

One other reasonably efficient non-opioid is available, with an analgesic activity superior to paracetamol. Nefopam has little potential for dependence, and any slight dependence is easy to overcome. It does not cause respiratory depression, and the side-effects of nausea, dizziness and excitement are uncommon if the dose is increased gradually. Its mode of action is still not fully clear, and its final place in pain therapy is still under evaluation. It does appear to be a useful intermediate between the opioids and paracetamol or non-steroidal anti-inflammatory drugs.

Weak narcotic analgesics

Opioid minor analgesics are codeine (normally used in combination with other mild agents in proprietary mixture), dextropropoxyphene (usually found in combination with paracetamol) and dihydrocodeine. These drugs are weak agonists at the opioid receptor sites. Some authorities class pentazocine (a drug which has a mixture of agonist and antagonist actions) as a minor analgesic.

Mixed agonist/antagonist drugs have an agonist action at opioid receptors when used alone, producing analgesia. When used with another opioid, they can antagonise analgesia. Two types of antagonism are seen: (1) a pure antagonism found at any dose typified by naloxone; and (2) a partial agonist group which does not show antagonism in low doses. There is a difference between potency and efficacy which must be understood when considering opioid drugs. A *potent* agent produces its effects at low doses, but some potent agents show a 'ceiling' effect in their administration, with increase in dose producing no increase in benefit. Other less potent agents continue to produce increasing benefit with increasing dose, and at higher doses therefore have a greater *efficacy* than the more potent agent which reached its ceiling of efficacy at low dose. An extremely potent drug has a high level of *affinity* for the receptors. Drugs with a high receptor affinity can displace from the receptors drugs with a lower receptor affinity.

It can be easily seen, therefore, that if a patient is gaining benefit from a relatively high dose of drug with moderate receptor affinity which is still below its ceiling of efficacy, the administration of another analgesic with a higher affinity will displace the original drug from the receptor sites. If the higher affinity drug is, at this dosage or pain level, a less efficacious one, then the patient will experience a return of pain. Drugs which can, under such circumstances, produce worsening of pain are referred to as partial agonists, because their action is not a pure agonistic one. The only one of the relatively weak opioids to show this partial agonist action is pentazocine.

Strong narcotic analgesics

These drugs include some of the oldest agents used in medicine. The type drug is morphine, a purified extract of the dried sap from the seed-pod of the opium poppy. Opium contains a complex mixture of alkaloids, with the most important constituent in both quantity and efficacy being morphine.

The medicinal use of opium was recorded in the 3rd century BC, and it was the drug used as 'nepenthes' to 'banish grief and trouble of the mind' from the followers of Odysseus in Homer's epic, written about events 3000 years ago. In various formulations, it was the standby of analgesia worldwide until the last century, when attempts to produce semi-synthetic and synthetic analogues with more analgesic potency and fewer side-effects were successful.

All the opioid agents act at various receptors within the central nervous system. Specific receptors appear to have specific actions—analgesia is covered by more than one type of receptor, while specific receptors appear to be responsible for side-effects, such as nausea and addiction. The current aim in pharmacology is to evolve a drug which is specific only to receptors which produce analgesia, without affecting the ones responsible for side-effects. Some success has been obtained, but the ideal analgesic does not yet exist in clinical practice.

Morphine and diamorphine are excellent agents in terminal care. They are efficacious agents over an extremely wide dosage range, and if the dose is titrated upwards carefully, the risk of the seriously depressant side-effects is extremely small. Diamorphine has long been claimed to have a greater incidence of dependence than morphine, but the evidence for this is anecdotal rather than scientific. Diamorphine may have a greater psychotropic effect, and therefore may produce a psychological dependence more readily than morphine, but the physical addiction potential of the two drugs seems very similar. Both drugs produce good analgesia with a similar incidence of virtually identical side-effects (nausea, constipation, sedation, rarely psychotropic). The great advantage of diamorpine is its solubility, which allows very high doses to be given without excessive volumes of solution.

Pethidine should have very little place in modern analgesia. Its incidence of psychotropic side-effects is unacceptable, its duration of action too short, and its advantages over other agents and techniques virtually nil.

A wide range of other agents is now available, although many are only formulated in injection form for anaesthesia or for acute use, e.g. in postoperative pain. Some of these drugs have relatively low respiratory depressant effects, e.g. meptazinol, nalbuphine, and are likely to gain in popularity. One, oxycodone, is only available in the UK as a suppository, but is a most efficient analgesic with a long duration of action.

Much has been made of the potential of the sublingually active drug buprenorphine. This absorbs very readily from the sublingual mucosa, but regrettably has a quite unacceptable incidence of nausea in the ambulant patient, although in the bedbound postoperative patient it is of value. In the author's pain clinic, 30% of patients have stopped this drug spontaneously, being unable to tolerate the nausea despite routine antiemetics, while 90% of patients report that nausea is a significant and disturbing effect. Despite claims to the contrary, it cannot be recommended for other than postoperative use for most patients.

Strong narcotics have a very limited role in non-cancer pain. There is an undoubted risk of dependence, although this is extremely small if the dose is correctly titrated against pain. There are, however, some patients for whom life is so intolerable that this risk is acceptable, after full discussion of the risks with the patient. There is no evidence that a therapeutically correct dose of opioid shortens life in terminal care, and some evidence to the contrary. It is not clear whether chronic pain patients differ in this respect from the terminally ill.

Research into analgesics is concentrating on finding specific agonists for the opioid analgesic receptors. There are many compounds under evaluation, and rapid developments are likely.

REFERENCES

Hannington-Kiff J. (1974). Intravenous regional sympathetic block with guanethidine. *Lancet*; **1**: 1019–20.

Huskisson E.C. (1984). Non-narcotic analgesics. In *Textbook of Pain* (Wall P.D., Melzack R., eds) Edinburgh: Churchill Livingstone.

Monks R.C. (1981). *The Use of Psychotropic Drugs in Human Chronic Pain: A Review.* 6th World Congress of the International College of Psychosomatic Medicine, Montreal, Canada.

Section II

Physiotherapy Modalities in the Management of Pain

Chapter 8

The Neuromuscular Facilitation of Movement

A. J. GUYMER

INTRODUCTION

Patients who seek medical assistance for musculoskeletal problems will almost always do so because of pain, either acute or chronic. The fact that they have loss of joint range and hence functional limitation is not usually of sufficient importance, by itself, for them to ask for treatment.

The origin of painful or noxious stimuli may be in the skeletal or muscular structures, or as is sometimes hypothesised, from venous distension or a combination of these. The fascia and connective tissue surrounding musculo-skeletal structures may also give rise to pain. The noxious stimuli will reflexly affect the degree of excitation occurring in the muscle fibres around the damaged structures. This reflex effect is explained in Chapter 2, Table 2.1 (p. 16).

Because proprioceptive neuromuscular facilitation (PNF) techniques can alter the degree of muscle excitation and inhibition they can sometimes be used very effectively when treating benign musculoskeletal problems.

MUSCULAR FUNCTION

The musculoskeletal system has to be able to respond to the needs of an individual in terms of postural control and coordinated movement. Unless there is good control of the background posture, i.e. joints fixed and origins of muscle controlled, it is not possible to produce movement that is smooth and efficient. In normal situations muscles must be able to perform in the following ways:

1. Tonic muscle fibres must control the position of one or more joints against any reasonable force. This means that muscles must be able to work isometrically at any point in the available range.

55

2. Activity in phasic muscle fibres must be able to produce coordinated movement, either through large or minute ranges, at varying speeds and against different forces. Movement will occur in any number of joints at one time. This requires the ability to produce phasic activity resulting in either shortening or lengthening of the individual muscles.

To function normally muscles must have:

1. full passive physiological length;
2. strength in tonic muscle fibres sufficient to control joints in all possible positions;
3. strength in phasic muscle fibres sufficient to move average loads in any direction;
4. endurance sufficient to maintain all postures and movements during a reasonable length of time.

In order to have full range in the physiological movements of a joint there must be a full range in the accessory movements. During active movement the latter are brought about by:

1. the contours of the cartilage at the articular interface;
2. the direction of the ligamentous fibres which will limit movement in specific directions while allowing freedom in others;
3. normal coordination of all muscles concerned—this means excitation of the agonists and synergists, together with inhibition of the antagonists.

The nervous control of muscles must be able to coordinate this activity in the various permutations and combinations of muscle fibres necessary to produce precision of movement at any normal speed. For the sportsman, of course, the efficiency of the cardiorespiratory and cardiovascular system in relation to muscle function is of vital importance.

In normal circumstances muscles are not concerned with exerting any limiting force on joint movement except in the use of two joint muscles. However, in the presence of abnormal hypermobility it is sometimes thought that they may have to contribute to this function.

Much research has been carried out on the plastic adaptation of muscle fibres to their environment and how their form, i.e. having the physiology of a phasic fibre or tonic fibre, will vary according to their neurological function. Plastic adaptation in the muscle fibres also occurs in response to their environment, e.g. during overuse or disuse, or when the muscle is held in a lengthened position for a long period of time, and of course during the ageing process (Rose and Rothstein, 1982). When the patient presents for treatment, there is of course no way of identifying clinically whether any changes have occurred at cellular level, but the physiotherapist needs to be very clear about the existing conditions under which the muscles have been working.

PAIN AND MUSCULOSKELETAL DYSFUNCTION

When considering treatment of patients by physiotherapeutic techniques, reference will only be made to the treatment of the benign musculoskeletal disorders. In such patients, all or some of these muscle functions may be abnormal. Most patients who have had a movement malfunction for some time have weakness, local or general, due to disuse. Following trauma, or due to a disease process, a patient may suffer pain which is either acute or chronic in type. Consequently, and over a period of time, they may develop antalgic postures or abnormal movement patterns so that the muscle fibres will be working either at an abnormally longer or abnormally shorter length. The movement abnormalities will also be of speed, coordination and strength and in addition the reversal of antagonists will be very slow.

In the presence of pain, many patients have an understandable reluctance to move, while in others there is such a high level of cocontraction in the muscles that movement cannot occur. The normal response to movement in any area of the body is a reflex irradiation of muscle activity to a varying extent. It is almost impossible for the individual to inhibit this, so it may result in an increased protective muscle spasm around a painful joint. There are situations in which the pain is so severe that the response is a neurological inhibition of muscle activity. One hypothesis is that this mechanism minimises the approximation or compression of the articular surfaces and thus prevents exacerbation of pain if this is of intracapsular origin.

The healing and repair process which occurs after tissue damage (Evans, 1980) results in the formation of new collagen tissue which eventually contracts. This may cause limitation to the extensibility of the articular and sometimes the muscular tissues, as well as preventing the normal mobility occurring between the structures and the different layers of tissue in the area of damage. It is often hypothesised that these collagenous adhesions may be one of the causes of pain.

When there has been trauma to the muscle or tendon itself, the formation of adhesions may cause pain when the muscle contracts. Sometimes this is only found on examination by placing the muscle in its lengthened range and then adding a strong isometric contraction.

The sensory feedback from muscles, tendons and joint structures will, if continued for long enough, 'convince' the central nervous system that this particular pattern of activity must be accepted as 'normal' (Fig. 8.1). Thus in re-education, not only must pain be reduced and passive joint range restored, but the normal realignment and coordination of muscle fibres must be facilitated and the central nervous system retrained through appropriate biofeedback.

Physiotherapists, knowing the effects and uses of PNF techniques, can use these skills when treating painful musculoskeletal problems, provided that they select the appropriate facilitating factors and techniques carefully in accordance with each patient's clinical picture.

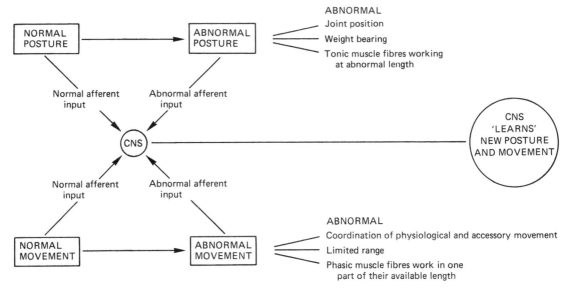

Fig. 8.1 Sensory feedback mechanisms and their effect on the CNS.

Muscle Spasm

A patient with a painful musculoskeletal problem may also have a varying degree of protective muscle spasm. The latter can be divided into three causes:

1. Mishandling the patient. So often people are already tense, anxious and perhaps frightened by the hospital or treatment environment and have often heard 'true' stories about 'treatment' from their friends and acquaintances.
2. Mishandling of the painful structures by the physiotherapist so that protective muscle activity is provoked (Fig. 8.2).
3. Reflex muscle spasm protecting the joint. This is unlikely to be affected until the cause of the pain is treated successfully. In all these categories it may be possible temporarily to reduce the muscle spasm, by extremely precise positioning of the affected part, but with the true reflex muscle spasm the patient often has so much pain that he may want to change positions continually.

ASSESSMENT

When considering the use of muscle techniques for the treatment of pain of musculoskeletal origin it has to be presumed that the patient has been given a very full, detailed examination in order to ascertain the precise area and direction of movement causing the pain, and then the final decision as to what treatment and what 'dosage' to give will be totally guided by continual

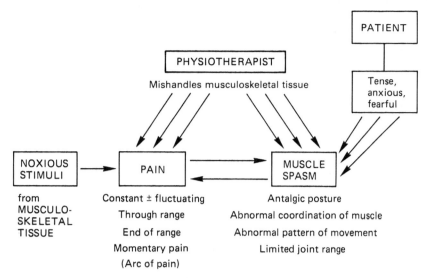

Fig. 8.2 Factors producing pain during physiotherapy.

reassessment of the patient's symptoms and signs both during treatment and between each attendance. The author uses Maitland's concept for examination, assessment and treatment, and so abnormalities of movement can be defined very precisely in movement diagrams (Maitland, 1986, pp. 365–72) (see also Chapter 1, p. 8). The diagrams enable physiotherapists to record different types of pain behaviour, as well as severity of symptoms, e.g. pain at rest, constant pain which may or may not fluctuate, through-range pain, end-of-range pain, momentary pain or 'arc of pain'.

In this concept pain can be described as having severity (from low to high) or irritability (from low to high). This latter defines whether the symptom is easily stirred to a high severity and then takes a long time to die down (irritable), or the opposite, being a symptom which may still be easily stirred up but which goes away *at once* when the provocation stops (non-irritable) (Maitland, 1986, p. 49).

PNF TECHNIQUES

The only effect that physiotherapists can have on muscle activity is to facilitate the excitation or inhibition of muscle fibres to a greater or lesser extent. The muscle techniques used by the author are proprioceptive neuromuscular facilitation (PNF) techniques and these are very completely described elsewhere (Voss *et al.*, 1985, pp. 298–306).

The facilitating factors used when applying PNF techniques must be carefully adapted when treating patients with pain. The main factors are as follows (Voss *et al.*, 1985, pp. 291–7):

1. *Patterns of movement.* Movement occurs in diagonal patterns which are

59

established along the line of the direction of fibres in the main agonist muscles. In the presence of pain the pattern chosen should use the least painful combination of muscles and therefore the least painful direction to start with. When working with an arm or leg it is important to clarify whether the patient works more efficiently with the middle joint flexed or extended.

2. *Hand holds*. These must be on the surface of the muscles working at all times, but particularly in the presence of pain these hand holds must not allow finger-tips to be used, they must be very large, comfortable hand holds avoiding painful bony points. The inability to place hand holds on one surface of a limb may force the physiotherapist to alter the choice of pattern and technique to be used.

3. *Stretch stimulus*. Starting position—normally with isotonic techniques, the pattern of movement starts when the agonist muscles are fully stretched in order to facilitate activity. In the presence of pain, the starting position often has to be modified and one or all of the component directions will be released slightly. The quick facilitating stretch technique uses the monosynaptic reflex arc, and cannot usually be used when there is pain.

4. *Traction and approximation*. The former is used to facilitate activity in flexor muscles and the latter for the extensor muscles. It is often far too painful to approximate the joint surfaces of these patients—similarly, traction for the acute pain problem is generally not used. Both could be used, with care, in the patient suffering from chronic pain.

5. *Appropriate resistance*. Where pain is the main limiting factor then both isotonic and isometric techniques are performed by facilitating a degree of muscle activity which will not provoke any pain. When aiming for inhibition of antagonists the same limiting criteria apply.

6. *Timing irradiation*. The order in which the muscle groups are brought into action can be varied by the physiotherapist's skills. When using isometric techniques, the muscles far away from the problem area are facilitated first and then irradiation into the local muscles can be exquisitely controlled up to the point of pain.

    When using isotonic techniques in a clinical situation involving chronic pain it should be possible to use normal timing from distal to proximal and to keep the irradiation of muscle activity to an acceptable level. This may be totally without pain or to an acceptable low level of pain.

7. *Verbal comments*. For isometric techniques the command word should be *'Stay'*, *'Don't move'*, *'Don't let me move you'*, etc. For isotonic techniques the command should be for movement, e.g. *'Pull'*, *'Push'*, *'Lift'*, or more detailed as appropriate to each patient. The better the handling skill of the physiotherapist the fewer words will be needed by the patient. In theory, PNF techniques can be used where there is a total language barrier! Naturally, the quality of the command is adapted to the acutely painful situation.

The Use of PNF Techniques for Acute and Chronic Pain

Before giving details of treatment it is worthwhile considering some of the hypotheses supporting the selection of muscle techniques for treatment, and to do this it is simplest to keep to two categories of patients:

1. *Acute pain*—may be severe and irritable and the behaviour may vary as shown in Fig. 8.2.
2. *Chronic pain*—may also be severe but usually only slightly irritable or non-irritable.

Acute pain

If the cause of this is trauma, then the tissues will go through the normal cycle of repair and healing (Evans, 1980) and the physiotherapist will therefore have some indication as to whether the repair collagen is still being laid down, or whether it is likely to have started contracting. The pain is often severe and it may manifest itself as a through-range pain, or an end-of-range pain and may be constant or fluctuating.

In acute pain, it is usually accepted that an increase in venous return from the part and blood supply to the part is therapeutic, and certainly muscle activity is known to help both these actions. Whether the intensity of the pain limits the muscle activity too much to bring this about, or whether the physiotherapist is able to use PNF techniques to produce this effect must remain a debatable point with each patient.

If the patient attends for treatment while the new collagen is being laid down, there may be a lot of protective muscle spasm and the aim of treatment is to reduce pain and muscle spasm and so regain a full range of movement as quickly as possible by gently facilitating inhibition in the antagonistic muscle of the required movement followed by gently facilitating excitation in the agonist muscles. This brings about further reciprocal inhibition in the antagonists, and it may then be possible to achieve the desired movement passively or by coordinated activity in the correct muscles. This normal coordination of muscles may produce the correct accessory movements at the articular interface, and so allow more physiological movement to occur. If isometric techniques are used it is possible for the physiotherapist to keep the inevitable irradiation of muscle activity below the pain threshold. This is more difficult to do with isotonic techniques and so the latter should be used with great caution. The result is to stress the newly formed collagen in all directions, so that at the time when collagen contraction starts to occur it will not interfere with the restoration of full function.

If the cause of the acute pain is an intra-articular disease process rather than trauma, then the approach may be as above or the aim of treatment may be to enable the patient to relax the muscles around the relevant joint in a position of minimum pain. It would seem a sensible hypothesis that this category of patient does not want to increase muscle activity and so cause greater compression at the articular interface. Similarly, this aim applies to the patient who has had plastic surgery and must remain in a very abnormal position for several weeks. They should be treated with techniques aimed at relaxing all muscles around the joints and so helping to reduce their postural ache. By using the reflex phenomenon of irradiation it is possible to produce minimal muscle activity around the affected joint, while achieving the effect of relaxation throughout the body. The physiotherapist merely applies her techniques as far away as possible from the area of acute pain. Needless to say there are always many situations in which acute pain is made worse by facilitation techniques, and then extremely gentle passive mobilising techniques or other pain-relieving modalities must be used.

Chronic pain

When this is the clinical situation following trauma, it is likely that the healing and repair of the tissues will have resulted in the formation of scar tissue and adhesions in various structures. Any limitation of movement may be due to pain more than resistance in the tissues, or resistance more than pain. Depending on the severity and irritability of the pain, muscle spasm may be provoked in some part of the available range.

The aim of treatment is as before, to increase movement without increasing the pain or provoking muscle spasm. The muscle techniques which are most effective are the same as those used for patients with acute pain, but it may be possible to produce greater irradiation of muscle activity within the limitations of pain and spasm and therefore greater excitation of agonists and inhibition of antagonists.

The question as to whether to develop strength in the presence of pain is difficult to answer out of the clinical setting. In the patient with acute pain, it is usually impractical to attempt to strengthen muscles until the pain is no longer irritable and severity is low. However, in the patient with chronic pain, where the physiotherapist is treating resistance of the tissues and where the pain is not severe or irritable, the aim of treatment is to re-educate muscle activity so that the agonists will have strength in their inner, shortened range. In the chronic pain patient, with the resistance as the main problem together with some end-of-range pain, manipulative techniques will be necessary to increase the range first and then facilitation techniques can be used to consolidate the passive range gained and so avoid any regression over a 24 h period.

Application of PNF Techniques

The techniques of PNF can be applied to many different combinations of muscles (i.e. patterns), but when treating patients with a pain problem, the author uses patterns which are most efficient for that patient, and starts with isometric techniques as it is then possible to control the extent of recruitment and irradiation of muscle activity and to keep within pain. However, in the patients with less pain, it is possible to progress to isotonic techniques, but only with great care. Eventually it is important to use the isotonic techniques, so that the movements in the affected joint may be coordinated again with all other joints on that limb, of between the limb and trunk.

The three most useful techniques are:

1. Hold relax.
2. Rhythmical stabilisations.
3. Repeated contractions.
4. For final re-education, slow-reversal and hold will be needed.

Hold relax

This technique (Voss *et al.*, 1985, pp. 298–306) facilitates isometric muscle activity in the antagonistic muscle of the required movement so that this may be followed by complete inhibition and relaxation of the same muscles. In the presence of pain, which is then the limiting factor to the irradiation, only a very small muscle contraction should be produced.

The affected joint is placed at the maximum range possible before pain, and then the technique is performed at this point on the muscle that is required to eventually lengthen out, i.e. the antagonist. Having achieved the relaxation of all muscles in that pattern, there are three alternative ways of achieving increased range:

1. The physiotherapist *passively* moves the joint further.
2. The patient gently and *actively* moves the joint further.
3. The physiotherapist gently *resists* the agonist pattern in order to produce greater reciprocal inhibition in the antagonists.

In Fig. 8.3*a*, *b* and *c*, this hold relax technique is being performed on the right shoulder, and there are examples of three different patterns being used to relax the sternal fibres of the pectoralis major:

1. Unilateral arm with elbow flexed so there is a short lever and irradiation from biceps and wrist flexors.
2. Unilateral arm with elbow extended—patients sometimes get less pain when the biceps is *not* included in the pattern.
3. Bilateral arm pattern when the command to the patient relates to the left arm (the normal arm) whereby irradiation to the right is smoother as the patient is not thinking of the affected joint.

Figures 8.4 and 8.5 demonstrate the alternative hand holds when the

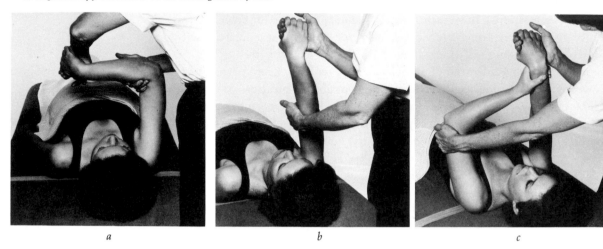

a   b   c

Fig. 8.3a,b and **c** Hold relax technique showing three different methods used to relax the fibres of the pectoralis major muscle: **a** = Hold relax to sternal fibres of the pectoralis major using unilateral pattern with elbow flexion (method A); **b** = Hold relax to sternal fibres of the pectoralis major using unilateral pattern with elbow extension (Method B); **c** = Hold relax to sternal fibres of the pectoralis major using bilateral pattern (Method C).

physiotherapist gently resists the agonist muscle—namely the middle fibres of the deltoid. In both instances, this is chosen to attempt to facilitate further relaxation of the sternal pectoral by reciprocal inhibition.

It will, of course, be necessary to carry out a similar technique on a pattern involving the latissimus dorsi as this muscle must fully lengthen to enable a painful shoulder to move into full flexion, adduction and external rotation range.

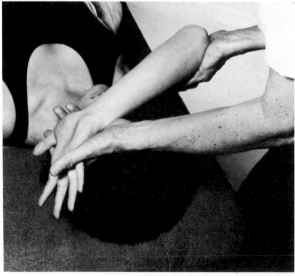

Fig. 8.4 Repeated contractions for inner range work to the middle fibres of the deltoid muscle (Method A).

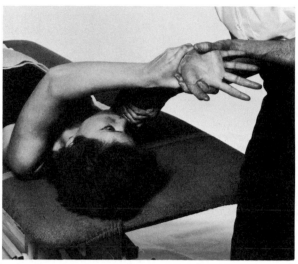

Fig. 8.5 Bilateral pattern using repeated contractions for inner range work to the middle fibres of the deltoid muscle (Method B).

Rhythmical stabilisations

This technique (Voss *et al.*, 1985, pp. 298–306) is based on the neurological phenomenon of the reversal of antagonists in order to build up the cocontraction between agonists and antagonists. The cocontraction is built slowly to the maximum possible before the onset of pain by alternating between agonistic and antagonistic patterns with *no* relaxation during the change over, thus the cocontraction continues to build in isometric strength until limited by pain. This is then followed by total relaxation of all muscles around the joint. The other effect of this technique is thought to be an increase in circulation by this alternating of muscle activity, with the result that waste products are removed and healing is promoted. Thus it is a useful technique for pain problems which result from tissue damage, but with acute, severe and irritable symptoms it needs to be performed with great gentleness. In fact, the physiotherapist may often get the desired result of relaxation by applying the technique as far away from the painful area as possible, e.g. at the feet of patients who have just had surgery around the hip joint.

Figures 8.6, 8.7 and 8.8 show rhythmical stabilisations performed at the maximum range of hip flexion. An isometric contraction for the gluteus medius (extension, abduction, internal rotation), hamstrings and dorsiflexors is followed by an isometric contraction for the psoas (flexion, adduction, external rotation). There is no relaxation of activity while changing from antagonistic to agonistic patterns. These two actions are continually alternated and the strength of the cocontraction built up to the point *before* pain starts.

When the resultant muscle relaxation occurs the physiotherapist can

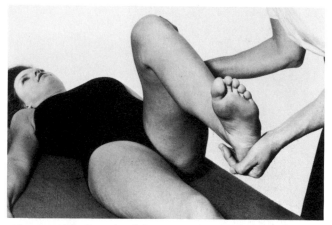

Fig. 8.6   Rhythmical stabilisation to the gluteus medius muscle.

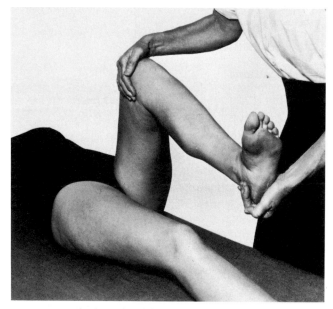

Fig. 8.7   Rhythmical stabilisation to the psoas-iliacus muscle.

passively take the joint through further range, or with the patient suffering from chronic pain it is often possible to finish with repeated contraction to facilitate inner range activity of the agonist patterns (see Fig. 8.8).

Repeated contractions

This is a series of isotonic contractions of through-range facilitated by gentle rotational stretch at the point where the contraction starts to diminish.

Figures 8.9, 8.10 and 8.11 show rhythmical stabilisation followed by repeated contractions being used to gain knee flexion beyond 90°. The aim here is to facilitate inner range work of the biceps femoris as a knee flexor

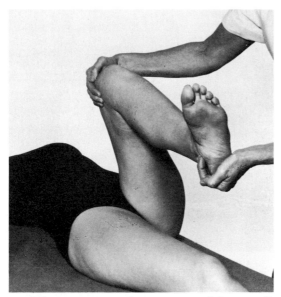

Fig. 8.8 Repeated contractions to the inner range of the psoas-iliacus muscle.

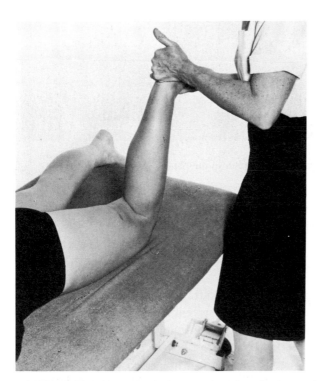

Fig. 8.9 Rhythmical stabilisation to the hamstrings stressing the biceps femoris as an external rotator of the tibia.

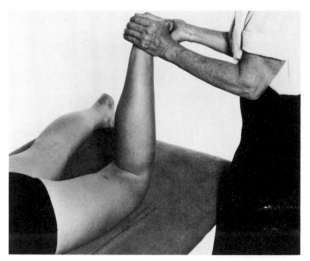

Fig. 8.10   Rhythmical stabilisation to the quadriceps stressing the vastus lateralis muscle.

Fig. 8.11   Repeated contractions to the inner range of the hamstrings stressing the biceps femoris as the external rotator of the tibia.

and external rotator of the tibia, while producing inhibition and relaxation of the quadriceps muscles, especially the vastus lateralis.

Slow reversal and hold

This is an isotonic contraction through-range of the stronger, more normal, or less painful pattern, finishing with an inner range isometric hold. This is then followed by an isotonic contraction through-range of the antagonistic pattern plus another inner range hold.

This technique may be useful with some patients when they are starting treatment immediately following trauma, as the healing tissue may respond to *very gentle* facilitation without any appreciable increase in pain.

With the patient who has chronic pain, this technique is used as a means of coordinating the joints of one limb again so that function may become normal.

In all muscle techniques used for re-education there is inevitably a greatly increased sensory, afferent feedback from the muscle and joint receptors and it is important that this should be an exaggeration of the norm for the central nervous system to relearn. PNF techniques are so useful in painful musculoskeletal disorders because there is a great variety of patterns of movement to choose from, and so the physiotherapist is able to 'tailor' the choice to the needs of each individual clinical situation. Similarly, the techniques available are very varied and although the author has suggested the use of certain techniques in this chapter, it is often the case that other patterns may produce better results in specific clinical situations.

The 'dosage' of each application of a technique is represented by:

1. the extent of the irradiation which is allowed to develop;
2. the amount of resistance given which will result in a desired level of muscle activity;
3. the time for which each technique is applied before retesting the result.

These techniques and principles for treatment may, of course, be applied to any joint or series of joints in the body.

All the examples mentioned so far are on peripheral joints; a review of the use of PNF for spinal problems can be found in Grieve (1986).

The principle of applying these techniques to spinal problems is the same, but the patterns used may be bilateral extremity patterns to irradiate into the trunk or direct trunk patterns, e.g. patients who have lumbar spinal canal stenosis syndrome need to learn to maintain a degree of lumbar flexion in order to minimise the pain. Thus, using bilateral leg patterns, the physiotherapist develops middle range strength in the abdominal and gluteus muscles.

A second example is the patient with a 'dowager's hump' in the upper thoracic level, with compensating hyperextension of the mid cervical area giving rise to the characteristic symptoms. These patients need to learn a correct posture and the muscles need to have their strength and endurance built up in their realigned position.

Another example is when a patient has had spinal surgery, then PNF techniques can be used to increase lumbar movement in all directions in a non-weight-bearing position in bed, as well as regaining full lengthening of the spinal canal structures.

Most musculoskeletal problems have abnormalities in both systems, and thus the best results are obtained by using these PNF techniques in close conjunction with manipulative techniques for the joint dysfunction. They can also be combined very effectively with such modalities as ice and TENS, but it must be remembered that such pain-relieving treatments do not give the physiotherapist licence to overdose with these highly potent PNF techniques!

REFERENCES

Evans P. (1980). The healing process at cellular level. *Physiotherapy*; **66(8)**: 256–9.

Grieve G.P., ed. (1986). *Modern Manual Therapy of the Vertebral Column*, Chapter 58, pp. 622–39. Edinburgh: Churchill Livingstone.

Maitland G. D. (1986). *Vertebral Manipulation*, 5th edn. London: Butterworths.

Rose S.J., Rothstein J.M. (1982). Muscle mutability. Part I: General concepts and adaptation to altered pattern of use. *Phys. Ther*; **62(12)**: 1773–87.

Voss D., Ionta M., Myers B. (1985). *Proprioceptive Neuromuscular Facilitation*, 3rd edn, Philadelphia: Harper and Row.

Chapter 9

Acupuncture

DAVID A. JACKSON

INTRODUCTION

Much interest has been expressed in recent years in the ancient practice of acupuncture. In particular, the recognition of pain management as a specialty in its own right has encouraged the exploration of this technique as a means of offering a non-toxic and a relatively non-invasive way of controlling pain. Acupuncture has much to commend it in this respect. In the correct hands, it is a safe technique which can sometimes be very effective when all else has failed. This is not to say that acupuncture should be used as a last resort only, on the contrary there is much to support the use of this modality as a first option. Acupuncture also has the advantages of being cheap and, as a physical procedure, it is readily acceptable and easy to incorporate into the physiotherapy department. Many patients with pain problems of the type which can be successfully treated by acupuncture are frequently referred to the physiotherapy department, and this is another good reason why the technique should be available there.

The practice of acupuncture consists of achieving a therapeutic effect by introducing needles into specific points on the surface of the body. An alternative method of stimulating these points is to apply local heat. This technique is called moxibustion and it is still used by those who adhere to the so-called traditional approach.

HISTORY AND DEVELOPMENT

Acupuncture has a long history. Certainly the practice dates back some thousands of years in ancient China when stimulation of the then known *points* would be achieved by using 'needles' made of bone, stone or bamboo.

It was noticed that certain medical problems seemed to improve significantly, or even completely disappear after sustaining a relatively minor discrete injury to the surface of the body. It became apparent that stimulation of certain specific areas on the surface of the body could produce changes which sometimes resulted in a beneficial therapeutic effect. This realisation was a major factor in encouraging the pursuit of greater knowledge in this area. It was only a matter of time before observation, and no doubt experimentation, revealed the existence of many such points.

As more points were revealed they were eventually grouped, perhaps as an *aide-mémoire* or because certain points exhibited similar properties, or possibly it was a combination of both these reasons. The groups were named and eventually organised to form the now well-known *meridian system*.

There are 14 main meridians, 12 of which are distributed bilaterally, the other two meridians being distributed along the anterior midline (the *conception vessel* or *Ren channel*), and the posterior midline (the *governor vessel* or *Du channel*). Each meridian is represented on the surface of the body by between 9 and 67 points.

Altogether there are approximately 700 points. Other useful points lying outside the traditional meridian system have also been discovered; these are known as *extra* points.

During the evolution of acupuncture interesting developments were taking place in the study of diagnostic techniques. The nature of society in ancient China was such that it was necessary for the doctor to employ techniques which relied upon observation, palpation, smell, etc. For example, by observing the patient's face carefully, the Chinese doctor was able to glean information which would help him to arrive at a 'diagnosis'. In this particular case he would look for changes in skin colour or texture, the presence of spots or blemishes and so on, all of which were said to give an indication as to the 'energy state' of the body. By observing the tongue, palpating the abdomen or the pulses and other similar procedures, the doctor could arrive at an overall picture of his patient's condition.

Having arrived at a 'diagnosis' (in Chinese terms), the doctor then had to somehow work out what to do about his patient's problem. Thus, various laws, rules, or principles were developed to assist him in this task.

It was noticed that certain acupuncture points seemed to have particular properties which could be used to an advantage in diagnosis. For example, each meridian system has a point called an *alarm* point, which sometimes becomes spontaneously tender on palpation when the patient's problem is related to that particular meridian.

In these ways much information was collected and assembled into the system of medicine which today we call acupuncture.

It is important to note the following:

1. Acupuncture has evolved within the framework of a total medical system, and itself forms only a part of that system.
2. Acupuncture was not (and is not today) limited to the management of pain only, but has useful applications in other areas of medical practice.

An increasing knowledge of pain pathways and mechanisms has led to a greater understanding of physiological mechanisms involved in the use of acupuncture for pain modulation. As a result, two general viewpoints have emerged regarding the practice of acupuncture, the so-called 'traditional' and 'Western' approach, and these two approaches are briefly mentioned below.

APPROACHES TO ACUPUNCTURE

The Traditional Approach

This approach is steeped in traditional Chinese philosophy. A person is regarded as being made up of three facets: body, mind and spirit. Each part is important and is closely related to the other two. Problems arising in one part can be manifested in either or both of the other two parts.

The body is regarded as a self-repairing, self-regulating, homeostatic mechanism. It is animated by a 'life force' or 'energy' called the *Ch'i (or Qi)* energy. In turn this energy is made up of two components, the *Yin* and the *Yang*. These energy forms are said to be balanced, but opposite in nature. The Ch'i energy is said to flow through the meridian system on a 24 h cycle, and illness is regarded as being the result of an obstruction to this flow of energy, such that an imbalance occurs. If this imbalance persists for any appreciable length of time then pathology results.

The approach to treatment is to locate the energy imbalance and to deal with it by treating the meridian points. By stimulating these points, the internal energy systems can be influenced and, hopefully, the 'blockage' can be rectified, which will ultimately allow the body to restore normal function. As the body is a closed system, an excess of energy in one part may be matched by a deficiency in another. Rarely, a total excess or deficiency may occur. It is a traditional concept that these energy imbalances can be brought about as a result of 'attack' from within the body or from outside. The internal factors are: joy, fear, stress, etc; the external factors are: cold, heat, damp, etc. The traditionally orientated acupuncturist would claim to be able to locate these energy changes and then to treat the appropriate points in order to bring about an acceptable energy balance.

The Western Approach

There is no doubt that stimulation of the body surface has consequences that can be measured objectively and appreciated subjectively, and a great deal of work has been carried out to explore the claims of traditionally orientated acupuncturists.

Some of the findings relating to the pain pathways and the modulation of pain mechanisms have already been reviewed in Chapters 2–5 of this book. The following observations have also been made by workers in this field relating to the effects of needle acupuncture. Their findings are noteworthy and may be compatible with modern pain theories.

1. Acupuncture points can be located on the surface of the skin by using

electrical means. The skin impedance drops significantly over an acupuncture point (Reichmanis and Becker, 1978).

2. There is a 71% correspondence between the traditional acupuncture points used for pain relief and well known trigger points used in the West for the treatment of pain in the same area of the body (Melzack *et al.*, 1977).

3. If spontaneously tender points are treated (these are points which are not necessarily known as 'trigger' points or acupuncture points), there is often an improvement in the patient's condition (Liao, 1978).

4. The analgesic effect of acupuncture is partially reversed by the administration of naloxone. As naloxone is a morphine antagonist, this would suggest that part of the pain relieving effect is achieved by the production of endogenous opiates (Liao, 1978). Further work has in fact shown this to be the case (Han and Terenius, 1982).

5. Local anaesthetic applied to an acupuncture point before its use, or an impaired afferent nerve supply from the point renders that point ineffective in its ability to produce pain relief. This obviously suggests that an intact afferent nerve supply is essential for the acupuncture point to be effective (Liao, 1978).

6. Histologically there seems to be a correlation between the acupuncture points and/or neurovascular bundles (Plummer, 1979, 1980).

7. Other changes have also been noted, (e.g. in levels of white cell counts, blood sugar, etc), as a result of needling acupuncture points.

A brief summary of the mechanisms proposed by modern research to explain the modulation of pain is given below:

1. The *pain gate control theory* (Melzack and Wall, 1965) (see also p. 30).

2. *Pharmacology/biochemistry*, i.e. the production of various substances within the body as a result of superficial stimulation which have the ability to modify the pain pathway and thus alter pain perception (Han and Terenius, 1982) (see also p. 28).

3. *Central biasing mechanisms*. The higher centres in the central nervous system project neural pathways back down the spinal cord to exert a 'biasing' effect upon transmission cells at a local level.

4. The *counterirritant effect*. This is well known, but the exact mechanism is not clear.

5. *Psychological effects*. Some would claim that the effects of acupuncture are mediated via some psychological mechanism—possibly the well-known placebo effect. Although this may go some way towards explaining the pain-relieving effect of acupuncture (or any other treatment), it cannot explain the effects seen in practice.

The general approach to the management of patients with a pain problem is obviously coloured by the viewpoint of the practitioner. The acupuncture approach described here leans towards the 'Western' approach but, at the same time, employs much derived from the 'traditional' school.

GENERAL COMMENTS REGARDING DIAGNOSIS

At the present time, the situation within physiotherapy is that acupuncture may only be used as a means of pain relief. (This applies to physiotherapists practising within the National Health Service.) In other words, the physiotherapist is not aiming to treat the underlying condition which is causing the pain. This being the case, it is important to have a clear diagnosis regarding the pathology involved, i.e. a 'Western' style diagnosis. Clearly it would be foolish, if not potentially dangerous, to the patient to indiscriminately treat painful complaints without having first fully investigated the possible cause. With this in mind it is important that the patient has had a good 'Western' type of diagnosis, which also means that there must be a good liaison between the physiotherapist and the patient's doctor at all times.

EXAMINATION AND ASSESSMENT OF THE PATIENT FOR ACUPUNCTURE

It is vital to examine and assess the patient fully before commencing treatment, recording carefully subjective symptoms including pain behaviour, and objective signs including a quantitative analysis of the pain by using the visual analogue scale (VAS) (*see* Chapter 2, p. 15).

The following is an outline as to how this examination and assessment should be conducted (adapted from Maitland, 1981).

Subjective Assessment

Establish why the patient has been referred for or sought treatment:

1. pain, stiffness, the 'giving way' of a joint, etc.;
2. postsurgical, trauma, manipulation under anaesthetic, pain, etc.

History

A detailed history must be taken, which includes the following areas of inquiry:

1. The history of this attack.
2. Previous history.
3. Socioeconomic history (where applicable).
4. Are the symptoms getting worse or better?
5. Any previous treatments? What was the effect of previous treatments?
6. Any contraindications?

The painful area

Is the disorder one of pain only, or does it also involve stiffness, instability or weakness? It is good practice to record this information on a body chart (*see* Chapter 1, p. 5). It is also useful to check other associated areas, such as:

1. the vertebral column;
2. the joints above and below the painful part;
3. any other relevant areas of the body.

Behaviour of symptoms

1. When are the symptoms present and how do they vary? Are they constant or intermittent? (If intermittent note the frequency.)
2. What type of pain does the patient experience? Is it sharp, burning, aching, etc?
3. What provokes and what relieves the pain/symptoms?
4. Is there any pain at night? Does the patient need to get up because of it? Is he able to lie on it? Is the night pain for mechanical reasons or e.g. inflammatory? Monitor the sleep pattern, as it often improves with acupuncture.
5. What are the symptoms like on first rising compared with the end of the day?
6. Carefully examine the functional limitations. Are they a result of pain stiffness, weakness, etc?

Special questions

Ask the patient questions concerning:

1. general health, including unexplained weight loss and his medical history;
2. any medication he is taking for this and other conditions, e.g. steroids, painkillers, anti-inflammatory drugs—monitor the drug intake, this may give a clue as to the effectiveness of treatment over a long period of time;
3. any changes of mood—it may be possible to ask a close friend or relative what is happening in this respect.

Objective Assessment

Observation

Observe the patient as he walks, undresses, gets onto the couch, etc.

Brief appraisal

Note any abnormalities of appearance, temperature, etc.

Active movements

Examine the active movements of relevant parts.

Passive movements

Examine the relevant parts by passive physiological and accessory movements.

Special Tests

Special tests, such as a neurological examination, can be carried out, if necessary, to test power, sensation and reflexes.

Palpation

Palpation is carried out to reveal:

    temperature
    swelling/wasting
    relevant tenderness
    position.

Careful palpation of the painful part and adjacent areas will occasionally reveal tender spots. These are worth noting and may be useful in treatment.

TECHNIQUE AND APPLICATION OF TREATMENT

Essentially the technique involved in acupuncture is very straightforward. The needles are inserted into the acupuncture points to a depth of 0·5–1·5 cm or even less, depending on the area being treated. Much controversy surrounds the subject of the depth of penetration. Some claim that the needle has to be inserted to a 'substantial' depth, which may be up to several centimetres, and then vigorously manipulated until a sensation is achieved called *De Ch'i* (or *De Qi*). This is also referred to as the 'needling sensation' and may be reported as being a feeling of warmth or numbness radiating from the site of the puncture. The sensation is sometimes quite uncomfortable to the point of being painful, but this is regarded as being acceptable. Those who advocate this approach stress that the needling sensation is essential for an effective treatment. It must be said that excellent results are often achieved without following this procedure.

Whether the diameter of the needle makes any significant difference to treatment results or not is doubtful. Likewise, the material that the needles are made of probably makes little difference to results, except when the patient is known to have an allergy to stainless steel, in which case gold or silver can be used.

77

Needling Technique

Three needling techniques are described here: sedating, stimulating, and draining.

Sedating

This consists of inserting the needle into the acupuncture point to a depth of 0·5–1·5 cm and leaving them in this position for 20 min. During this time the needle is not manipulated. After 20 min the needle is removed.

Stimulating (Supplying, Tonifying)

This is a brief technique. The needle is inserted and is rolled to and fro between the thumb and forefinger for a short time (usually up to about 1 min) until the patient experiences some sort of needling sensation. The needle is then withdrawn.

Draining

The needle is inserted as above. It is left in place for about 5 min after which it is manipulated as described in the section on stimulating above. When the needling sensation is achieved the manipulation is stopped and the needle is left in position for a further 5 min, after which time it is manipulated again. This procedure is repeated. After the third manipulation the needle is left *in situ* for a further 5 min and is then withdrawn. The whole process takes approximately 20 min.

A further technique is occasionally used by some practitioners and is mentioned. This is called 'periosteal pecking' and consists of inserting the needle to a depth where it impinges on the joint capsule or the periosteum. The needle is then applied to these structures with a thrusting movement. It must be stressed that the needle is not pushed through these structures. This procedure is carried out for a short time only and then the needle is withdrawn.

Treatment Regimes

The initial treatment should be straightforward and simple, i.e. only about five acupuncture points should be treated, and the needles should not be manipulated. Vigorous needle technique may exacerbate a patient's pain, especially if the presenting situation is acute.

After this initial treatment decisions can be made as to how to proceed. If a beneficial result is achieved then it would be appropriate to continue using the same approach, gradually spacing out the treatments until the patient can be discharged.

If an unpleasant 'reaction' results, i.e. the symptoms are exacerbated to an unacceptable degree, then several options are open:

1. Use fewer needles.
2. Use points which are not in the immediate vicinity of the pain.
3. The use of local points can be abandoned altogether, distant points only being needled. Alternatively the equivalent points on the opposite side of the body may be used.

Usually any reaction experienced by a patient is tolerable and subsides quickly, generally within 24 h.

If, after the initial treatment, there is no response then one of the following approaches could be used:

1. More points could be stimulated.
2. The needles could be manipulated, i.e. the supplying or sedating techniques described above (p. 78) could be employed. This would be applied together with the 'rules' described later (p. 79–80). The draining technique is usually used in cases of stubborn resistance to treatment.

Initially a patient would be seen one to three times a week, the frequency gradually being reduced until discharge. Some patients may return for a repeat treatment every few months. This particularly applies to those whose pain is a result of gross pathology, e.g. advanced osteoarthritis of the knee joint, or where there is some disorder such as migraine.

It must be emphasised that acupuncture treatment, as with any other physiotherapy treatment, must be accompanied by a programme of self-help from the patient. Patients should be encouraged to get involved in their own treatment and rehabilitation, and it must be stressed that they have to accept responsibility in this area.

PRINCIPLES OF ACUPUNCTURE POINT SELECTION

Given a particular pain situation and a clear diagnosis, the first major problem facing the practitioner is how to decide which acupuncture points to use. There are several 'rules' or general principles which offer guidance in this matter.

Some of the main rules are as follows.

Local Points

Acupuncture points located in the painful area are selected and used. In every situation it is worth noting the origin of the pain (if known) and considering the inclusion of some points in that area if it is remote from the painful site.

Local and Distant Points

Local points are selected as above, and to these are added certain distant points. It is believed that certain distant points can reinforce the effects of the local points. For example, Colon 4 (in the web between the thumb and the first finger, on the posterior aspect) is known to be helpful in the treatment of head, facial or jaw pain (Fig. 9.1) and so may be used in conjunction with local points around the face in the treatment of toothache, for example.

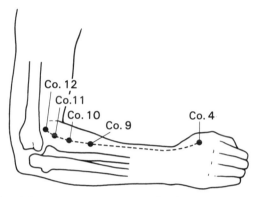

Fig. 9.1   Local and distant acupuncture points for the treatment of a painful elbow.

There is a special group of points called the Ho points. These are all located around either the elbow or the knee. Each meridian has its own Ho point (therefore there are 12 altogether). It is traditionally accepted that if several local points are used which are all on the same meridian, then the Ho point of that same meridian can be used to enhance their effectiveness. A good example of this approach is demonstrated when treating the shoulder (Fig. 9.2). It is possible that one might use three Colon points running over the point of the shoulder, (Co. 14, 15 and 16). The Ho point of the Colon meridian is at the elbow (Co. 11) and could be added to enhance the local effect. Also, when using this relationship, it is sometimes desirable to modify the needle technique. In the above example, if the shoulder pain was very acute, one would employ a sedation technique with the local needles; at the same time the Ho point would be stimulated. The reverse procedure could be carried out if one felt that the shoulder problem was of a 'cold' chronic nature, i.e. the local points would be stimulated and the Ho point sedated. This type of needle technique is only applicable when using this Ho point relationship.

Points in Opposition

In certain circumstances it may not be possible or desirable to insert needles into the local points, e.g. in an extremely painful, inflamed joint, or in the case of an amputee who is experiencing phantom limb pain in a now non-

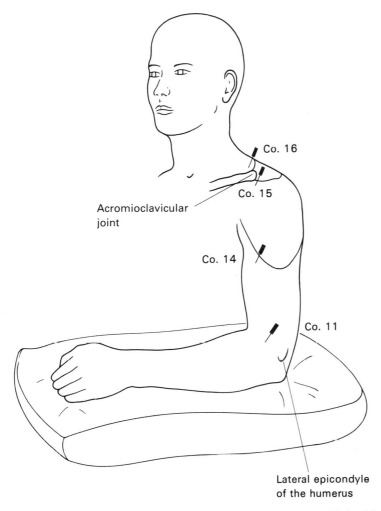

Co. 16

Co. 15

Acromioclavicular
joint

Co. 14

Co. 11

Lateral epicondyle
of the humerus

Fig. 9.2 Local acupuncture and Ho points for the treatment of a painful shoulder.

existent joint. In this case, it is quite acceptable to use the equivalent points
on the other side of the body (Fig. 9.3*a–e*).

Points in Line

A series of adjacent points on a meridian may be used over a painful area,
e.g. the shoulder points of the Colon meridian described above.

Spontaneously Tender Points

In the West, these points are often referred to as myofascial or trigger
points. It is worthwhile carefully palpating the local painful area and the
extremities of the same limb to detect any of these painful points. Often they
will coincide with well-known trigger points, but occasionally tender points

81

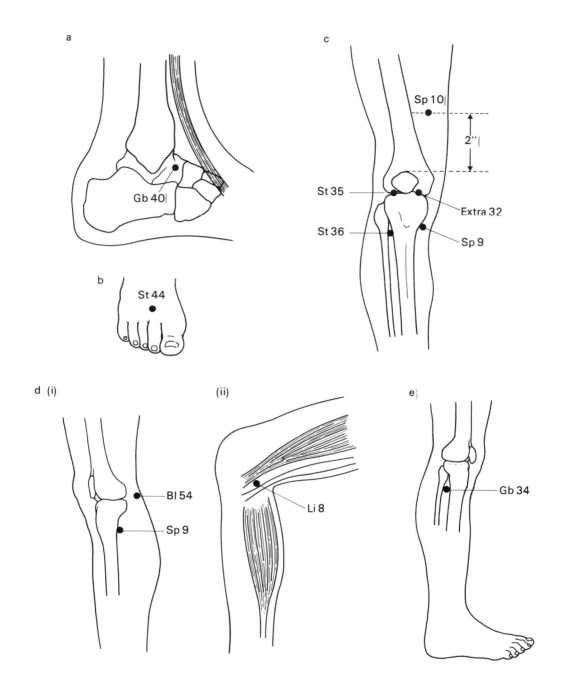

Fig. 9.3 Points which may be used in the treatment of pain on the opposite side of the body, e.g. phantom limb pain. *a*= Lateral aspect of the right ankle. *b*= Ventral aspect of the right foot. *c*= Anterior aspect of the right knee. *d* (*i*) and (*ii*)= Medial aspect of the right knee. *e*= Lateral aspect of the right leg.

may be present where one would not expect them. For example, with back pain it is preferable to palpate down the legs (especially over acupuncture points), and also carefully around the foot and ankle. Any tender points located in this way may be incorporated into the treatment plan providing that the practitioner is satisfied that they are not suspicious in any way, e.g. infectious nodules.

The use of myofascial trigger points is well accepted and is known to be beneficial in the treatment of painful conditions (Frampton, 1985).

THE EFFECTS OF ACUPUNCTURE

It is important to be aware of some of the effects that may be produced as a result of needling. These are briefly summarised below.

De Ch'i (De Qi)

This is a sensation of tingling and/or warmth which radiates from the point being needled. This sensation may change during the treatment time. Some practitioners regard this sensation as being essential for a successful treatment, although in practice this is not found to be the case.

Erythema

A small erythema usually develops around the needle. Occasionally, however, a much larger erythema or even a weal may develop in the area being treated and this is acceptable.

Gripping of the Needle

Occasionally the tissue may 'grip' the needle even to the extent that it is difficult to withdraw it from the skin. This will happen particularly if the needle is manipulated for a time. Presumably this is a result of muscle fibres in the tissue going into spasm. If the needle is left alone for a short period of time it is usually easier to withdraw.

Lightheadedness

The patient may become lightheaded and this may possibly be due to the production of endorphins in the CNS.

Fainting

As with any treatment procedure this will sometimes happen, and usually occurs in young men!

83

Reaction

Sometimes the patient may experience a temporary exacerbation of their symptoms. This lasts only a short time and is nothing to be concerned over unless it is very persistent and severe.

Delay in Results

The remedial effect of acupuncture treatment may take some time to be effective. This may prove to be a problem in these days of the 'instant' society. It is worth persevering for a time before abandoning the treatment.

INDICATIONS FOR ACUPUNCTURE

Physiotherapists are often involved in the treatment of essentially 'painful' conditions. This obviously covers a wide range, but it will usually involve the physiotherapist in the management of the following types of situations:

1. *Soft tissue/locomotor problems.* These are the 'usual' conditions seen in a typical out-patients' department. They include soft tissue inflammatory conditions, e.g. tennis elbow, and acute shoulder problems as well, conditions such as 'backache', radiating neck pain, etc.
2. *Degenerative conditions.* These may be acute or chronic, e.g osteoarthritis.
3. *Recent injuries*, i.e. acute strains, sprains, etc.
4. *Chronic severe pain problems.* This type of problem is often seen in pain clinics and includes pain originating from, e.g. carcinoma, migraine, neuralgias.
5. The *pain experienced during childbirth.*

Acupuncture has a part to play in the management of painful conditions as seen above; however, it must be noted that those conditions involving gross pathology, or those that are very longstanding, will normally be more difficult to treat than those with minor pathology. Also in these situations there is a tendency for the pain to recur so that the patient may require repeat treatments from time to time.

SAFETY, DANGERS AND CONTRAINDICATIONS

The dangers involved in using acupuncture are fairly limited and are relatively simple to avoid. Broadly speaking they fall into three categories:

1. Those involving the spread of infection.
2. Those related to the structures pierced by the needle.
3. Those related to the type of patient being treated.

These categories are dealt with in more detail below.

Infection and Sterile Technique

The possibility of spreading bacterial and viral infections is a hazard with any invasive technique. In particular, viral hepatitis (types A and B) and AIDS make it imperative that acupuncturists maintain the highest possible standards as regards hygiene and sterile procedures, e.g. the use of disposable needles and gloves. Whether known carriers of the above-mentioned diseases should be treated with acupuncture is a matter of personal decision on behalf of the acupuncturist, but certainly if there is the slightest risk then only disposable needles should be used.

Two types of needle are usually employed:

1. Presterilised disposable needles.
2. Reusable needles. These are rarely used nowadays, but if they are then a foolproof routine needs to be established to avoid any risk of contaminated needles causing any complications. After use the needles should be cleaned and then packed in readiness for autoclaving. Anything less than the minimum requirements operating within the NHS regarding autoclaving is unacceptable. Another disadvantage of using this type of needle is that they are blunted by the process of autoclaving.

Needles are also available in many sizes, both in length and diameter. It is wise to have at one's disposal say two different lengths of needle, one 2.5 cm (1 inch) and the other 1.26 cm ($\frac{1}{2}$ inch). The shorter ones are useful for needling skin which lies over bony parts (e.g. hands, feet, head) and also for the ears. It is an advantage if the shorter needles are thinner than the longer ones. This makes them more comfortable to use in these very sensitive areas.

The actual technique of inserting the needle into the skin should be aseptic. The skin should be cleaned with an alcohol impregnated swab before puncture. Also all the usual aseptic precautions regarding the administration of an invasive procedure should be observed, i.e. a high standard of hygiene (clean hands, clean premises, etc).

Dangers Relating to Body Structures

There are many structures which should not be pierced with an acupuncture needle. A list of these is given below:

1. anywhere near the carotid bodies;
2. the lungs or pleura (special care should be taken when points around the apex of the lung are being used);
3. eyeballs, nipples, gonads;
4. bumps, lumps or any tissue that may harbour infection;
5. skin which exhibits eczema or psoriasis;
6. veins, arteries, nerves, tendons;
7. joints capsules and periosteum (see the section concerning 'periosteal pecking', p. 78).

Dangers Relating to the Type of Patient Being Treated

The following types of patient should not be treated with acupuncture:

1. Those who are pregnant (?risk of abortion).
2. Those with heart implants (valves or pacemakers). There is a risk of these patients developing bacterial endocarditis following acupuncture treatment.
3. Those with epilepsy. If the patient should have an epileptic fit while the needles are in place, this could have dangerous consequences.
4. Children.
5. Overanxious/agitated patients.

Great care should be exercised when treating the following types of patients:

1. Diabetics and patients with peripheral vascular disease. Certainly avoid using the peripheral points in these patients.
2. Haemophiliacs and those taking anticoagulants. Check the clotting time and confer with the referring doctor.
3. Those patients who are suffering from immunosuppressive diseases, e.g. SLE, AIDS, or those taking high doses of immunosuppressive drugs, e.g. steroids. Confer with the referring doctor.
4. Those with allergies to stainless steel (use silver or gold needles).
5. Patients with, or carrying, the hepatitis or HIV virus. Treating these patients is potentially hazardous to the practitioner. Only disposable needles should be used.
6. Blood donors. Use disposable needles only.

As well as the above, there are other considerations to bear in mind regarding safety:

1. Do not penetrate the skin too deeply.
2. Do not push the needle into the tissue 'up to the hilt'. The weakest part of the needle is at its junction with the handle.
3. In the event of a needle breaking in the tissue, mark the point of insertion immediately.
4. If the needles are very painful then remove them immediately. (*Note*: be sure to distinguish between *pain* and the acceptable *needling sensation*, see p. 77).
5. Discard bent or corroded needles.
6. Do not allow the patient to move around after needles have been inserted.
7. Warn patients not to exert themselves if the treatment removes their pain.
8. Be aware of patients who may become lightheaded as a result of treatment, especially if they are operating machinery or driving.
9. It is probably a good idea to avoid using the heart and heart constrictor

points in patients who have had a heart attack or stroke or those with a history of heart disease.

10. It is probably a good idea to avoid using those points which have traditionally been designated as being 'forbidden' points for needling.

THE FUTURE OF ACUPUNCTURE

Acupuncture has much to offer in the management of painful conditions, but it has to be stressed that, like other modalities, it has its limitations.

Although, at present, the use of acupuncture by physiotherapists within the NHS is limited to the management of pain, there is a much wider field of application opening up. Some other areas where acupuncture is found to be useful are:

1. in the treatment of drug addiction;
2. in the treatment of upper motor neuron-type spasticity;
3. in the treatment of chest conditions;
4. in the treatment of skin conditions.

A great deal of research needs to be undertaken, not only in connection with specific conditions, but also in investigating the relationship between acupuncture and other types of treatments, e.g. connective tissue massage, reflexology, and the development of 'hot-spots' in painful conditions (Middleditch and Jarman, 1974). Also, a careful examination of the traditional Chinese theory needs to be undertaken in order to interpret it in the light of modern research findings.

It may be concluded that acupuncture is a valuable tool in the hands of the trained physiotherapist. It is not a panacea, but it does make a useful contribution to the management of painful conditions. Every effort must be made to explore the uses of this therapy, particularly in view of its relative simplicity of application, low cost and effectiveness. In particular, acupuncture must develop as a treatment of first choice rather than being used as a 'last resort' procedure, when all else has failed.

REFERENCES

Frampton V.M. (1985). A pilot study to evaluate myofascial or trigger point electro-acupuncture in the treatment of neck and back pain. *Physiotherapy;* **71(1)**: 5–7.

Han J.S., Terenius L. (1982). Neurochemical basis of acupuncture analgesia. *Ann. Rev. Pharmacol. Toxicol;* **22**: 193–220.

Liao S.J. (1978). Recent advances in the understanding of acupuncture. *Yale J. Biol. Med;* **51**: 55–65.

Maitland G. D. (1987). *Musculo-skeletal Examination and Recording Guide,* 4th edn. South Australia: Lauderdale Press.

Melzack R., Wall P.D. (1965). Pain mechanisms: a new theory. *Science;* **150**: 197–9.

Melzack R., Stillwell D.M., Fox E.J. (1977). Trigger points and acupuncture points for pain: correlations and implications. *Pain;* **3**: 3–23.

Middleditch A., Jarman P. (1974). An investigation of frozen shoulders using thermography. *Physiotherapy;* **70(11)**: 433–9.

Plummer J.P. (1979). Acupuncture points and cutaneous nerves. *Experientia;* **35(11)**: 1534–5.

Plummer J.P. (1980). Anatomical findings at acupunture loci. *Amer. J. Chinese Med;* **VIII(2)**: 170–80.

Reichmanis M., Becker R.O. (1978). Physiological effects of stimulation at acupuncture loci: a review. *Comparative Med. East and West;* **6(1)** 67–73.

Chapter 10

Transcutaneous Electrical Nerve Stimulation and Chronic Pain

VICTORIA FRAMPTON

INTRODUCTION

The ancient Egyptians were the first to apply electric currents therapeutically, using electric eels in the treatment of headaches and gout. Throughout the centuries there have been references to the use of electrical stimulation for pain relief, though these were not taken seriously by the medical profession. By the late 1950s and early 1960s, research into the pathological changes which occurred in nerves after injury indicated that there might be a scientific justification for applying electrical impulses to such nerves to modify their response. These and other findings led Melzack and Wall (1965) to formulate their hypothesis of *gate control* to explain pain modulation. Although this has been revised since, it still remains the basis for much of our understanding of pain mechanisms and may explain the therapeutic value of electrical nerve stimulation.

When fast-conducting, large afferent sensory fibres are stimulated they produce some form of presynaptic inhibition, which effectively blocks further transmission in the smaller, slower-conducting afferent fibres (the nociceptive afferents) which may be carrying noxious information.

Electrical stimulation can be given transcutaneously or by directly implanting an electrode on the nerve. Direct implantation requires a difficult invasive procedure with many possible complications. Cutaneous nerve stimulation or transcutaneous electrical nerve stimulation (TENS) is much easier to apply and less hazardous. An electric current is transmitted to the body through the skin by means of electrodes on the skin surface. This technique exploits the concept of the gate control theory in that long-term stimulation produces presynaptic inhibition of noxious information in the small diameter afferent nerves. Similar inhibition can, of course, be produced by rubbing and vibration, but these modes are not easy to use for the prolonged periods necessary to achieve good results.

THE APPLICATION OF TENS

A vast amount of literature exists on the subject of TENS. Much of the material is American and the authors are predominantly physicians or academics. Mannheimer and Lampe (1984), both American physiotherapists, provide the most comprehensive textbook review of the subject. The constantly changing concepts of pain mechanisms and the difficulties of establishing conclusive placebo trials, still leave TENS among the group of modalities that are not yet sufficiently widely accepted. In the UK and other countries with nationally sponsored health care, physiotherapy departments may have difficulty in funding large numbers of TENS equipment. This is unfortunate as the cost and maintenance of these machines is small compared with many pain-relieving drugs, which are often themselves of unproven reliability in pain relief and, of course, are not reusable.

If we can effect pain relief by modulation of normal physiological pathways, it is vital that we understand how these have been damaged or are 'behaving' abnormally, so that the appropriate treatment can be selected and then applied in a logical and comprehensive manner. This is of particular importance with regard to TENS. The abuse of TENS in some centres quickly led to much sceptical criticism, and this cheap, practical apparatus almost fell into disrepute.

This chapter discusses the use of TENS in a variety of painful conditions, reflecting the author's personal experience of this modality over a number of years. Treating in-patients with chronic pain in a rehabilitation setting and working as a physiotherapist in a multidisciplinary pain clinic provided the opportunity for a comprehensive approach to the control of pain by modulation of normal physiological pathways. Monitoring, evaluation, and short- and long-term follow-up have led to the evolution of the method of application of TENS which will be described here.

Pain mechanisms and pain pathways have already been discussed in Section I of this book. It is obvious, therefore, that pain can be approached in many ways. The technique for the use of TENS can best be illustrated by examining normal physiological pathways following nerve damage (see Chapter 6, pp. 40–1).

As discussed in Chapter 6, there are profound peripheral and central effects following nerve damage (Fig. 10.1*a*). One might argue that the barrage of abnormal peripheral discharges leads to the consequent changes and effects that occur at spinal level and higher centres. These central changes may, in themselves, produce further abnormal peripheral nerve discharges. The circle of events has to be interrupted at more than one point to modify chronic pain (Fig. 10.1*b*).

A-beta fibres provide the vehicle for TENS. These large, fast-conducting fibres are highly susceptible to electrical stimulation, and will conduct the electrical impulse quickly to the spinal cord. Slower-conducting, non-myelinated C fibres are thus unable to pass on their message of noxious

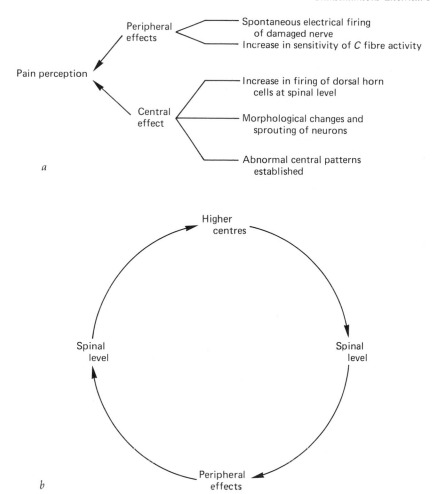

Fig. 10.1 *a* = A summary of peripheral and central effects following nerve damage. *b* = The autonomous circle of peripheral and central effects of nerve damage.

stimulation, as the synapse has already fired and allowed the electrical stimulus carried by the A-beta fibres to pass on to the dorsal horn of the spinal cord; presynaptic inhibition has occurred. This over simplified summary of the gate control theory (as already described in Chapter 5, p. 30), allows the logical application of TENS as, obviously, the closer to the damaged area TENS can be applied the more likely it is that inhibition of noxious stimuli will be effected at the appropriate level. In the case of peripheral nerve damage, experimental work (Wall and Gutnik, 1974) has shown that proximal application of vibration or electrical stimulation 'dampens', or stops the abnormal firing that occurs at the damaged end of the nerve or neuroma (see Chapter 6, p. 40) and along the length of that nerve. So TENS may have a 'mechanical' effect on damaged nerves to 'subdue' or lessen the abnormally firing, excited damaged nerve. This hypothesis can be compared with the pathology that may be occurring in damaged nerve roots. Long-term irritation or pressure on, for example, the L5 root can lead to chronic firing at the site of irritation and along its length (Wall and Devor, 1981). TENS may also play a part in restoring an artificial input when the normal afferent supply is cut off.

Previous experiments (Loeser and Ward, 1967) have demonstrated that following severance of the trigeminal nerve of the cat, the cells in the dorsal horn fired spontaneously. The frequency of this abnormal firing increased over a 3 week period until the cells were firing almost continually. This barrage of abnormal firing could result from the loss of normal afferent input from the nerve that has been divided. After all, much of the input to the spinal cord results in central inhibition, and its loss leads to the unsuppressed firing of cells in the dorsal horn. In the author's clinical experience, many patients with avulsion lesions of the brachial plexus complain of severe pain of a characteristic nature (see Wynn Parry, 1980); however, the pain does not necessarily occur immediately but up to 2–3 weeks post-injury (Wynn Parry, 1981). This clinical observation is certainly compatible with the experimental findings. One might argue that application of TENS, artificially restores an afferent input to the spinal cord. Thus TENS may well be working in one or several ways to inhibit or relieve pain:

1. by presynaptic inhibition;
2. by direct mechanical inhibition on an excited, abnormally firing nerve;
3. by restoring an artificial afferent input.

A lack of understanding of the ways in which TENS may work to inhibit or relieve pain has led to its random application. A greater understanding of these mechanisms provides the physiotherapist with a more logical baseline from which to apply TENS, and from the examination and assessment of the patient how best to judge where to focus treatment.

TENS can only form part of the whole treatment programme for patients suffering from chronic pain (Frampton, 1982). As has been described by Withrington and Wynn Parry (1984) central changes that have occurred must be reversed or modified. A full programe of normal functional activities must be employed in conjunction with TENS, so that normal use can be restored to the affected part once the pain has been reduced or relieved. Many clinics have reported poor results with TENS for pain relief. This may be due to their failure to consider the management of pain as part of a comprehensive rehabilitation programme. Short-term treatment with TENS may be inadequate to modify the complex changes that result in a chronic pain state, whereas shorter periods may be adequate for more acute pain.

THE APPARATUS AND WORKING OF TENS

Despite the large number of machines on the market, the electronic specifications do not vary enormously. Although larger stimulators are available, these are predominantly found in the United States where the use of TENS began. These machines are not portable and are much more expensive. With the present theories based on longer term stimulation and the need for patient freedom and independence to complement stimulation with functional activities, these larger machines have little value and are rarely seen in the United Kingdom. The small portable battery operated stimulators are much cheaper and more practical. The wave form may be described as an asymmetrical, biphasic modified square wave; there is a zero net DC component (Fig. 10.2) the area of the positive wave portion is equal to the area within the negative portion. Therefore, there are no net polar effects to cause long-term positive–negative ion concentrations within the tissues beneath each electrode (Mannheimer and Lampe, 1984), and adverse skin reactions to polar concentrations are avoided.

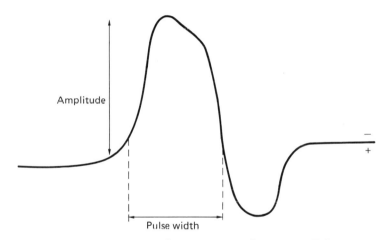

Fig. 10.2   Biphasic asymmetrical square wave with a zero net DC component.

Amplitude of the Current Output (OP)

This can be adjusted between 0–50 mA (milliamperes) into an electrode impedance of 1 kΩ (kilo-ohms). This range is standard for almost all TENS machines and does not vary from one manufacturer to another. It must be noted that amplitudes (i.e. current strengths) producing only a mild paraesthesia are required (see p. 96).

The Pulse Width (PW)

This, in many machines, is fixed usually at 200 μs (microseconds), however other machines provide a variable pulse width ranging usually from 50–300 μs. The relationship of the PW and amplitude dictates the net potential output or strength of stimulus that is produced (Mannheimer and Lampe, 1984). That is, the strength of stimulus can be increased either by increasing the OP or the PW. However, by increasing the PW, motor nerves are more likely to be recruited, and this is not desirable. The greater the intensity of the current the more nerve fibres will be recruited. As the objective of the stimulation is to activate large diameter, fast-conducting afferent fibres, high OP or long PW are not necessary. This is often misunderstood by patients, and occasionally physiotherapists, who mistakenly assume the stronger the current the better the pain relief. Although high intensity currents may provide a 'counterirritant' effect, this is achieved by different physiological mechanisms, e.g. 'hyperstimulation analgesia' (Melzack and Wall, 1982). There are other much cheaper methods of providing counterirritation!

Pulse Frequency or Rate (R)

This is variable on almost all machines, varying from 15–200 pulses/s or H_z (Hertz). The sensation of the variable rates can be expressed as a slow 'ticking' pulse (slow rate) and a continuous buzz (high rate) (Fig. 10.3a).

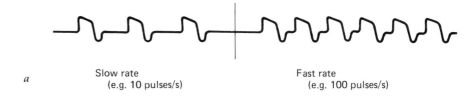

a

Slow rate
(e.g. 10 pulses/s)

Fast rate
(e.g. 100 pulses/s)

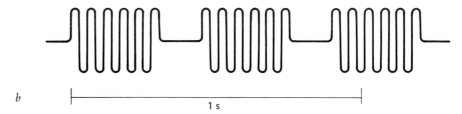

b

|———————————————————————|
1 s

Fig. 10.3   *a* = Impulse frequency or rate of impulse expressed in 1 s (not drawn to scale). *Note:* the pulses demonstrated do not necessarily represent 10 pulses/s or 100 pulses/s, they merely represent the difference between fast and slow. *b* = 'Burst' waveform—low frequency additional 'burst-type' output. In this example, 2.3 bursts/s are shown. *Note:* amplitude, pulse width, and rate of individual impulse does not alter from the initial settings (the impulse has just been interrupted).

Pulsed or 'Burst' Type Output

This variable was introduced more recently and claims to help occasionally in overcoming patient 'accommodation' during long periods of stimulation (Fig. 10.3b). This method is also used in obstetric TENS.

Adjustment of Parameters

Little clinical evidence exists that one specific parameter setting is better than another. One major difficulty is that without an oscilloscope to monitor the wave form, an estimation of each output parameter has to be made assuming that the variable range is linear (Mannheimer and Lampe, 1984). The dial settings may be marked 1–5, 1–10 or 1–50. An estimation has to be made with a variable amplitude, e.g. of 0–50 mA that on mark 5 of a dial (settings 1–10) that the current output is 25 mA. These are obviously estimates which can only be made if the parameter distribution is linear. As machines vary, comparison of clinical results is very unreliable. More recent work suggests that low rate stimulation is more effective in producing the release of endogenous opiates and high rate stimulation activates the more 'mechanical gate' effect (Baxter, personal communication, 1985). In the author's experience, there is no specific pattern of parameters that is more effective in the treatment of any one painful condition, but rates of between 30–50 Hz are most frequently used. As a result, parameter settings must be made on a one-to-one basis, and adjustments based on careful monitoring and recording of results, so that one variable is altered separately and evaluated before altering another parameter; simultaneous altering of more than one parameter at a time makes evaluation impossible. The operation and application of the stimulator will be discussed on p. 96ff.

Lead Wires and Electrodes

The stimulus from the machine is delivered to the patient transcutaneously via lead wires (or cables) and conductive electrodes. Some machines have single leads with separate output sockets, others have a single output socket and bifurcated leads into a single plug. Most units are issued with a pair of black silicon rubber carbon-impregnated electrodes. Although these are available in two sizes, manufacturers issue the small 5 × 5 cm electrodes as standard. This often results in the stimulator being abandoned as unsuccessful, when the use of larger pads, and thus a greater afferent input, may have resulted in a successful treatment.

There are a variety of different electrodes available. Those of most note are the self-adhesive electrodes. The carbon rubber electrodes require an electroconductive gel (which is supplied as standard) to transmit the current through the skin, and they have to be fixed in place with tape or adhesive patches. Self-adhesive electrode pads dispense with gel and tape but usually incur greater cost as they are not indefinitely reusable and some only last for one application. As electrodes often provide the greatest problems in TENS application due to allergic responses to the tape or gel, it is important to familiarise oneself with the available alternatives, such as electroconductive gum pads which provide another medium to electroconductive gel and tape. Other available electrodes are small button electrodes for stimulation of small difficult areas.

95

It is essential to emphasise the importance of using the correct electro-conductive gel. Experience has shown that the use of EMG gel has produced severe allergic responses, as it was designed only for short-term use. Other mediums, such as KY jelly, are also unsuitable as they do not possess the cohesive properties of the TENS gel, and following a relatively short period, the gel contracts to cover only the centre of the electrode pad. The electroconductive TENS gel has high-conductive, non-allergic and cohesive properties which make it suitable for use with the TENS equipment.

Although many manufacturers are now producing a wide range of accessories, adaptability and improvisation are still necessary skills of the physiotherapist. The use of the 'Prembaby butterfly' ECG electrodes provides an excellent solution for the treatment of areas with uneven or difficult contours, such as the fingers, where conventional carbon rubber electrodes are inadequate on account of the inability to maintain a good fixed contact with the skin.

OPERATION OF TENS

The concept of an electric current is sufficient to prevent many people using TENS. It is essential to explain to patients the working of the machine, what the stimulus feels like and that the current can do no harm regardless of the intensity used. Accidental knocking of the OP dial can give a strong jolt but no personal permanent damage! Once the site of stimulation and the size of pad has been selected, one surface of the pad is completely covered with electrode gel and secured well to the skin and connected to the stimulator via the lead wires. All dial settings must be on zero, or the lowest setting; the amplitude is then switched on and increased until a mild buzzing or a pulsation sensation of the impulse is felt. The rate (R) should then be altered from the minimum setting to the maximum to demonstrate the range to the patient; this should then be set at mid-range and any further alterations in R or OP should be monitored so that the optimum settings for comfort and pain relief are obtained. It is important to explain to the patient that he will feel a slow pricking or tickling sensation on a low rate, whereas on maximum pulse frequency the sensation is one of continuous buzzing. It should be emphasised that only a mild sensation of the stimulus is required and that the stimulation should not be strong or painful, that TENS is effective only with mild stimulation and is not counterirritant. There is a tendency for patients to feel that the stronger the stimulus the more pain relief they will obtain. However, the objective is to stimulate the large, fast-conducting low-threshold A-beta afferent fibres, and higher amplitudes are not necessary.

As mentioned previously, the PW is often fixed; the author has found limited use of a variable PW, the exception being in the management of brachial plexus lesions when areas of diminished skin sensation may require higher pulse widths in order for the patient to perceive the impulse

(Frampton, 1982). Many of these patients have denervated muscles and therefore stimulation of motor nerves at these higher PW settings does not result in muscle contraction, which in normally innervated areas would be contraindicated and unpleasant.

Principles of Electrode Placement

These are based on the aforementioned physiological pathways, and an understanding of the pain mechanisms involved; if deafferentation is the predominant feature, then one large pad should be placed over the appropriate damaged dermatome (provided there is some residual afferent input). The other pad may be placed over the nerve trunk of the appropriate root level of damage (Fig. 10.4, 4a,b,c, and e). Alternatively, with peripheral nerve damage, such as carpal tunnel syndrome or ulnar nerve neuritis these may be best treated directly over the affected nerve with one electrode proximal to the site of damage where the affected nerve is nearest the surface (Fig. 10.4, 1 and 2). Small pads may be adequate for these stimulations.

The fundamental guidelines to follow are that the pads should be placed:

1. over the affected nerve where it is most superficial;
2. over the affected dermatome or the adjacent dermatome;
3. over the nerve trunk;
4. above and below the painful area;
5. not over anaesthetic areas;
6. over areas which will still allow functional use of the limb or part.

One or more of the above principles of placement may be employed in one treatment, e.g. stump and phantom limb pain, one pad may be placed over a painful neuroma, the other over the adjacent dermatomes to the deafferented limb (Fig. 10.4, 6e).

The reasons for poor results are related to either patient, technique or equipment. A summary of these is mentioned on p. 100.

Fig. 10.4, 1–11 Body chart showing alternative electrode position placements for different conditions. (The electrodes are either placed in position *a* or *b*, etc.) **1***a*–*b* Median nerve injury. **2***a*–*b* Ulnar nerve injury. **3***a*–*b* Sudeck's atrophy. **4***a*–*g* Brachial plexus injuries. **5***a*–*f* Phantom limb and stump pain in above knee amputations. **6***a*–*f* Phantom limb and stump pain in below knee amputations (position similar to 5 can be used). **7** Painful neuroma following amputation of digit demonstrating the use of the butterfly electrode. **8** Painful menisectomy scar. **9** Post-herpetic neuralgia involving the T4 dermatome. **10** Trigeminal neuralgia and facial pain—two alternative positions. **11***a* and *b* Low back pain (single channel unit). **11***c* and *d* Low back pain L5 root pain (single channel unit). **11***e* Low back pain S1 root pain (single channel unit). **11***f* Back pain following laminectomy and painful scar over bone graft donor site. **11***g* Low back pain and left leg pain (dual channel unit). **11***h* Low back pain and bilateral leg pain (dual channel unit).

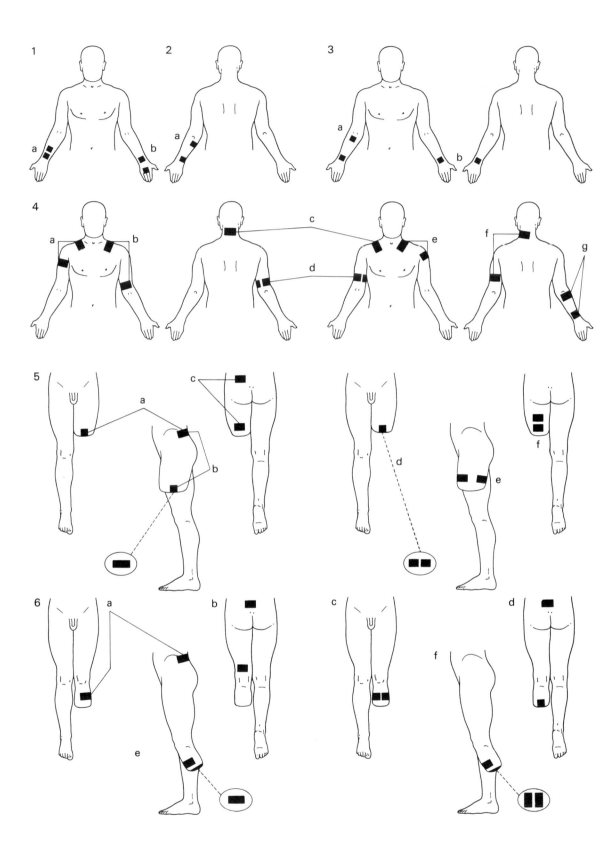

7

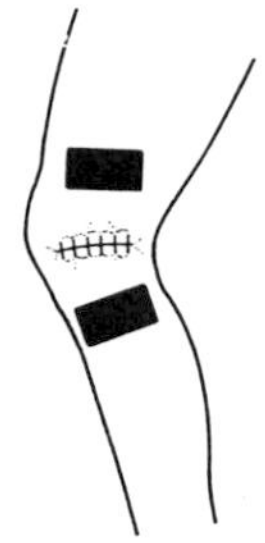

8

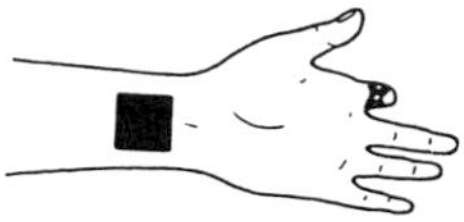

9

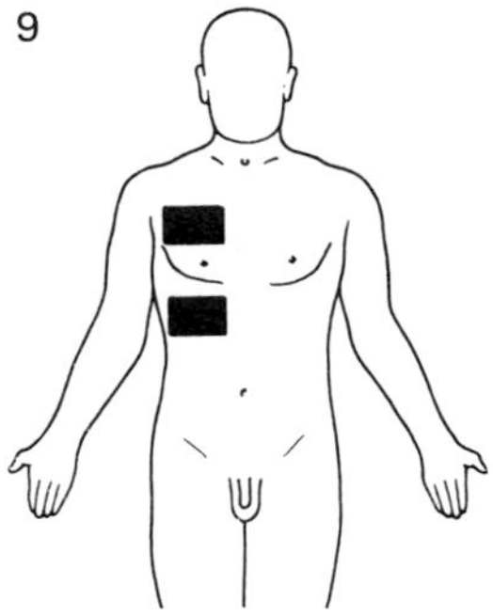

10

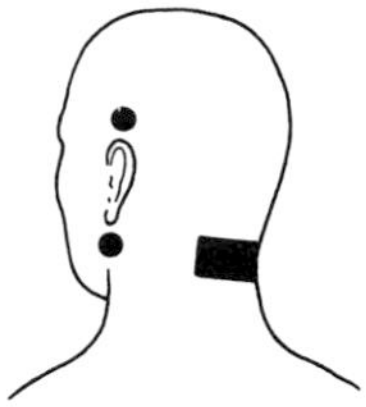

11

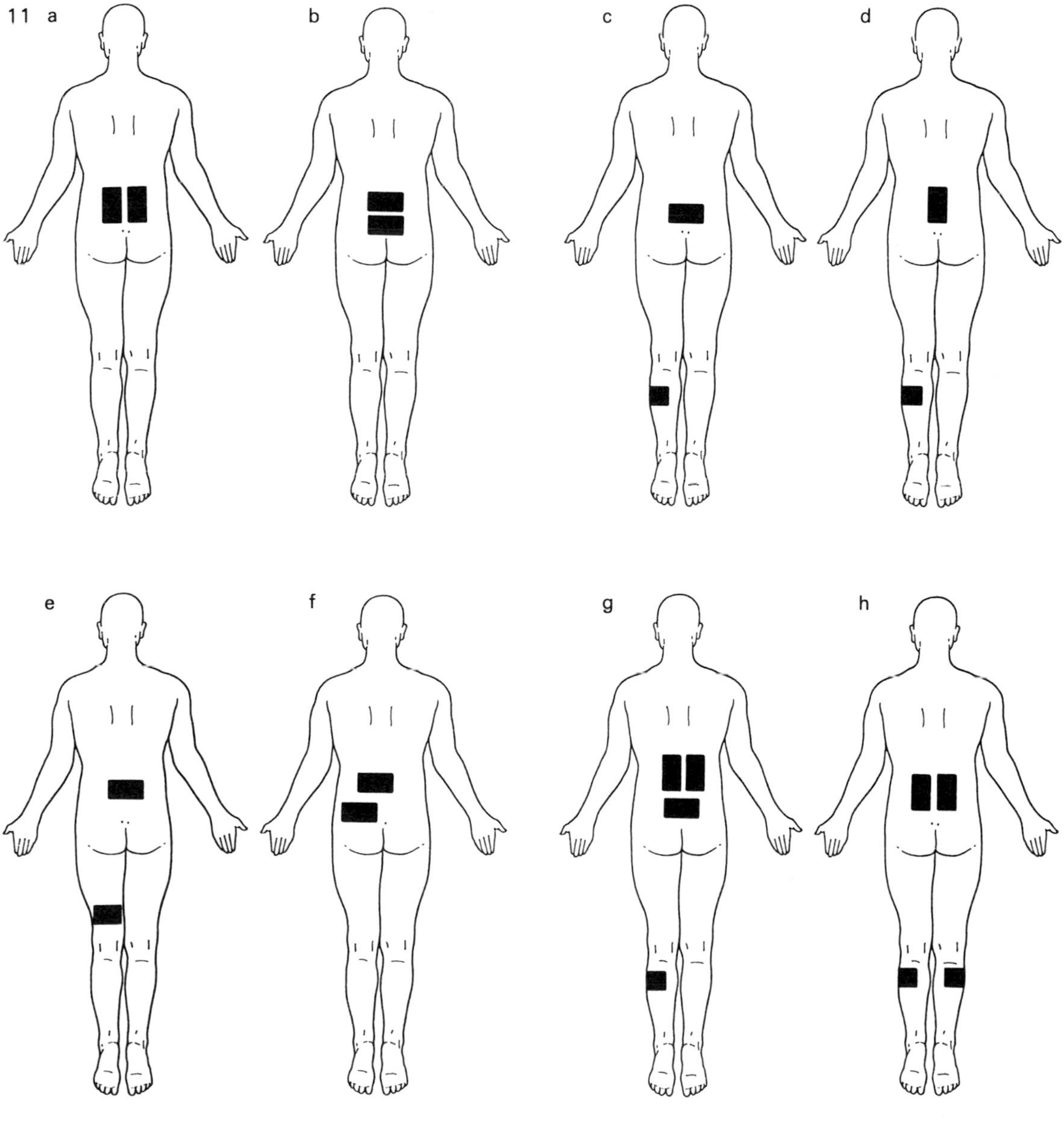

1. inappropriate patient selection, e.g. an hysterical patient, or an unreliable patient;
2. inappropriate placement of electrodes, e.g. over anaesthetic areas;
3. inadequate coverage or too much electroconductive gel on the pad;
4. inadequate securing of electrodes;
5. failure to explore different placements of electrodes in consecutive manner or alternative electrode sizes;
6. failure to explore various parameters of stimulation comprehensively and sequentially;
7. application of flimsy cables that break easily;
8. the use of flat batteries;
9. poor battery connection of the wires with the machine;
10. failure to replace the carbon silicon electrode pads when life of the original pad has expired;
11. failure to try a dual output machine (see below);
12. inadequate monitoring of results and documentation for comparative evaluation and follow-up;
13. inadequate treatment time.

It can be seen that poor results can be attributed to many different factors, ranging from patient treatment techniques to basic technical faults. These may seem trivial in isolation, but a combination of these problems are most frequently the cause of the TENS application being abandoned as unsuccessful. It is worth re-emphasising that poor results may be attributed to failure in considering TENS as part of a comprehensive rehabilitation programme.

Single and Dual Channel Units

So far only single channel TENS units have been described, i.e. a unit with a single amplitude parameter and one pair of electrodes. In most cases where one site of pain is identified, a single channel is adequate; the rationale of treatment must include ease of application and operation and cost effectiveness. Why complicate the situation with a dual channel machine (which is more expensive) if a single unit is effective in providing adequate pain relief? Indications for use of a dual channel unit are when two sites of pain need to be treated or the pain is widespread and a single unit is not sufficient, e.g. a patient suffering with back and leg pain may find that a single channel unit will only relieve one pain, in either his leg or back, but not in both depending on where the pads are placed (Fig. 10.4, 11c and d. In this case a dual output machine would enable back and leg pain to be treated to maximal effect (Fig. 10.4, 11g and h.

Criteria for the Selection of Machines

As already discussed the parameters vary little between manufacturers, so the following suggestions must act as a guide to the physiotherapist enabling selection of the machine which best suits her needs. Obviously, the ultimate choice is a balance between what the machine offers in relation to its cost. The following features are useful to consider when making a selection:

1. a small compact size;
2. a robust casing;
3. a functional low profile clip;
4. dials that are easy to operate with a moderate turning resistance to avoid accidental knocking and a consequent sudden increase in current;
5. a unit with a single amplitude output socket with bifurcated lead wires;
6. a variety of electrode sizes and types;
7. robust leads;
8. a lightweight unit;
9. a good back-up service and maintenance facility;
10. a choice of dual or single channel units (good to have both!);

Other features to consider are:

11. a variable pulse width;
12. a burst or pulsed mode facility.

Other machines for specialist use are the obstetric TENS units (see Chapter 18, p. 294), which have been modified to meet the needs of acute spasmodic pain and are based on a different principle.

ASSESSMENT, MONITORING AND EVALUATION

Successful treatment will depend on an accurate assessment of the patient, and whether that patient is a suitable candidate for TENS (see case histories, p. 107). All patients with pain must be thoroughly examined. There is a great temptation to omit conventional assessments with chronic pain patients on the grounds that they have been referred for the 'treatment of pain'. There may be many contributing factors associated with the pain and these must be identified. In some cases, however, an effective objective examination is almost impossible and a subjective and functional assessment is the only baseline that can be obtained. The author uses the pain charts illustrated in Figs 10.5 and 10.6. A quantitative analysis using a 10 cm horizontal visual analogue scale (VAS) (see Chapter 2, p. 15) and a behavioural analysis (Fig. 10.6) of pain provide a baseline of information which can be compared with subsequent measures following treatment by TENS. For example, a patient with a brachial plexus lesion has intense shooting pain. Following TENS the frequency of the spasms may be reduced from 10 every 5 min to once every hour. But the background burning pain that frequently exists may remain unchanged and therefore the patient's score on the VAS remains unchanged.

It is the evaluation of both the behavioural and quantitative analysis of pain which assists in the management of TENS, together with other objective signs from the original examination. The chart of the VAS allows a score to be taken before and after stimulation. It is important that records are

Name:	**Medical record number:**	**Date:** . . . .

Date: . . . .

Before stimulation

No pain   Maximum pain

After stimulation

No pain   Maximum pain

Date: . . . .

Before stimulation

No pain   Maximum pain

After stimulation

No pain   Maximum pain

Date: . . . .

Before stimulation

No pain   Maximum pain

After stimulation

No pain   Maximum pain

Date: . . . .

Before stimulation

No pain   Maximum pain

After stimulation

No pain   Maximum pain

Date: . . . .

Before stimulation

No pain   Maximum pain

After stimulation

No pain   Maximum pain

Date: . . . .

Before stimulation

No pain   Maximum pain

After stimulation

No pain   Maximum pain

Date: . . . .

Before stimulation

No pain   Maximum pain

After stimulation

No pain   Maximum pain

Fig. 10.5 Visual analogue scale chart. On a full-sized VAS chart the scale measures 10 cm in length. This enables the physiotherapist to obtain accurate data of the patient's pain after each treatment session.

```
PAIN

Onset

Increasing/static/decreasing

Nature

Distribution

Frequency of pain in one day

Daily pattern

Aggravates

Eases

Drugs

Sleep disturbance

                        COMMENTS
```

Fig. 10.6 Pain behaviour chart.

kept for at least 1 week's trial, as very often pain relief is not immediate due to one of the reasons mentioned on p. 100. A data and body chart (Figs. 10.7 and 10.8) record all relevant information regarding the parameters used, type of machine and length of treatment time. The body chart provides a quick way of recording electrode positions, which can be numbered and then recorded in the data chart; thus, on any one treatment session an immediate comparison can be made between the parameters used, the position of electrodes and length of treatment time with the VAS and pain behaviour. The comments column allows information regarding drug intake to be recorded. Frequently large doses of analgesics are taken and a reduction in dose may be another indicator to successful treatment with TENS.

Many people have expressed a disappointment in the less dramatic effect of TENS. All too often the chronic pain patient comes in looking for the 'cure', anticipating immediate relief with TENS. Objectives must be clearly set prior to treatment. It must be explained to the patient that TENS may only reduce the pain at first and not obliterate it, and that the overall effect may only be to allow the discontinuation of all analgesics, which in some cases may be narcotic, and if this goal alone is achieved some success of treatment must be claimed. This attitude results in different goals being set for different conditions, e.g. a patient with an 11 year history of back pain is not going to have the same outcome as a patient with post-herpetic neuralgia with single root involvement.

Above all, the patient's expectations must be rationalised but without damping their hope, which may already be at its lowest level. The need to encourage and motivate the chronic pain patient is an extremely important facet of treatment and the need to gain the patient's confidence is vital. TENS can provide an excellent tool in the total management of these patients who, once pain is relieved to some degree, are encouraged to participate in their own treatment.

DURATION OF TREATMENT

This is one of the most frequent reasons for poor or unsustained pain relief with TENS. Work has shown that TENS can have a cumulative effect (Sjölund and Ericksson, 1979). Certainly, the need for prolonged periods of stimulation are compatible with the evidence of the profound peripheral and central effects chronic pain has had on the central nervous system. On the basis of a comprehensive rehabilitation programme once pain has been relieved, normal functional stimulation must be fed back into the spinal cord so that abnormal central patterns can be replaced by more normal ones. Exact recommendations are impossible to make as each patient varies considerably, but the following provides a helpful baseline from which to work:

1. Use continuous stimulation for a minimum of 8 h/day.

Date	Tens Make & Number	Time on	Time off	Total h Stimulation	Electrode Position/ Size	Most Effective Position			Comments
						Output	Frequency	Pulse Width	

Fig. 10.7 TENS data chart.

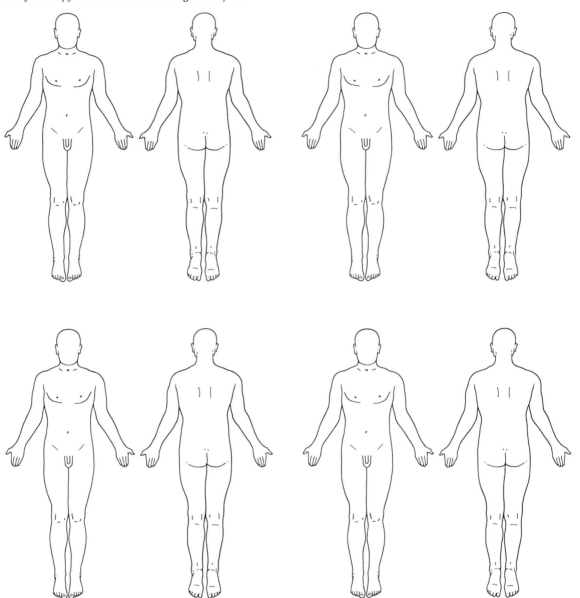

Fig. 10.8 Body chart for the physiotherapist to complete with the electrode positions used. Examples of the completed chart are shown in Fig. 10.4.

2. Continue experimenting with TENS for at least 1 week before abandoning it as unsuccessful.
3. Continue a regime of 8 h for 3 weeks and then reduce the treatment gradually if it is helping.
4. If less than 4 h of TENS stimulation a day results in returned or increased pain, return to 4 h a day for a further week or so.
5. Continue to reduce the treatment until no stimulation is required.

6. Keep the TENS machine for a further 2–3 months before returning it to the department.
7. Stimulation for 24 h may be necessary in some cases.
8. Complete cessation may not be possible, and the patient may require 2 h TENS stimulation in the morning or at night.
9. In some cases, such as amputation, the need to wear a prosthesis is obvious not only for function but also to restore afferent stimulation to the stump. In such a case TENS may be used for the required 8 h, either overnight (when pain is often the most intense) or in the evening when the prosthesis is removed.

The author is aware that not all physiotherapists are working in the 'ideal' environment and shortage of machines results in more patients being treated at the sacrifice of length of treatment. One might argue that this is not going to promote the need for more machines. Evidence of successful treatments on a regular basis will prove the need for more machines.

THE USE OF TENS IN SPECIFIC CONDITIONS

TENS can be used in acute and chronic pain; the most common use in acute pain is in the management of labour pain (see Chapter 18, p.294). Chronic pain may present most commonly in the following cases (Frampton, 1982):

1. chronic back, leg or neck pain (see case history 1);
2. post-herpetic neuralgia;
3. brachial plexus lesions (see case history 2);
4. peripheral nerve injuries (PNI) including painful neuromas and Sudeck's atrophy;
5. stump and/or a phantom limb pain (see case history 3);
6. trigeminal neuralgia.

Some case histories illustrating the use of TENS in specific conditions, e.g. low back pain, brachial plexus lesions and stump pain/phantom limb pain, are given below.

Case History 1

In August 1982 a 34-year-old lady developed acute low back pain. The previous day, she had carried her sick child around 'on her hip' all day. She was treated initially with bedrest for 3 months, with only marginal improvement in her pain. She subsequently received two epidural injections weekly for 8 weeks. Over the next 6 months, she developed leg pain and was referred for physiotherapy. She received traction and mobilisation and finally was put in a plaster of Paris jacket.

In May 1983 EMGs showed denervation in the L4–L5 roots, and the patient proceeded to a laminectomy of L4–L5. Relief of pain lasted 6 weeks and then returned as intensely as before. One year later a spinal fusion was performed and 2 months later the pain was significantly worse. In 1985, the patient was referred to a pain clinic and from there to an in-patient rehabilitation ward for assessment and management of her pain.

The lady was distressed and depressed, she showed little faith in the prospect of any further successful treatment. She complained of a constant dull ache in her back, with intermittent shooting pain down her right leg. Pain was present at night and was increased when standing for longer than 15 min, sitting for 10 min and sustained flexion, and walking 18.2 m (20 yd). Pain was relieved by lying flat and painkillers (Diconal × 6 a day; Distalgesic × 8–10). She was stiff and painful in the morning and the pain gradually increased towards the end of the day. Movement was restricted in all directions and she had a bilateral 40° straight leg raise. Her abdominal and back extensor muscles were very weak.

On the visual analogue scale she scored 9 out of 10. She was counselled and encouraged to make a fresh start on treatment. On the following day, a single channel TENS unit was tried with large pads, size 2 × 4. As she had both back and L5 root pain into her leg, position 11*d* (Fig. 10.4) was selected. After 2 h, she had some relief from leg pain and noticed an increase in walking distance. Following 1 week of 8 h TENS a day, she had 50% reduction in her leg pain and was walking 91 m (100 yd). Also, in this first week, she had commenced gentle mobilisation in the hydrotherapy pool, and Maitland mobilisations to L3–L4 proximal to the fused segment, which was painful. As her back pain continued to be a problem, a dual channel unit was selected in the second week and position 11*g* (Fig. 10.4) was tried, and this successfully relieved her back pain.

Mobilisation and monitoring of all activities was continued, and on discharging her 3 weeks following admission, her VAS was 3 out of 10 for back and leg pain. She was walking 273 m (300 yd) and could sit up for 1–2 h, and she had completely stopped all analgesics and felt much happier and 'back to normal'.

At a 3 year follow-up she was still using TENS 8 h a day; this may seem a limited successful result. However, the patient was very happy not to be taking analgesics; she was leading a normal and full life, and also had a part-time job.

Case History 2

In October 1982, an 18-year-old man was involved in a motorcycle accident while travelling at 66 km/h (40 mph). The front wheel of the motorcycle hit a hole in the road and he came off the machine and hit a telegraph pole. The patient sustained a right brachial plexus lesion (BPL) involving roots of C5–T1. C5 and C6 were diagnosed as post-ganglionic lesions and C7 and C8–T1 as preganglionic lesions. Two weeks later he developed a constant, severe, burning pain in all his fingers and the ulnar border of his forearm, with sharp shooting pain in his middle, ring and little fingers occurring every 5–10 min. Although the pain varied little, he found that distraction was the only means of providing some degree of relief, as drugs had no effect.

His life was affected dramatically by the pain, preventing him from concentrating on any activity as he had to stop to grip the arm with every stab of pain. He had been fitted with a flail arm splint (Frampton, 1984a and b) to restore some function to his paralysed arm but was unable to use it because of the pain.

Following sensory assessment, he was found to have sensation to light touch proximal to the elbow, but no sensation below that level and his VAS score was 10 (the maximum). It was decided to apply TENS and position 4*b* in Fig. 10.4 was used. After only a few hours' stimulation, he had obtained good relief of pain. He was then encouraged to use his flail arm splint to restore some afferent input from the deafferented side. He was discharged 3 weeks later using TENS 8 h a day. Although he still had the constant burning pain, the frequency of the stab of pain was reduced to once daily and his VAS score dropped to 2. After 2 months he was using TENS one morning per week and had ceased using it altogether at the 7 month follow-up. When seen 2 years after his accident, he was not using TENS and was working full-time as a television engineer.

Case History 3

A 72-year-old diabetic man had undergone a below knee amputation for gangrenous toes. Preoperatively he had complained of severe continuous pain which was almost intolerable. It had been present on waking and had increased during the day, reaching its peak at night, as a result of which he had difficulty sleeping. Although the pain in his phantom foot decreased over the first postoperative month, as expected, he still had sufficient pain to interfere with mobilisation. Therefore TENS was applied in position 6e in Fig. 10.4. The patient used the machine for 8 h per day and obtained almost immediate relief. After 2–3 weeks, the pain was almost gone and he progressed to wearing his prosthesis all day and only using the TENS machine at night. Eventually he no longer needed to use TENS.

In the category of peripheral nerve injuries (PNI) one may include ulnar neuritis, median nerve neuritis following carpal tunnel decompression or painful digital neuromas (Frampton, 1985b). The most common symptom of a painful PNI is one of hyperpathia. This abnormal painful response of the patient to light touch makes normal functional use impossible. TENS must be applied to affect the nerve but allow the hand to remain free to participate in a subsequent desensitisation programme. In such cases, combination treatments may be necessary (Withrington and Wynn Parry, 1984). A guide to electrode placements for different conditions and alternative placements can be seen in Fig. 10.4.

Other conditions, such as osteoarthritis, rheumatoid arthritis, strains and sprains and other sports related injuries are not discussed here. There is no doubt that TENS is widely used as a pain-relieving modality on painful joints prior to or in conjunction with other treatments. Other modalities are of course available and may be more appropriate to treat joint conditions as TENS is most effective in treating conditions of a neurogenic origin. However, if TENS is to be used to treat joint conditions shorter periods of stimulation would in these cases be indicated.

No reference to acupuncture or the use of TENS on acupuncture points has been made. Although the author uses the Western approach to acupuncture, it is in accordance with myofascial or trigger point methods. However, it is interesting to note that frequent successful treatments have been achieved using TENS by placing electrodes over trigger points (Frampton, 1985a).

CONTRAINDICATIONS TO THE USE OF TENS

Manufacturers quote several contraindications which are listed here:

1. TENS should not be used to treat patients with pacemakers.
2. TENS should not be used to treat patients with known myocardial disease and arrhythmias (except on the recommendation of a physician following evaluation of the patient).
3. TENS should not be used in the area of the carotid sinus and mouth.
4. TENS appliances should be kept out of the reach of children.
5. TENS should not be used while operating vehicles or potentially hazardous equipment.
6. Application or removal of electrodes should always be carried out with the appliance switched off.
7. Electrodes must not be placed over broken skin sites.
8. One side-effect can be a skin irritation or a rash developing beneath or around the electrode in prolonged application. Care of the skin and electrodes is therefore important. It is necessary to wash the area of application and the electrodes following stimulation, in the first case to prevent skin rash, and also to prevent the rubber perishing.
9. TENS must not be used in/over anaesthetic areas of skin.
10. Some manufacturers state that the safety of TENS during pregnancy has not been established. However, there has been no research, so far, to support this claim. Obstetric physiotherapists feel strongly that its use during pregnancy and lactation is preferable to strong analgesic medication. It appears manufacturers include this to avoid litigation. As a result it is advisable to avoid placing the electrodes directly on the abdomen, but there is no reason why TENS should not be used for the treatment of limb, back or neck pain (Mannheimer and Lampe, 1984). The use of TENS in pregnancy is an area of research that needs urgent investigation.

Common sense must prevail when considering these contraindications, as many are for the purposes of insurance. For example, when driving a car it is obvious that if the driver knocks the dials the sudden jolt may cause him to have an accident. Apart from cases of skin irritation and allergic responses there are few reasons why anyone may not use TENS. The allergic response to the tape and gel can be overcome by the use of hypoallergic self-adhesive pads. It is important to look out for the chronic pain patient who is unobserved at home and returns to the outpatient department with what appears to be an allergic response under the pad itself. Frequently, this can be caused by a current that was too intense and the rash is an electric burn. Patients often deny this, and the only remedy is close supervision with the physiotherapist altering the dials. More often the patient presents with a white unaffected skin area under the pad and a red inflamed area around it. This is the common allergic response from tape.

RESEARCH AND FOLLOW-UP

As has already been outlined in the earlier sections, controlled double blind trials and reliable evaluations of parameters are not easy (Wynn Parry, 1981). The author has based her method of treatments on retrospective studies over the last 9 years of patients whose records have been maintained through follow-up (Frampton, 1982). Following discharge all patients are reviewed at the pain clinic and a behavioural and quantitative analysis of their pain is taken. Each patient has their own card with this updated information. All the cards are filed together and colour coded according to their diagnosis. A separate card system for each TENS machine is kept so that at any time one can see at a glance where any particular machine is and this can be cross referenced with the patients' cards. This system has been in operation at the hospital where the author worked since the introduction of TENS in 1976, and although initially time-consuming is certainly time-saving in the long run, and allows an on going monitoring system for evaluation.

TENS is just another tool for the physiotherapist in the range of treatments for patient care. Properly used and evaluated, it provides one of the cheapest electrical modalities available. However, on occasions it is prescribed like a 'tablet' and patients are told to 'go away and try it for a while' without proper instruction. If this is the case, TENS will fail to be considered as part of a complete rehabilitation programme and a valuable piece of equipment will be lost to the chronic pain sufferer.

ACKNOWLEDGEMENTS

The author would like to thank Dr C. B. Wynn Parry for his untiring inspiration and encouragement, Dr Robin Withrington for his invaluable help in preparing this chapter, the physiotherapy staff of the Royal National Orthopaedic Hospital for their enthusiasm and support, and finally Mrs A. J. Frampton for her secretarial assistance.

REFERENCES

Frampton V.M. (1982). Pain control with the aid of transcutaneous nerve stimulation. *Physiotherapy*; **68 (3)**: 77–81.

Frampton V.M. (1984a). Management of brachial plexus lesions. *Physiotherapy*; **70(10)**: 388–92.

Frampton V.M. (1984b). Treatment note: brachial plexus flail arm splint. *Physiotherapy*; **70(11)**: 428.

Frampton V.M. (1985a). A pilot study to evaluate myofascial or trigger point electro-acupuncture in the treatment of neck and back pain. *Physiotherapy*; **71(1)**: 5–7.

Frampton V.M. (1985b). Conservative management of pain in the upper limb amputee. *Brit. Assoc. Hand Therapists Newsletter*; **2**: 17–21.

Loeser J.D., Ward A.A. (1967). Some effects of de-afferentation on neurons of the cat spinal cord. *Arch. Neurol;* **17**: 629–36.

Mannheimer J.S., Lampe G.N. (1984). *Clinical Transcutaneous Electrical Nerve Stimulation.* Philadelphia: F.A. Davis.

Melzack R., Wall P.D. (1965). Pain mechanism: a new theory. *Science;* **150**: 971–8.

Melzack R., Wall P.D. (1982). *The Challenge of Pain.* London: Penguin Books.

Sjölund B., Ericksson M.B.E. (1979). The influence of naloxone on analgesia produced by peripheral conditioning stimulation. *Brain Res;* **173**: 295–301.

Wall P.D., Devor S. (1981). The effect of peripheral nerve injury on dorsal root potentials and on transmission of afferent signals into the spinal cord. *Brain Res;* **209**: 95–111.

Wall P.D., Gutnik M. (1974). Properties of afferent nerve impulses originating from a neuroma. *Nature;* **248**: 740.

Withrington R.H., Wynn Parry C.B. (1984). The management of painful peripheral nerve disorders. *J. Hand Surg;* **9B(1)**: 24–8.

Wynn Parry C.B. (1980). Pain in avulsion lesions of the brachial plexus. *Pain;* **9**: 41–53.

Wynn Parry C.B. (1981). *Rehabilitation of the Hand.* London: Butterworths.

FURTHER READING

Hannington-Kiff J. (1974). Intravenous regional sympathetic block with guanethidine. *Lancet;* **1**: 1019–20.

Loh L., Nathan P.W. (1978). Painful peripheral states and sympathetic blocks. *J. Neurol., Neurosurg., Psychiat;* **41**: 664–71.

Noordenbos W., Wall P.D. (1981). Nerve resection fails to relieve chronic peripheral nerve pain. *J. Neurol. Neurosurg. Psychiat;* **44**: 1068–73.

Ochoa J., Torebjörk H.E. (1981). Paraesthesiae from ectopic impulse generation in human sensory nerves. *Brain;* **103**: 835–53.

Rasminsky M. *et al.* (1978). Conduction of nervous impulses in spinal roots and peripheral nerves of dystrophic mice. *Brain Res;* **143**: 71–9.

Symposium on Pain (1979). *Int. Rehab. Med. J;* **1(3)**: 98–116.

Wall P.D., Devor S. (1978). Physiology of sensation after peripheral nerve injury regeneration and neuroma formation. In *Physiology and Pathology of Axons* (Waxman S.G., ed.). New York: Raven Press.

Wall P.D., Gutnik M. (1974). Ongoing activity in peripheral nerves. The physiology and pharmacology of impulses originating from a neuroma. *Exper. Neurol;* **43**: 580–93.

Wallin G., Torebjörk E., Hallin R.G. (1976). In *Sensory Functions of the Skin* (Zotterman Y., ed.). Oxford: Pergamon Press.

Woolf C.J. (1984). Transcutaneous and implanted nerve stimulation. In *Textbook of Pain* (Wall P.D., Melzack R., eds) pp. 679–90. Edinburgh: Churchill Livingstone.

Wynn Parry C.B. (1981). Recent trends in surgery of peripheral nerves. *Int. Rehab. Med. J;* **3(4)**: 169–73.

Wynn Parry C.B., Withrington R.H. (1984). The management of painful peripheral nerve disorders. In *Textbook of Pain* (Wall P.D., Melzack R., eds) pp. 395–401. Edinburgh: Churchill Livingstone.

Chapter 11

Shortwave Diathermy, Microwave, Ultrasound and Interferential Therapy

JOHN L. LOW

SHORTWAVE DIATHERMY, MICROWAVE AND ULTRASOUND

INTRODUCTION

There is sometimes an element of mystery about the application of therapeutic high frequency energy. The relief of pain, occasionally dramatic, after the application of ultrasonic energy, or the gentle comforting heat of shortwave diathermy produced from electrodes which do not become hot and do not touch the skin may seem rather magical. It may, at least, provoke some feelings of awe for the technology. How far such beliefs are appropriate for the patient can be a matter of opinion, but they are totally and absolutely inappropriate for the physiotherapist applying the treatment, a point that has been emphasised by Scott (1957).

High frequency energy is completely comprehensible and behaves in a predictable way. Its effects, such as the relief of pain, can be explained rationally. In the past, electric and magnetic phenomena have been studied from many different standpoints which led to different ways of expressing the same concepts. Thus, radiations may be described in terms of either wave or particle motion. Furthermore, energy released in the tissues by the passage of electric currents may be confused with the energy liberated due to electromagnetic radiations.

ELECTRIC AND MAGNETIC FIELDS

The electric force exerted between protons and electrons leads to the presence of an electric field between objects and this is measured in volts; the motion of electric charges described as an electric current is measured as the rate of flow in amperes. This motion of charges, be they electrons orbiting atomic nuclei, currents in a wire, or ions moving in fluid, causes a *magnetic force* (magnetic field) to act at right angles to the direction of motion of the charges.

Steady continuous currents have been used therapeutically for many years, e.g. in the treatment of non-united fractures, where it is considered as effective as bone grafting and safer (Brighton *et al.*, 1981) also for iontophoresis. Magnetism has also been used as a treatment for various conditions with rather less justification since magnetic forces pass easily through the tissues and there are no evident effects. High intensity magnetic fields do not seem to damage animal or human tissues, and, indeed, there is evidence that some birds, at least, can utilise the vertical component of the earth's magnetic field as a navigational aid. It follows that there must be some physiological mechanism for recognising these extremely weak magnetic fields, and this is currently being investigated. There have also been suggestions, and some supporting evidence, that man has a similar capability.

It must be recognised that the concept of a *static* magnetic, or *steady* electric field applied to the tissues is rather too simple. Since there is a continuous movement of particles all the time in the tissues, e.g. in blood flow, any magnetic or electric field is bound to interact with moving charges leading to complex effects.

Alternating Currents

If the direction of the electric field is repeatedly reversed a current, which varies in direction and intensity, results and at low rates of reversal is called a *low frequency alternating current*. Such currents produce similar varying magnetic fields. The number of such cycles in each second is referred to as so many *cycles per second*, but more properly as *Hertz* (Hz). Thus 1000 cycles/s is 1 kilohertz (kHz) and 1 000 000 cycles/s is 1 megahertz (MHz).

High Frequency Currents

At higher frequencies, over 500 000 Hz or 0.5 MHz, such currents are usually called *oscillating currents*, but may also be referred to as alternating (Fig. 11.1).

Electromagnetic Phenomena

Constantly varying electric and magnetic fields generate an electromagnetic disturbance which propagates energy through space and is recognised as *radiowaves* and at higher frequencies as *radiation*. All electromagnetic energy travels in space at a constant velocity of 300 000 000 m/s (3×10^8 m/s) which is the product of the frequency and the wavelength

$$V = f \times \lambda$$

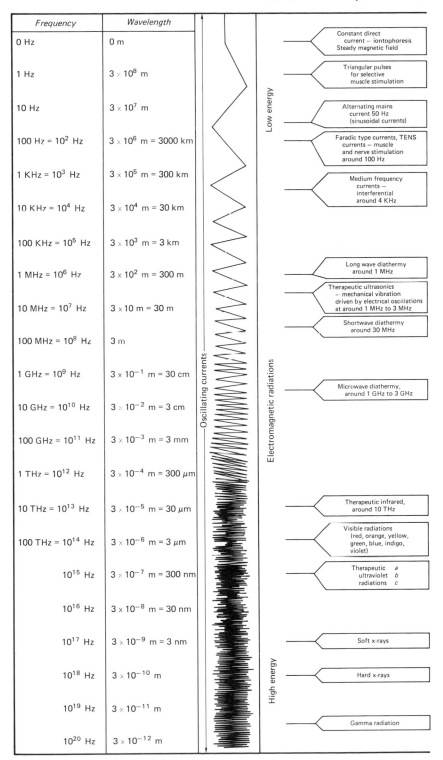

Frequency	Wavelength		
0 Hz	0 m		Constant direct current – iontophoresis Steady magnetic field
1 Hz	3×10^8 m		Triangular pulses for selective muscle stimulation
10 Hz	3×10^7 m		Alternating mains current 50 Hz (sinusoidal currents)
100 Hz = 10^2 Hz	3×10^6 m = 3000 km		Faradic type currents, TENS currents – muscle and nerve stimulation around 100 Hz
1 KHz = 10^3 Hz	3×10^5 m = 300 km		Medium frequency currents – interferential around 4 KHz
10 KHz = 10^4 Hz	3×10^4 m = 30 km		
100 KHz = 10^5 Hz	3×10^3 m = 3 km		
1 MHz = 10^6 Hz	3×10^2 m = 300 m		Long wave diathermy around 1 MHz
10 MHz = 10^7 Hz	3×10 m = 30 m		Therapeutic ultrasonics – mechanical vibration driven by electrical oscillations at around 1 MHz to 3 MHz
100 MHz = 10^8 Hz	3 m		Shortwave diathermy around 30 MHz
1 GHz = 10^9 Hz	3×10^{-1} m = 30 cm		Microwave diathermy, around 1 GHz to 3 GHz
10 GHz = 10^{10} Hz	3×10^{-2} m = 3 cm		
100 GHz = 10^{11} Hz	3×10^{-3} m = 3 mm		
1 THz = 10^{12} Hz	3×10^{-4} m = 300 μm		
10 THz = 10^{13} Hz	3×10^{-5} m = 30 μm		Therapeutic infrared, around 10 THz
100 THz = 10^{14} Hz	3×10^{-6} m = 3 μm		Visible radiations (red, orange, yellow, green, blue, indigo, violet)
10^{15} Hz	3×10^{-7} m = 300 nm		Therapeutic ultraviolet radiations a b c
10^{16} Hz	3×10^{-8} m = 30 nm		
10^{17} Hz	3×10^{-9} m = 3 nm		Soft x-rays
10^{18} Hz	3×10^{-10} m		Hard x-rays
10^{19} Hz	3×10^{-11} m		
10^{20} Hz	3×10^{-12} m		Gamma radiation

Fig. 11.1 Electric and magnetic fields—electromagnetic radiations. kHz = kilohertz; MHz = megahertz; GHz = gigahertz; THz = terahertz.

where V = velocity, f = frequency and λ = wavelength. Such radiations differ only in their frequency and wavelength, thus it is only necessary to describe the radiation in terms of either. In the past, many radiations were described by their wavelength, e.g. long, medium and shortwave radio emission, 12.5 cm *microwave*. Nowadays frequencies are often used, and these relationships are shown in diagrammatically form in Fig. 11.1. The therapeutic modalities are also indicated here and are discussed below.

THERAPEUTIC MODALITIES

Longwave Diathermy

At oscillating frequencies of a 1 000 000 cycles/s (1 MHz) the electric and magnetic effects can be recognised as electromagnetic radiations, i.e. *radiowaves*. When such currents are passed through the body tissues, via pads wetted with salt water, they cause heating in the pathway of the current. These were quite extensively used to give heat treatments in physiotherapy about 40 years ago, and are known as *longwave diathermy*. Diathermy was a term coined in 1907 from the Greek meaning 'through heating'.

Ultrasound

If oscillating currents are used to produce mechanical oscillation these ultrasonic vibrations can be passed into the tissues to produce heating and other effects. Ultrasonic treatments are given at various frequencies between 0.5 MHz and 3 MHz.

Shortwave Diathermy

Higher frequencies, around 30 MHz, have the advantage that they can be applied to the tissues across an air gap without the need for wet pads. By international agreement 27.12 MHz has been designated, with other frequencies (13.56 and 40.68 MHz), for medical and scientific use; virtually all shortwave diathermy machines are manufactured to operate at the 27.12 MHz frequency. When the body tissues are included in the output circuit of these shortwave diathermy machines heat produced as energy is absorbed by the tissues.

Microwave

At still higher frequencies microwave radiations (*radar*) can be used to heat the tissues. These radiations, often at a frequency of 2450 MHz, are 'beamed' into the tissues and cause heating as they are absorbed.

Heating

Figure 11.1 indicates the relationship of modalities in terms of their frequency and wavelength. They convey energy to the tissues in different ways. Thus when electromagnetic radiations like microwave radiations, or high frequency currents like shortwave diathermy, or mechanical waves of compression and rarefaction, such as ultrasound, are passed through the tissues energy is absorbed in the tissues. The particles that make up all matter are in constant irregular motion which is recognised as heat, the greater the motion the higher the temperature. Thus all the modalities lead to heating (see Fig. 11.3a, p. 119). Of course it is only recognised as such by patients if it causes the temperature of the tissues to rise sufficiently to be perceived as heat. Even the most trivial absorption of energy must lead to some temporary local increase in temperature, but this may not be felt. Such low intensity treatments are often not regarded as 'heat' treatments. Low intensity shortwave diathermy treatments are sometimes called 'athermic' or 'subthermic', obviously a somewhat inaccurate term. Similarly, because ultrasonic therapy often gives rise to no detectable heating it is often not regarded as a heat treatment. However some authorities emphasise the significance of ultrasonic heating by calling these treatments *ultrasonic diathermy* (see e.g. Lehmann and de Lateur, 1982).

Since all these modalities can produce significant detectable heating in the tissues, it may be asked whether there is anything to choose between them, or for that matter between them and any other form of tissue heating, such as a hot water bottle.

Skin is an organ concerned with the control of body temperature, and therefore heat applied to the surface of the skin, either as radiation or by conduction, will have only a limited effect on the deeper tissues. As the skin surface is heated vasodilatation occurs rapidly dissipating the local heat; furthermore, the subcutaneous fat acts as efficient thermal insulation preventing much heat passing to the underlying tissues by conduction. This is not to say that there will be no transfer of heat to the deeper tissues but that the skin can exert thermal control over heating methods like infrared or conduction heating due to hot water or hot air, the natural sources of heat. On the other hand, shortwave, microwave and ultrasonic diathermy are able to generate heat throughout the tissues thus, in a sense, being able to bypass the thermal barrier of the skin. Certainly, in most therapeutic situations using shortwave diathermy or microwave the skin is made hotter than the subcutaneous tissues, but deeply placed tissues are also directly heated in patterns which depend on the modality and the structure of the tissues; this is discussed later. Thus direct heating of the deeply placed tissues is similar to normal metabolic heating, heat being generated within the tissues, which is some justification for heating in this way.

117

EFFECTS OF THERAPEUTIC MODALITIES

The Penetration of Electromagnetic Radiations and Sonic Waves

When these radiations pass through the tissues energy is absorbed so that the transmitted energy decreases with distance. As the amount absorbed at any point depends upon the total energy at that point it follows that the decrease must be exponential (Fig. 11.2). The actual amount of energy absorbed depends on the nature of the tissues and the frequency of oscillation.

It is not possible to determine a point at which all the energy is absorbed, i.e. a point to which the modality penetrates, so it is usual to specify the *half value depth*. This is the depth at which half the initial energy has been absorbed. In the example in Fig. 11.2, the radiations penetrate to 3 cm before losing 50% of their energy, at 6 cm 25% remains and even at 12 cm over 6% of the original energy remains. This, of course, is an idealised example; in real tissues the penetration and absorption would be much more irregular.

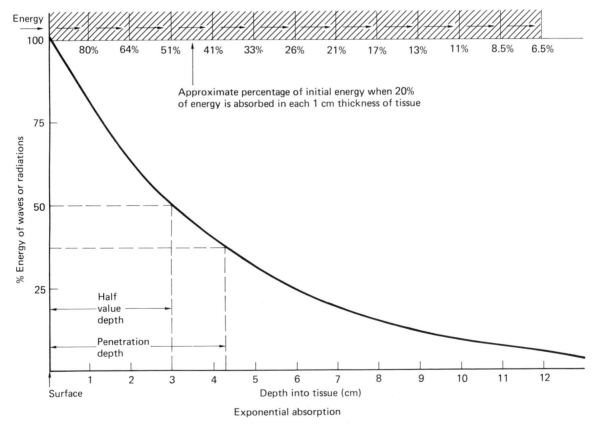

Fig. 11.2 The percentage of energy waves (radiations) absorbed by the tissues at different depths. Suppose 20% of energy is absorbed in each 1 cm of tissue, the approximate percentage of initial energy at each 1 cm layer is given.

The same concept is sometimes expressed as the *penetration depth*, the distance travelled until the energy is reduced to 37% of the original. At twice the penetration depth the energy is reduced to 37% of 37%, i.e. 14% of the original energy and so on.

$$\text{Penetration depth} = \text{Half value depth} \times 1.44$$

and

$$\text{Half value depth} = \frac{\text{Penetration depth}}{1.44}$$

Other Effects

At ultrasonic, shortwave and microwave frequencies it is claimed that almost all the therapeutic effects can be accounted for by the heating (Fig. 11.3a). For many years this view has been disputed, and effects such as the reduction of inflammation and acceleration of healing were claimed to be specific effects; this has led to the interest in *pulsed diathermy*.

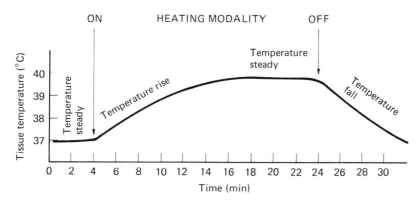

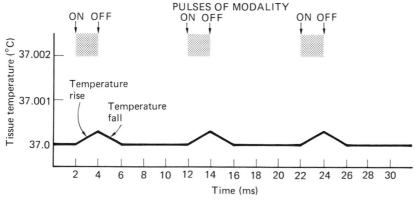

Fig. 11.3 *a* = A representation of tissue heating. As heat is added the local temperature rises, but at the same time the body's thermoregulatory system reacts removing heat until a steady state is reached at a new, higher temperature. (The temperature changes shown in these figures are not based on actual measurements.) *b* = A representation of tissue heating due to a pulsed modality. The small, negligible temperature rise due to each pulse is dissipated during the pulse intervals. (Note the different time and temperature scales of Fig. 11.3*a*).

Pulsed Diathermy

Ultrasonics, shortwave, and microwave can all be pulsed, that is delivered to the tissues as a series of discrete 'bursts' of energy. The time between pulses allows the heat generated by each pulse of energy to be dispersed thus there is no significant overall heating, the effects being due to 'mechanical' or 'biological' changes. In a way this is simply a low frequency cycle superimposed on the diathermy frequency. The idea is shown diagrammatically in Fig. 11.3*b*. Various pulse lengths and pulse frequencies are used and will be described in more detail on p. 149. There is considerable evidence supporting the efficacy of pulsing these modalities (see e.g. Bentall and Eckstein, 1975; Dyson and Suckling, 1978). It must be recognised, however, that heat is still generated, albeit at very low intensities, so that some effects could still be accounted for by heating.

The Use of Heat in Pain Control

Heat seems to have been used for the relief of pain throughout history and is used at present in a large number of painful conditions, especially musculo-skeletal conditions. This is almost entirely on an empirical basis as there is surprisingly little experimental evidence on the matter. It has been shown that heating the body tissues can raise the pain threshold and a number of suggestions have been made about the mechanism involved (Lehmann *et al.*, 1958). These include the effect of heat on reducing muscle spasm, or in relieving local ischaemia which has sometimes been considered a cause of pain. A widely endorsed view is that the heat alters the sensory input to the nervous system diminishing pain sensations by means of the *gate control mechanism*. It can also be accounted for by the release of endorphins.

There is much evidence that pulsed shortwave or pulsed ultrasonics can accelerate resolution after injury (see e.g. Bentall and Eckstein, 1975; Dyson and Suckling, 1978; Goldin *et al.*, 1981). One suggested reason for this is the increased rate of phagocytosis that occurs on gentle agitation of the tissue fluid which increases the number of chance cell contacts (Evans, 1980). Hastening resolution would lead to earlier reduction of local oedema and hence to diminution of pain. It is also possible that the mild agitation of the tissue fluid particles encourages more rapid motion through cellular membranes and intercellular spaces, e.g. the capillary wall, thus lessening the mechanical distortion of the tissues which contributes to the pain (Fig. 11.7 p. 130) and see also the section on therapeutic effects of shortwave diathermy below).

SHORTWAVE DIATHERMY

Treatment due to the electric and magnetic fields at radio frequencies between 10 and 100 MHz is traditionally called 'shortwave' because these frequencies are in the shortwave radio band. The patient is placed in the circuit so that energy is released in the tissues by the oscillation of electric charges. The radiation generated by these machines is largely incidental. Virtually all therapeutic sources operate at 27.12 MHz and thus a wavelength of 11.0619 m.

Production of Shortwave Diathermy

High frequency current is generated by a circuit called the *oscillator circuit*, the dimensions of which are such as to allow electrons to oscillate at precisely 27.12 MHz. The part to be treated is included in a separate circuit, either between two electrodes or close to an induction coil, which must be tuned so that it has the same natural frequency as the oscillator circuit. Thus high frequency electrical energy is transferred to the tissues.

Effects of High Frequency Currents on the Tissues

Tissue molecules are influenced in three ways by a varying electric field. Inductothermy causes a varying induced electric field like that produced between the capacitor plates in the condenser field method (below). High frequency currents affect the tissues in the following ways:

1. *Ionic motion*. Masses of positive and negative ions in the tissues are accelerated under the influence of the electric field. As they move rapidly to and fro they collide with other particles and in this way electrical energy is converted to heat. The actual distance moved by each ion is very small at this frequency, more like a vibration, but it is sufficient to generate heat (Fig. 11.4*a*).
2. *Dipole rotation*. Molecules that have a relative positive charge at one end and negative charge at the other (e.g. water) and will orientate themselves appropriately in the field and thus rotate back and forth as the field alternates. The frictional forces generated between these polar molecules and others cause heating (Fig. 11.4*b*).
3. *Distortion of electron 'clouds'*. Molecules that are not polar have the paths of their orbiting electrons distorted by the electric field thus becoming temporarily polarised alternately in each direction. This causes some molecular movement and heating (Fig. 11.4*c*).

All three mechanisms lead to heating but (1) is likely to be the most efficient at converting electrical energy to heat and (3) the least efficient (Ward, 1980).

Application of Shortwave Diathermy

The electric field (electrostatic field) is applied either by rigid metal plates enclosed in plastic cases called *space plates, rigid electrodes* or *plate electrodes*; or

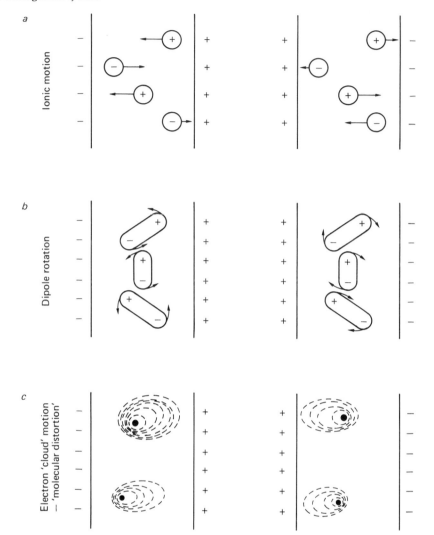

Fig. 11.4 The effects of oscillating high frequency electric fields on the molecules and ions in the tissues. *a*=Ionic motion—positive and negative ions move to and fro under the influence of an oscillating electric field. *b*=Dipole rotation—polar molecules rotate to and fro as the electric field oscillates. *c*=Electron 'cloud' motion (molecular distortion)—the paths of orbiting electrons are distorted first in one direction then in the other as the electric field oscillates.

by means of flexible metal sheets encased in thick rubber, called *flexible electrodes* or *malleable electrodes*. This is known as the *condenser field* method.

A cable or coil consists of a flexible tubular conductor insulated with thick rubber. When coiled around the part in a helical manner or coiled and laid flat on the skin surface, a so-called *pancake coil*, it generates an electromagnetic field through the tissues which induces eddy currents causing heating as already described. The coil also produces an electric field between the ends and adjacent turns which has been shown to play a major part in heat production. Such treatments are called *inductothermy*. Some machines have a drum-shaped electrode, sometimes called a *monode*, which contains a flat rigid coil and parallel capacitor enclosed in a plastic case. It produces an electromagnetic field like a small pancake coil.

In all these methods the electric field must not be concentrated when passing into the tissues so an air gap of a few centimetres is necessary between the metal electrode and the tissues. Air does not become heated by the electric field, similarly the plastic and rubber covers of the metal electrodes have little effect. The gap is usually maintained by felt pads for the malleable electrodes and several layers of towelling with the coil, but other suitable materials can be used.

Controlling and understanding the pattern of the electric field is central to the application of shortwave diathermy. The factors involved are summarised below and illustrated in Fig. 11.5.

1. The electrodes
   size
   shape
   distance from the skin
   distance from each other
   orientation to skin
2. The part being treated
   size
   shape
   nature of tissues
   arrangement of tissue layers

It is usually best to use electrodes a little larger than the part to be treated in order to give a more uniform field, also to use the widest spacing possible. Spacing is limited by the output of the machine, if the electrode–skin distance is greater than about 7 cm (2.5 in) the field is so dispersed that no significant heating can occur with most shortwave diathermy machines. Even relatively uniform shortwave fields cause more heating in the skin than elsewhere; this contributes to the safety of shortwave diathermy since the skin is temperature sensitive.

Of the other tissues, fat tends to be particularly heated with shortwave diathermy not because of its dielectric properties but because the field becomes 'squeezed' or channelled into blood vessels causing considerable local heating. The field will preferentially heat areas of high conductivity and high dielectric constant where parallel pathways are offered, thus coplanar treatments or applications in the long axis of a limb tends to heat the vessels or the muscle tissue (Ward, 1980; Scott, 1957).

Techniques in Application of Shortwave Diathermy

Various electrode positions are illustrated in Fig. 11.6. It is important that the part to be treated is fully supported in an appropriate and comfortable

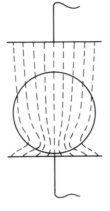

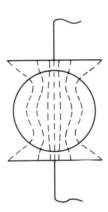

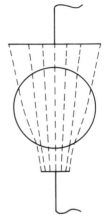

Unequal spacing of electrodes
giving superficial heating under
the close electrode

Closely spaced electrodes giving
superficial heating

Different sized electrodes
give superficial heating under the
small electrode

a Spacing of electrodes

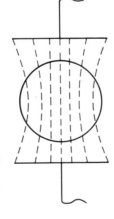

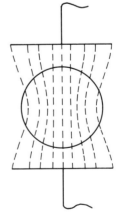

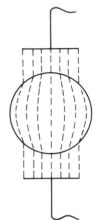

Normal electrode spacing giving
a uniform field and thus more
even heating

Electrodes smaller than body part gives
superficial heating because the field
spreads out in the tissues

b Size of electrodes

Electrodes a little larger than the
body part gives a uniform field
and thus more even heating

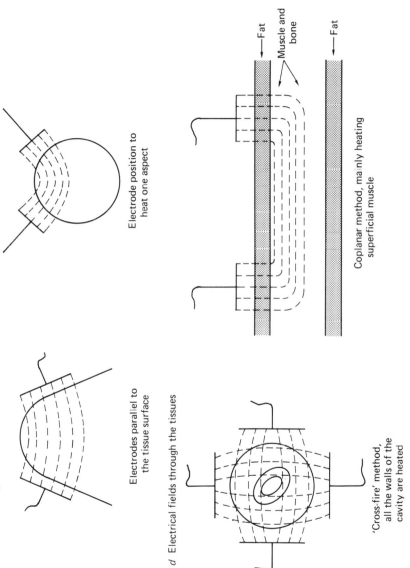

c Positioning of electrodes

Electrode position to
heat one aspect

Electrodes parallel to
the tissue surface

d Electrical fields through the tissues

'Cross-fire' method,
all the walls of the
cavity are heated

Coplanar method, mainly heating
superficial muscle

Fat

Muscle and
bone

Fat

Fig. 11.5 Electric fields through the tissues. **a** = Spacing of electrodes. **b** = Size of electrodes. **c** = Positioning of electrodes. **d** = Electrical fields through the tissues.

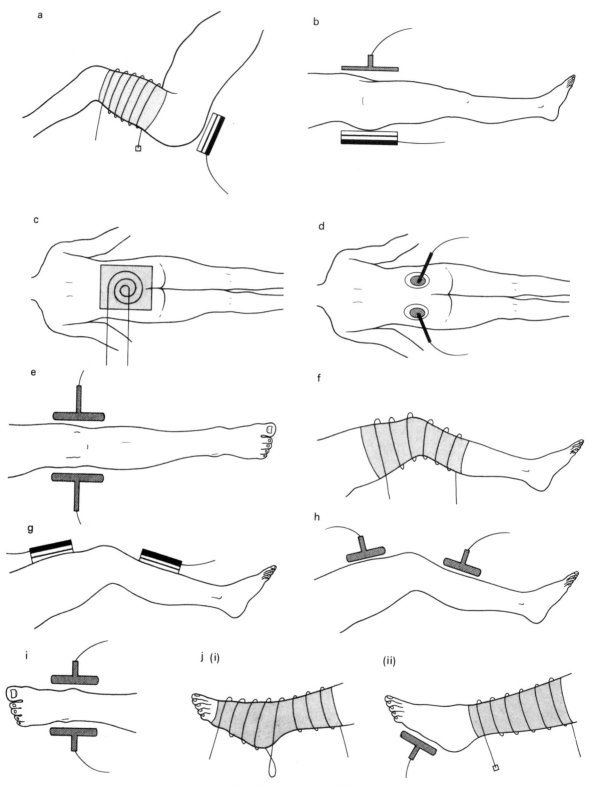

Fig. 11.6a–j (see p. 128).

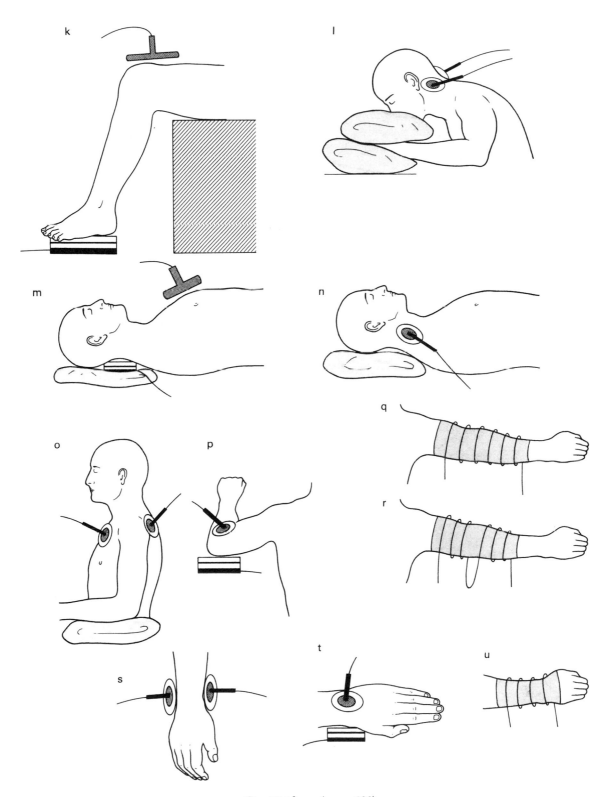

Fig. 11.6*k–u* (see p. 128).

position since any movement detunes the circuit. After suitable explanation, the patient should be instructed not to move and to describe both the intensity of heating and sites where it occurs; he must also be warned to call out if any burning or painful sensations are felt. It is therefore essential to ascertain that the skin areas treated have normal thermal sensation. The only knowledge of what heating is occurring comes from the patient so that full and proper communication is essential to regulate dosage. The heating may alter during the treatment and may need adjustment. At the end of the treatment palpation of the surface and the presence of any erythema can indicate the heating achieved.

Dosage

Increasing the tissue temperature depends on introducing energy at a faster rate than it is being dissipated but, of course, not at such a rate as to cause damage. As the temperature rises the heat regulating mechanisms of the body react until the heat input is once again the same as the heat loss when a new, higher, local temperature becomes steady (see Fig. 11.3a). It usually takes some 15–20 min for these vascular adjustments to take place, although it can take up to 1 h. Most treatments are therefore given for periods of 20–30 min (Wadsworth and Chanmugam, 1980). The heating rate can only be ascertained by the patient's perception, as already noted, so that descriptions such as: 'comfortable', 'definite warmth' for 'normal' heating—moderate heating; 'mild', 'gentle warmth' for mild heating; 'I can only just feel the heat' for minimal perceptible heating and 'I feel no heating' for no perceptible heating are used to quantify the intensity of heating. (The terms subthermic and athermic are best avoided.) Apparently, similar energy inputs cause widely differing heat perceptions; this is mainly due to differences in blood flow, and Scott (1957) quotes some evidence concerning this point.

Therapeutic Effects of Shortwave Diathermy

The effects of continuous shortwave diathermy are usually considered to be entirely due to the local heating that occurs. The physiological effects of

Fig. 11.6 Some techniques with shortwave diathermy. *a* = Hip joint: 1 malleable electrode and the coil as a 'cuff' electrode—'Scott technique'. *b* = Hip joint: 1 rigid and 1 malleable electrode. *c* = Lumbar spine: 1 coil electrode as a flat spiral—'pancake'. *d* = Lumbar spine: 2 rigid electrodes. *e* = Knee: 2 rigid electrodes. *f* = Knee: 1 coil electrode. *g* = Knee: 2 malleable electrodes. *h* = Knee: 2 rigid electrodes. *i* = Ankle: 2 rigid electrodes. *j* = Ankle: (i) Coil and loop electrodes (ii) Rigid and cuff electrodes. *k* = Ankle: 1 rigid and 1 malleable electrode. *l* = Cervical spine: 2 rigid electrodes. *m* = Cervical spine: 1 rigid and 1 malleable electrode. *n* = Cervical spine: 2 small rigid electrodes, one on either side. *o* = Shoulder: 2 rigid electrodes. *p* = Elbow: 1 rigid and 1 malleable electrode. *q* = Elbow: 1 coil electrode. *r* = Elbow: 1 coil electrode with a centre loop, giving a mainly capacitive field. *s* = Wrist: 2 rigid electrodes. *t* = Wrist: 1 rigid and 1 malleable electrode. *u* = Wrist: 1 coil electrode.

local heating considered below would, of course, pertain to any other form of local heating.

Local heating produces an interrelated set of physiological responses which occur markedly at temperatures above 40°C and below 45°C; continued heating above 45°C would lead to tissue damage. The direct effects can be summarised as:

1. increased metabolic activity;
2. increased blood flow, capillary pressure and permeability of cellular and vessel walls;
3. decreased viscosity of all fluids, including blood;
4. increased extensibility of collagenous tissues;
5. effects on neuronal activity.

All metabolic activity is temperature dependent so that quite small increases in temperature will cause considerable changes in cellular activity, such as greater leucocyte motility and phagocytosis or rates of cell growth. The increase in blood flow is due to reflex effects on arterioles, the consequences of increased metabolism, as well as the reduced viscosity. This is evident on the skin and has been demonstrated in muscle and other tissue (Millard, 1961). This increase may not occur where inflammatory disease, and hence hyperaemia, are already present (Harris, 1963). A consequence of increased activity and capillary pressure changes is a greater exchange across cell membranes and capillary walls. All these can assist the resolution of acute and chronic lesions. Collagen extensibility has been shown to increase at high, but therapeutic, levels of heating allowing a greater range of joint motion (Lehmann *et al.*, 1970). Similarly joint stiffness is reduced by heating (Wright and Johns, 1961).

Stimulation of sensory nerves by heat can lead to activation of the axon reflex as well as provoking the sensation of heat. Afferent nerve stimulation by heat may have an analgesic effect due to the gate control mechanism (see Chapter 5, p. 30), such an effect was formerly described as a counter-irritation mechanism (Gammon and Starr, 1941). Some evidence has been produced to show that stimulating heat receptors has an inhibitory effect on neurons conveying nociceptive impulses in rats, and it is believed that this mechanism may account for the analgesic effect of local heating (Kanui, 1985). Muscle spasm is reduced by heating and it has been suggested that this is due to the heating of secondary afferent muscle spindle nerve endings and Golgi tendon endings (Lehmann and de Lateur, 1982). Patients have been found to sleep easily during and after heat treatment, a sedative effect. This could be due to pain relief but it is pointed out that skin temperature rises just before the onset of sleep so that the sedative effect could be a reflex phenomenon (Lehmann and de Lateur, 1982).

Pain Relief

That heating leads to the relief of pain is well-recognised but not equally well researched. The pain threshold has been shown to rise during some forms of heating (Lehmann *et al.*, 1958) and there is some evidence that patients choose intermittent heating to diminish their pain (Gammon and Starr, 1941). The suggested reasons for pain relief are the analgesic effect and reduction of muscle spasm already noted, the raised blood flow reducing any ischaemic pain, the reduced joint stiffness, the accelerated resolution of injury and possibly the sedative effect. These responses and their inter-relationships are shown in a somewhat simplified form in Fig. 11.7 in which the immediate direct effects are linked to the therapeutic effects.

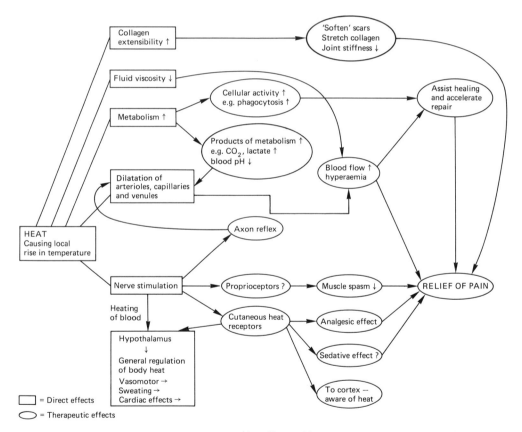

Fig. 11.7   The effects of heat.

Clearly local effects do not occur in isolation from the general effects that maintain the constant body temperature. While local heating is taking place heat is constantly dispersed and lost from the rest of the body by vasomotor adjustment under the control of the hypothalamus.

Potential Dangers with Shortwave Diathermy

The principal danger to the patient is that of a tissue burn. This can occur if:

1. The patient is unaware of the heat either due to defective skin sensation or unconsciousness, e.g. epilepsy or fainting during treatment. Occasionally a strong-minded or mentally unbalanced patient may stoically suffer a burn because of inadequate explanation and warning.

2. The shortwave field becomes 'concentrated' so quickly that the ensuing burn happens before the patient can react. This can occur as a consequence of many things including:

    (a) Defective positioning of electrodes.

    (b) Electrode leads too close to the patient's skin.

    (c) The presence of a low resistance pathway between the electrode and the skin, such as metal or water. All metals will act in this way even when enclosed in plastic (e.g. the metal in the plastic arms of spectacles) or metal buried in clothing like zip fasteners. What matters is the shape of the piece of metal and how it is orientated in the shortwave diathermy field. Thus if the long axis of a slender pointed metal object such as a key is parallel to the lines of the field with the point touching the skin, then current passes through the metal and will cause a burn where it touches the skin. Water droplets, such as sweat, provides a similar low resistance pathway.

    (d) Metal implanted surgically, such as a metal arthroplasty or fracture fixation by plate or wire, or metal accidentally embedded in the tissues, such as shrapnel, can provide a low resistance pathway leading to a burning at the junction of the metal and the tissues. The magnitude of this effect depends on the size and orientation of the metal. Thus small round tooth fillings embedded in dentine are insignificant, but a large long intramedullary nail is highly dangerous (Scott, 1957).

    Cardiac pacemakers can be affected by the electromagnetic fields produced by various kinds of electrical equipment. The 'triggered' or demand type pacemaker is much more likely to be affected than the fixed rate type. Reported causes of pacemaker dysfunction (Jones, 1976) include a number due to shortwave diathermy as well as numerous other sources of electromagnetic energy such as electric razors. These dysfunctions, which include stopping the pacemaker and altering its rhythm, occur most frequently when the patient is within 30 cm (1 ft) of the machine but have also been reported occurring at greater distances.

    It is therefore important to keep patients with implanted pacemakers away from shortwave diathermy and microwave machines, as these effects could occur not only if the patient were being treated but also if he or she were simply close to the machine. Although there seem to be no reports of interference due to pulsed shortwave diathermy or microwave it can be inferred that this could happen.

An entirely separate danger arises by applying shortwave diathermy, microwave, or ultrasound to the region of the implanted pacemaker. As well as interfering with its function, excess local heat may be produced causing a burn in the same way as with other metal implants.

Hearing aids and other electronic devices may be affected by both pulsed and continuous shortwave diathermy. This may only cause temporary buzzing noises but could also lead to permanent damage to the hearing aid.

MICROWAVE RADIATION

Microwaves are electromagnetic radiations extending from approximately 300 MHz (1 m wavelength) to 30 GHz (1 cm wavelength) found between radiowaves and infrared radiations (see Fig. 11.1). They are well known as radar radiations. They behave like visible or infrared radiations in that they travel in straight lines, are reflected by metal, and can be refracted.

In Europe three frequencies are available for therapeutic sources but only the first is in widespread use (Table 11.1).

Table 11.1 Frequencies of Microwave Radiation

Frequency (Hz)	Approximate Wavelength (cm)
2450	12.25
915	33
433.9	69

The Production of Microwaves

A beam of electrons controlled by a strong magnetic field is made to pass over a number of resonant cavities causing high frequency oscillations. This device is called a *magnetron*. The principle is similar to causing sound vibrations by blowing across the top of a bottle. The oscillations are conveyed by a coaxial cable to an antenna. The output can be controlled by varying the power to the magnetron, but the frequency is fixed by its dimensions.

A reflector is mounted behind the antenna, and the whole assembly is called a *director* or *emitter*. These can be made in various shapes and sizes which usually give a diverging beam of differing intensity in its cross section as described in the manufacturer's literature.

Effect of Microwaves on the Tissues

The high frequency electromagnetic field due to microwaves causes heating in the tissues by provoking the movement of ions, rotation of dipoles, and electron orbit distortion in the same way as described for shortwave diathermy (see Fig. 11.4, and p. 121). In the case of microwaves the energy is 'beamed' onto the skin and passes into the body. It might be expected that heating would be greatest at the surface and diminish progressively; however, it is not quite that simple.

Microwaves are strongly absorbed by water so that highly vascular tissues, such as muscle, are preferentially heated. Fat and bone on the other hand, absorb less radiation and thus both have much larger half value penetrations than muscle. For 2450 MHz radiations the half value depth for fat and bone is about 3.4 cm and for muscle about 0.7 cm. It can be seen that much of the energy will pass through the superficial fat and be absorbed rapidly in the underlying muscle causing heating (Fig. 11.8a). What tissue is heated clearly depends on the thickness and relationships of the various tissues; thus joints with little overlying muscle tissue, like the knee, may be quite successfully heated but not joints, such as the hip, which are deep and covered with thick muscle. The heating pattern also depends on the frequency; it can be shown that the lower frequencies, 434 and 915 MHz, will give even less heating of the fat and thus much better heating of deep muscle and other structures (Fig. 11.8b) (Ward, 1980). That microwave heating is 'only effective to a depth of 3 cm' is a statement hallowed more by repetition than accuracy. It is clear that microwaves will strongly heat skin, subcutaneous fat, and, particularly, superficial muscle but could still have a significant effect on deeper structures.

Absorption of microwave energy also depends on reflection at interfaces which leads to irregular absorption, 'hot spots' are likely to occur. This depends in a complex way on the thickness of the fatty layer particularly for 2450 MHz microwaves so that actual heating patterns are likely to vary greatly from patient to patient. It also means that quite large amounts of radiation are reflected from the skin surface. The therapeutic effects are due to the heating and have been considered in connection with shortwave diathermy on p. 128 (see also Fig. 11.7). Microwave diathermy sources can also be pulsed; the effects are probably similar to other pulsed modalities.

The Application of Microwaves

The patient should be comfortably supported so that the part to be treated can be fully and conveniently exposed. The procedure and the nature of the treatment should be explained to the patient and the patient's thermal sensation tested. The emitter to be used, determined by the size of the 'target' being treated, is adjusted to ensure that radiations strike the surface at right angles. The emitter–skin distance is important in determining both the size of the area treated and the intensity. A diverging beam leads to a large area treated with a low intensity at greater distances and *vice versa* at smaller distances. Many emitters give an appropriate heating pattern at

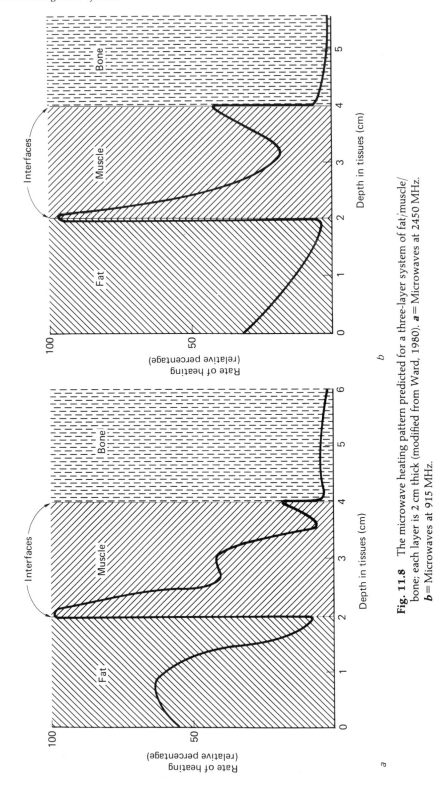

Fig. 11.8 The microwave heating pattern predicted for a three-layer system of fat/muscle/bone; each layer is 2 cm thick (modified from Ward, 1980). *a* = Microwaves at 2450 MHz. *b* = Microwaves at 915 MHz.

10 cm, approximately the width of a hand, but closer application, 2 cm, is used and recommended. The intensity control on the machine is used to adjust the heating and will thus compensate for different distances up to a point.

The required heat level, 'normal' or mild warmth, should be described to the patient who must also be warned to call out if excessive heating, pain, or any acute discomfort occur. This is essential since knowledge of heating in the tissues depends entirely on sensations felt by the patient; the output of the machine is usually shown by a meter but this gives no indication of tissue heating which varies with distance, nature of the tissues and blood flow as already noted.

Normal treatments are usually given for about 20 min to allow time for the vascular adjustments to occur (see Fig. 11.3*a*). The deeper parts take longer than the superficial tissues to reach their maximum steady temperature; at depths greater than 2 cm the temperature is still rising after 10 min (Boyle *et al.*, 1950).

Potential Dangers with Microwaves

Effects of metal

Metal reflects microwaves, so any metal on the surface will shield the underlying tissues. Overheating due to reflection into the part could also occur, e.g. placing the treated part close to large metal surfaces that could turn the scattered radiation back into the tissues. Similarly metal implants can cause overheating. This is much more likely with superficial rather than deep implants.

Eyes

Microwaves are strongly absorbed by the water of the eye, as the lens does not dissipate heat easily; also cataracts have been provoked in animal experiments. It is therefore not advisable to allow microwaves to enter the eye. If the beam is to be applied close to the eye then protective goggles should be worn; these are either glass with a thin metallic film or 2 mm wire mesh, both of which are almost impervious to microwaves. (It must be clearly understood that these are *not* interchangeable with ultraviolet goggles.)

Testes

Although quite small temperature increases can interfere with spermatogenesis in mammals, it is thought that very high doses would be needed to produce testicular damage in man. Nonetheless, it is sensible to avoid the testes because they are close to the surface and there is some evidence that microwaves may be more damaging than other forms of heating.

General Safety with Microwaves

Many patients, familiar with microwave ovens, may feel some alarm. It should be explained that microwaves reflected in an enclosed oven will be applied to, and absorbed by, the food from all sides. As the heat cannot be dissipated it will increase the temperature rapidly thus cooking the food. In the living body microwaves applied to one area, as in therapeutic application, cause local heating which is passed to other areas and lost to the atmosphere so that no increase in total body heat will occur. It is generally accepted that the human body could easily dissipate $10 \, mW/cm^2$ of radiation which is the permitted maximum continuous exposure for general purposes (higher levels are permitted for temporary exposure). These limits do not apply to the therapeutic application of microwaves under medical supervision.

Stricter limitations apply in the USSR and other Eastern European countries. This is based on research which was reputed to indicate an association between microwave radiation and various ill-defined symptoms such as headache, insomnia and buzzing in the ears; this work is not entirely accepted in the West.

The safety of microwaves in physiotherapy has been investigated (Scowcroft *et al.*, 1977; DHSS, Medical Scientific Services, 1980) and is considered perfectly safe provided that the radiation is confined to the treatment site. Based on measurements with various emitters it was found that the physiotherapist was quite safe for short periods near the emitter and was safe for indefinite periods at 1 m from the front and 25 cm from the back of the emitter. Radiation monitors are recommended to delineate microwave patterns.

ULTRASOUND THERAPY

Ultrasonic waves are mechanical vibrations in the form of longitudinal pressure waves. They are called ultrasonic because they are beyond the frequency recognised as sound by the human ear.

1. Infrasound or infrasonic waves, 0–30 Hz, are felt as a vibration.
2. Sound waves have a frequency of approximately 30 Hz–20 kHz.
3. Ultrasonic waves have a frequency of approximately 20 kHz–10 GHz.
4. Therapeutic ultrasonic frequencies are 0.5–3.5 MHz.
5. Commonly used therapeutic frequencies are 0.75 MHz, 0.87 MHz, 1.0 MHz, 1.5 MHz and 3.0 MHz (see Fig. 11.1).

Sonic waves are distortions of the medium through which they pass. They are waves of particle compression and rarefaction moving continuously in the direction of travel. Ultrasonic waves can travel through solids, liquids, and gases. At megahertz frequencies they cannot be seen or felt. Low frequency 'standing waves' can be made visible on the surface when ultrasound is passed in water and reflected from the wall of a container. This is a useful way to demonstrate the presence of an ultrasonic output in the clinical situation. This mechanism accounts for the 'buzzing' sensation sometimes experienced by patients during ultrasound treatment.

Velocity of Sonic Waves

There is a simple relationship between the velocity, frequency and wavelength of sonic waves.

$$\text{Velocity (m/s)} = \text{Wavelength (m)} \times \text{Frequency (Hz)}$$

Since ultrasonic waves distort the medium through which they travel their velocity depends on the nature of that medium. Thus ultrasonic waves travel at different velocities in different tissues as shown in Table 11.2 below.

Table 11.2 **Approximate Velocities for Sonic Waves (m/s)**

Air	343
Water	1480
Blood	1560
Muscle	1585
Fat	1450
Bone	3360

Passage of Ultrasonic Energy in the Tissues

At the interface of different types of tissue, the ultrasonic beam can be reflected or refracted. This is made use of in ultrasonic imaging for diagnosis where reflections from interfaces are picked up and displayed. Through any given volume of tissue some ultrasonic energy will be absorbed and the rest transmitted.

Heating of the tissues depends both on the rate at which energy is absorbed (see Fig. 11.2) and the amount of reflection from these interfaces within the tissues. This latter depends on the difference in the nature of the tissues at the junction. Actually it is the difference in acoustic impedance of the tissues, the acoustic impedance depending on both the density and elasticity of the tissues. In the tissues differences between fat, muscle and other soft tissue are very small so little reflection occurs; however, differences between bone and soft tissues are larger.

As fat does not absorb ultrasonic energy readily, little heating occurs in subcutaneous fat and much more energy is absorbed by muscle which is therefore heated. When the ultrasonic beam impinges on bone the energy is absorbed almost at once. Additionally there will be reflection from the muscle/bone interface causing further heating. This calculated large temperature elevation in the periosteal region is believed to account for the deep

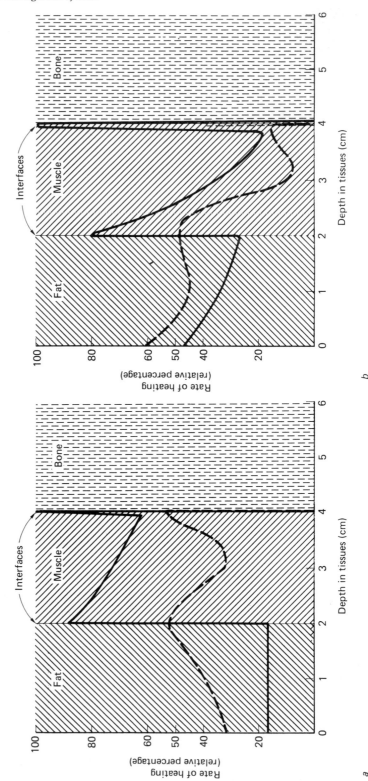

Fig. 11.9 The ultrasonic heating pattern predicted for a three-layer system of fat/muscle/bone; each layer is 2 cm thick (modified from Ward, 1980). — = Initial heating pattern. ∙∙ = Heating pattern suggested when thermal conductivity and blood flow are considered. (Note that this line only illustrates the change of pattern and is not based on any

138

'bone' pain which is sometimes experienced when high doses of ultrasound are used. This is illustrated diagrammatically in Fig. 11.9*a* for 1 MHz ultrasonics, and in Fig. 11.9*b* for 3 MHz ultrasonics, which has a lower half value depth of penetration and therefore gives a different pattern of heating. However, other factors are involved, notably the rate of heating which is influenced by the blood flow. In highly vascular tissues, such as muscle, the heat would be rapidly dissipated preventing a large rise in temperature. Fat and dense connective tissue, being less vascular, become relatively more heated leading to a more even distribution of heat between the various tissues. This is suggested in the dotted line on Fig. 11.9*a* and *b*. There is evidence that ultrasonic therapy preferentially heats collagenous tissues.

The wavelengths at a velocity of 1500 m/s and the approximate half value depths of penetration (the result of absorption in a mixture of tissues) are given below in Table 11.3 and depend on the frequency as shown.

Table 11.3   Frequency, Wavelength and Published Half Value Depth of Penetration for Ultrasonics at 1500 m/s in Tissues

Frequency (MHz)	Wavelength (mm)	Half Value Depth (cm) (from different published sources)		
0.75	2	10		
0.87	1.724	9		
1.0	1.5	6.5	5	4
1.5	1.0	5.5		
3.0	0.5	3	1.5	2.5

The ultrasonic beam passing through the tissues diverges somewhat, more especially with lower frequencies and smaller transducer heads. Furthermore, in the area close to the transducer, the *near-field* or *Fresnel zone*, the ultrasonic beam is very irregular; in the *far-field* or *Fraunhofer* zone it becomes more uniform but this is of little consequence since in most therapeutic situations the tissues are in the Fresnel zone, the extent of which depends on

$$\frac{\text{Radius of transducer head}^2}{\text{Wavelength}}$$

The tissues that are heated by therapeutic ultrasonics cannot be determined with great precision due to this irregularity.

Effects of Ultrasound Therapy

The biological effects of ultrasonics are those due to heating and those due to the other, mainly mechanical effects.

Thermal effects

As a direct consequence of the heating and as a result of the metabolic changes there will be an increase in blood flow, dilatation of blood vessels, and more rapid exchanges across capillary walls and cell membranes. Such changes are believed to hasten the resolution of chronic inflammatory processes; this may account for the pain relief often experienced when chronic lesions are given ultrasonic treatment (see Fig. 11.7).

Heating fibrous tissue structures such as tendons, ligaments or joint capsules can cause an increase in their extensibility. This also applies to scar tissue. Hence ultrasonic treatment coupled with active movement or passive stretching can lead to an increase in joint or tissue mobility in conditions such as Dupuytren's contracture or joint adhesions.

The advantages of using ultrasonics for therapeutic heating lie in the fact that it preferentially heats collagen-rich tissues as well as the periosteal region. Thus it is possible to achieve significant temperature increases in deeply placed joint capsules or intramuscular fibrosis without overheating the skin or other overlying tissues.

Non-thermal effects

Cavitation

This is due to the activity of bubbles under the influence of an acoustic field, and is of two kinds. Stable cavitation involves minute gas bubbles (a few microns) moving to and fro with the ultrasonic pressure waves and occurs during ultrasonic treatment. It is believed to contribute to changes observed in the cell membrane of nerve and muscle which could be involved in the relief of pain (Dyson, 1985). Transient cavitation, on the other hand, appears to occur only at ultrasonic intensities greater than those used therapeutically and describes rapidly growing bubbles which implode violently causing cell destruction. The essential point about cavitation is that it concentrates ultrasonic energy locally.

Acoustic streaming

The rapidly oscillating ultrasonic pressure waves cause a regular to and fro movement of particles. It also causes continuous particle motion in one direction; this latter is acoustic streaming. It occurs at boundaries such as the cell membrane.

Pulsed Ultrasonics

The principle of pulsed treatments has already been described on p. 120 (see Fig. 11.3*b*). In ultrasonic therapy the pulses are described as either: (1) the *duty cycle*, which is the ratio of time *on* to total time, usually expressed as a percentage; or (2) the *mark–space ratio*, which is the ratio of *on* to *off* time. Thus if the output were *on* for 2 ms and *off* for 8 ms the duty cycle would be 20% and the mark–space ratio 1:4; the pulse frequency would be 100 Hz. The effect is to reduce the energy applied to the tissues to one-fifth. The same total energy could be applied if the pulsing treatment were given for five times the duration at the same intensity or at five times the intensity for the same duration. However, tissue heating will depend on the rate of energy absorption not on the total energy because of heat dissipation in the tissues (see Fig. 11.3*b*). Thus pulses will generate 'bursts' of mechanical disturbance in the tissues without significant local heating, so higher intensities can be safely used. It is reasonable to suppose that there is a threshold below which mild mechanical agitation has no effect, however long-continued, whereas short bursts of vigorous agitation can produce marked effects. It has been found that rates of ion diffusion across cell membranes are increased by ultrasonic application (Dyson, 1985). This is thought to be due to increased particle movement on either side of the membrane and perhaps to increased motion of the phospholipids and proteins which make up the membrane. The use of a flour sieve or garden riddle provides an analogy. Some particles are pushed through the sieve by gravity, but many more drop through if the sieve is gently vibrated, like the effect of continuous ultrasonics. However, there comes a time when none of the remaining particles will pass through the mesh and gentle vibration is ineffective no matter how long-continued. If the sieve is now shaken vigorously a further shower of particles is produced. So that intermittent vigorous agitation has a different effect from continuous gentle vibration.

It is also possible that the frequency of the pulsing cycle (often 100 Hz as in the example above) may have some special effect. Pain relief has been achieved in other modalities such as interferential and transcutaneous nerve stimulating currents using frequencies in the region of 100 Hz. Many studies showing increased rates of healing have used pulsed ultrasonics, (e.g. Dyson and Suckling, 1978). For a full discussion of these mechanisms see Dyson (1987).

Therapeutic Effects and Indications

After tissue injury the acute inflammatory processes are accelerated by mild doses of ultrasonics. This may be due to the gentle agitation of the tissue fluid causing increased phagocytosis or the increased motion of other particles or cells, it may also be due to increased histamine release from mast cells which has been shown to occur (Dyson, 1987). Local oedema is believed to be decreased but it is not known by what mechanism, and it may account for the reduction of pain that occurs. Very low intensity pulsed ultrasound has been shown to reduce swelling and pain after tooth extraction (Hashish *et al.*, 1986). During tissue healing the synthesis and secretion of collagen by fibroblasts is an important process that has been shown to be accelerated by ultrasonic treatment (Harvey *et al.*, 1975). It may also assist repair by increasing the blood flow (improved blood flow has been found to occur in ischaemic muscle after ultrasonic treatment). In the later stages of repair, remodelling of the scar tissue is improved by ultrasonic treatment making it somewhat stronger and more resilient.

Ultrasonic treatment has been clearly shown to increase the rates and strength of skin healing in several situations by the mechanisms described above. It seems reasonable to suppose that other soft tissues behave similarly. Experiments have indicated that the early stages of fracture healing are also accelerated (Dyson, 1985).

Thus ultrasonics can be successfully used to aid the resolution of soft tissue injuries (see e.g. Binder *et al.*, 1985), but especially those involving collagenous tissues. As the reparative processes are increased and fibrous tissue rendered more flexible so degenerative processes, such as tendon calcification or degenerative arthrosis, will benefit. Lehmann *et al.* (1958) applied ultrasonic therapy to the region of the ulnar nerve in 10 volunteers and found a statistically significant rise in pain threshold over the little finger; this suggests that ultrasonic therapy applied to the nerve had a true analgesic effect. (He also achieved similar results with infrared radiation.) Such effects on peripheral nerves could account for the benefits claimed in the treatment of neurogenic pain or phantom limb pain by ultrasound, although these have usually been achieved with much lower doses than those used by Lehmann *et al.*

Increased flexibility and extensibility of fibrous tissue results from ultrasonic application; hence it is useful in the treatment of scarring, joint contractures, adhesions, Dupuytren's contracture, scleroderma and other conditions involving inflexibility of collagenous tissues. While the mechanisms of these changes remain unclear, therapeutic levels of ultrasonics have been shown to increase protein synthesis in fibroblasts (Harvey *et al.*, 1975). For a recent critical evaluation of the efficacy of ultrasonic therapy see Partridge (1987).

Production of Therapeutic Ultrasonics

The high frequency mechanical vibration needed to produce ultrasonic waves is provided by the reversed piezo-electric effect exhibited by certain crystals. If an oscillating electric field is applied at a frequency which matches the natural resonant frequency of the crystal maximum amplitude is achieved. The crystal is bonded to a metal plate which therefore also vibrates and this assembly, enclosed in a metal case, forms the transducer or treatment head. Sustained electrical oscillations are produced to drive the crystal by means of an oscillator circuit.

Some therapeutic ultrasonic sources operate on one frequency only, often 1 MHz, in others different frequencies can be chosen and this may involve using a different transducer. Many allow more than one pulsing pattern, e.g. 1:1 and 1:4 mark–space ratio, and the power output is displayed in total watts (W) and W/cm² on a meter. Apart from mains and ultrasonic output indicator lights, some machines have a useful additional indicator which shows whenever the treatment head is not in full contact with the tissues.

Methods of Applying Therapeutic Ultrasonics

In order to transmit ultrasonic energy to the tissues it is necessary to provide a *couplant*. Virtually no transmission occurs through air, the treatment head simply heating up as energy is absorbed at the transducer/air interface. Ultrasonic energy is absorbed by air bubbles so degassed water is best if water is being used as the couplant.

When the treatment head is applied to the skin a couplant must be interposed. As the skin is not flat the air pockets must be filled with fluid (Fig. 11.10), and this fluid has to be sufficiently viscid to stay in place. Thixotropic gels are semisolid substances that become fluid on vibration and are thus ideal for this purpose. They are available under various trade names, or may be made in a hospital pharmacy. Glycerine or various oils such as liquid paraffin or arachis oil can also be used but are less efficient transmitters than either thixotropic couplants or water. Compensation for transmission loss can be made by increasing the intensity but heating of the skin may limit the treatment when oil is used. The fluid couplant also provides lubrication for movement of the treatment head over the skin.

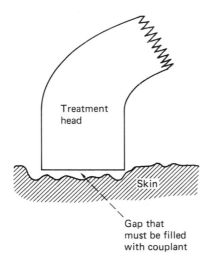

Treatment head

Skin

Gap that must be filled with couplant

Fig. 11.10 A cross-section of a transducer on the skin surface.

A way of applying treatment to very irregular areas that cannot be submerged in water is to use a rubber or plastic bag filled with water (Fig. 11.11). Couplant must be used between the bag and the skin and between

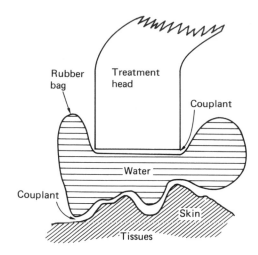

Fig. 11.11 A cross-section of a transducer and water bag on the skin surface.

the bag and the treatment head. The treatment head can be moved by either sliding over the surface of the bag or by deforming the bag so that the head moves relative to the skin. Only a minimal depth of water should separate the treatment head from the tissues.

Technique of application

The skin of the area to be treated must be examined. Inflammatory skin lesions or open wounds are avoided. The nature of the treatment should be explained to the patient. In many ultrasonic treatments the patient will feel no sensation so that there is no check on the output. It is therefore advisable to test the machine by putting the transducer just below the surface in a bowl of water and observing the standing waves which appear. High frequency vibrations are reflected from the side of the bowl interfering with one another to produce waves of large amplitude and low frequency which are visible on the surface.

Direct contact treatment

Couplant is placed on both the area of skin to be treated and the treatment head which is then pressed upon the skin before the output is turned on. The transducer can be damaged if high intensities are applied while it is in air. The treatment head is moved over the area with a pressure sufficient to maintain even contact between the whole surface area of the head and the skin. Much skill in applying ultrasound lies in performing this movement correctly. The ultrasonic beam emitted is very irregular and is unevenly absorbed. Moving the treatment head ensures uniform treatment of the target tissue and obviates the risk of damage due to local high intensities.

The speed of this movement must be slow enough to allow the skin and superficial tissues to deform and thus remain in contact with the rigid treatment head as it moves; if it is too slow the physiotherapist has difficulty maintaining an even pressure. Rates of movement of between 2 and 5 cm/s are appropriate.

The pattern of movement of the treatment head can be a series of overlapping circles, figures-of-eight or parallel overlapping strokes. This latter is likely to give less even treatment due to the longer time taken changing direction at each end of the stroke (Fig. 11.12). It is essential to keep the treatment head flat on the surface and in contact at all times. Altering the angle will lead to scattering and marked energy loss and if an air gap forms transmission is completely prevented.

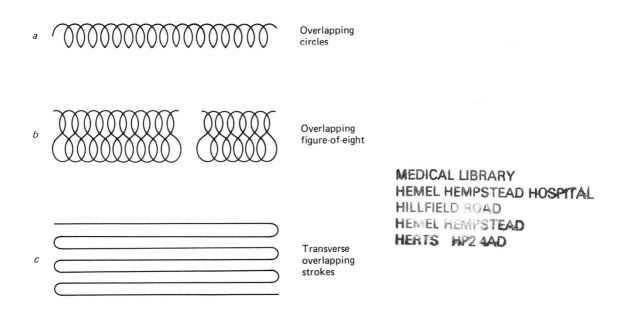

Fig. 11.12   Patterns of movement of the ultrasonic transducer on the skin surface.

Supporting the part to be treated in a suitable position is obviously important in view of the need to apply even pressure during movement of the transducer. If possible the treatment head should be applied downwards and moved horizontally. This is less tiring for the physiotherapist as the weight of the treatment head contributes to the pressure and it is easier to move at a constant rate; also the couplant does not tend to flow downwards away from the area. It is important that patients are not in such a position that they have to oppose the pressure of the ultrasonic head with their own muscular effort. Apart from the discomfort and fatigue, this is likely to lead to a less constant pressure.

Water bath technique

The water temperature should be above skin temperature and comfortable for the patient. The position of the bath and the patient should be so adjusted that the hand, forearm, ankle or foot can be rested comfortably in the bath with the patient sitting. The treatment head should be moved parallel and about 2 cm away from the surface following the surface contour as far as possible. The transducer face and the skin surface should be wiped clear of bubbles at intervals because bubbles will absorb ultrasonic energy. Using degassed water reduces bubble formation.

The main advantage of this method is that very irregular surfaces can be treated; also tender areas are not touched by the treatment head. Little additional energy is absorbed by the water.

Water bag method

Ordinary rubber balloons can be used in this method, and plastic containers have also been recommended. In each case the bag is filled with warm water, preferably degassed, and as much air as possible is excluded before the bag is sealed. Couplant is smeared onto the bag, skin and treatment head. It is often necessary to have an extra pair of hands, sometimes the patient's, to hold the bag in position. The treatment head is pressed into the bag so that an appropriate thickness of water separates it from the irregular surface. Movement of the head can be effected both by deforming the bag and sliding on its surface. Considerable energy losses are likely to occur at the various interfaces so that the intensity must be increased considerably (by about 75%) to compensate (see Fig. 11.11).

Dosage

The energy absorbed in the target tissues depends on:

1. the *frequency* (Hz). As already noted, lower frequencies penetrate further, thus of the commonly used frequencies for therapeutic ultrasonics: 3 MHz penetrates least and is therefore absorbed superficially; 1.5 MHz penetrates further; 1.0 MHz penetrates further still and 0.75 MHz penetrates furthest and is thus absorbed in both superficial and deeper tissues (see Fig. 11.2, and Table 11.3).
2. the *intensity* (W/cm^2). Since the output is very irregular this is more correctly the space averaged, time averaged intensity. It may be shown on the meter in total W, W/cm^2 or both, usually to a maximum of 3 W/cm^2.
3. *pulsing pattern*—duty cycle or mark—space ratio, e.g. 1:4.
4. total *time of the treatment*.
5. the *size of the area being treated*.
6. nature, size and position of the *'target' tissue* to be treated. Since the actual

intensities absorbed at any point in the tissues cannot be known dosage is, to some extent, a matter of judgement. It is first necessary to decide which is the target tissue and what effect is required, and then consider:

(a)	*Depth of the target from the surface*	*Superficial* →	*Deep*
	Frequency (see Table 11.3)	3 MHz	0.75 MHz
	Intensity	0.1 W/cm²	3 W/cm²
(b)	*Size of the target area to be treated*	*Small* →	*Large*
	Time	3 min	15 min
(c)	*Condition*	*Acute* →	*Chronic*
	Intensity	0.1 W/cm²	3 W/cm²
	Time	3 min	15 min
	Pattern	Pulsed	Continuous
(d)	*Heating required*	*No heat* →	*Heat*
	Intensity	0.1 W/cm²	3 W/cm²
	Time	3 min	15 min
	Pattern	Pulsed	Continuous

Each—(a), (b), (c), and (d) of the above—can vary independently so that the choice of intensity is influenced by (a), (c), and (d) and the time controlled by (b), (c), and (d). Clearly these modifications can sometimes cancel each other out. Thus a lesion may warrant a low intensity treatment because of its acute nature, but a higher intensity because it is deeply placed. It is important to remember that what matters is the ultrasonic energy delivered at the target tissue.

There seems to be little agreement on how much to vary these treatment parameters. Structures within 1 cm or so of the surface (i.e. skin, subcutaneous tendons or ligaments, etc.) are considered superficial and treated with 3 MHz ultrasound, deeper structures being treated with lower frequencies. If only one frequency is available (e.g. 1 MHz) it must be recognised that treatment will still lead to considerable energy absorption in the superficial tissues (see Fig. 11.2).

Increasing the intensity to compensate for ultrasonic energy losses due to absorption and scattering at greater depth is a reasonable adjustment. Adding 0.25 W/cm² intensity for each centimetre of depth can be used as a rough guide.

The area covered by the moving treatment head must, obviously, be the main determinant of the time taken by the treatment. A useful guide is 1 min for every 10 cm² (1.5 in²), thus an area such as the palm of the hand (about 50 cm²) would be given 5 min treatment. Treatment of even the smallest target is likely to cover 20–30 cm² so that 2 or 3 min are regarded as the shortest reasonable treatment times. Usually, 15 min is considered the longest appropriate treatment time.

When using pulsed ultrasound, which, as already noted, would produce no heating (see Fig. 11.3*b*), it is usual to compensate for the reduced energy input by increasing both the intensity and time of treatment. Intensities of 1 or 2 W/cm² are often used; this is the pulse intensity, not the average intensity which would be very much lower. Increases in the time of pulsed treatments are usually not such as to completely compensate for the pulse intervals.

Theories of Therapeutic Mechanisms for Ultrasonics

There have been two schools of thought for some time. One, which might be called the American view, emphasises the importance of heating. This approach recommends quite high intensities and sees little value in low intensity and pulsed treatments; the term *ultrasonic diathermy* is often used. The other, mainly European, is more impressed with neural and low intensity mechanical effects and uses low doses that are often pulsed. To some extent the historical development of these differing views, well described by Fyfe and Bullock (1985), has contributed to the lack of agreement over ultrasonic dosage. Other factors are the calibration inaccuracies of ultrasonic sources, uncertainty over how the energy spreads in the tissues and a lack of clinical research (Partridge, 1987).

Potential Dangers with Ultrasonics

There seems to be no reported evidence of damage due to therapeutic ultrasonics, but reasonable presumptions and some experimental evidence to suggest the following. Ultrasonic therapy should not be applied to:

1. Neoplasms, because it may accelerate growth and cause metastases.
2. Tissues recently treated with x-ray or other ionising radiation, because it could lead to further damage and possibly neoplastic changes.
3. Areas where haemorrhage might be provoked, e.g. an enlarging haematoma or recent haemarthrosis, or in uncontrolled haemophilia.
4. Acute infections, because the infection might spread.
5. Severely ischaemic areas, e.g. local arterial disease, because of the diminished heat transfer and possibly greater risk of arterial thrombosis.
6. Tuberculous lesions, because of the risk of reactivating encapsulated lesions.
7. The pregnant uterus; it is suggested that there might be some risk to the rapidly dividing tissues of the fetus from larger therapeutic doses. (Diagnostic ultrasonics uses very low intensities which are quite safe.)
8. Over recent venous thromboses where part of the clot might be freed causing an embolus.
9. The eye, since the fluid-filled chamber may allow good transmission damaging the retina.

There are some other circumstances where high doses should be avoided; notably anaesthetic areas because the patient may be unaware of pain and thus allow damage to occur. It must be realised that the pain commonly produced by overdosage is deep periosteal pain and that thermal sensation can only be felt on the skin. High doses have been shown to damage cells in the central nervous system, but only when applied directly. There seems to be no danger normally, and large therapeutic doses have been applied to the tissues around the spinal cord for many years without ill effects; but circumstances where the CNS is exposed, e.g. in spina bifida, should be avoided. Rapidly dividing tissues, such as the gonads and even epiphyseal plates have been considered to be at risk but without evidence. Similarly, treatment over the vagus nerve and cervical ganglia in cardiac disease is considered dangerous by some. Treatment over an implanted cardiac pacemaker should not be given as it may affect the pacemaker's stimulating frequency.

Surgical metallic implants cause reflection of the ultrasonic beam at their interface with the tissues causing increased energy absorption in this area. This does not, however, lead to a temperature rise in the implant or the surrounding tissues because the high thermal conductivity of the metal allows heat to be rapidly conducted to cooler untreated areas. Experiments have been done with implants (in pigs) without ill effects. It is therefore suggested that metal implants present no hazard when giving ultrasonic treatment (Lehmann and de Lateur, 1982). However, the effects might well be different with superficially placed and smaller implants so that cautious low doses are advisable in these circumstances.

High density polyethylene or other plastics used in replacement surgery should be avoided because their effect on ultrasonic energy absorption is, as yet, unquantified.

PULSED HIGH FREQUENCY RADIATIONS—PULSED SHORTWAVE DIATHERMY

The output of a shortwave diathermy source can be pulsed in the same way as ultrasonics and with the same consequence, i.e. negligible heating. Although considerable interest in this therapy has developed in the past 15 years its origins can be traced to work done in the 1940s by Abraham Ginsberg which led to the Diapulse machine being developed. Many firms have since produced similar sources but most of the significant research has been done with Diapulse.

The Production of Pulsed High Frequency Radiations

High frequency oscillations at 27.12 MHz are produced in a conventional shortwave diathermy machine controlled by a timing circuit which allows the high frequency oscillations to be produced for a very short time, 65 μs in the case of Diapulse. These are repeated at intervals depending on the repetition rate. Thus at 100 pulses/s, each 65 μs pulse would be separated from the next by a gap of 9935 μs (a duty cycle of 0.654%). Each pulse is, of course, a series of high frequency oscillations, actually 1762.8 in this case. Other sources have other pulse lengths and repetition rates, some sufficient

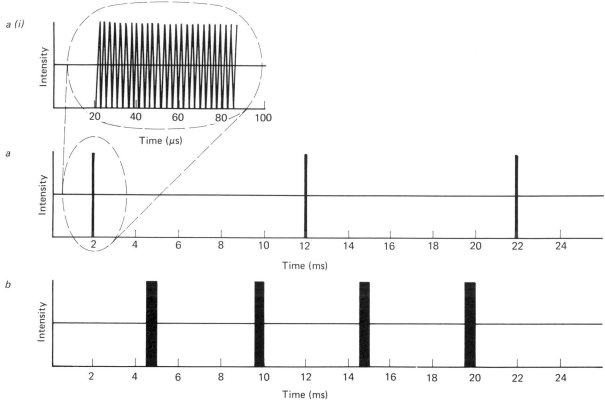

Fig. 11.13   *a* = 65 µs pulses of 27.12 MHz oscillations repeated 100 times/s at 100 Hz. *a(i)* = Approximately 1800 oscillations during a 65 µs pulse. *b* = 400 µs pulses of 27.12 MHz oscillations repeated 200 times/s at 200 Hz.

to produce mild heating (Fig. 11.13*a* and *b*). Pulsed high frequency energy can be applied to the tissues by any of the conventional shortwave diathermy methods, but the Diapulse and others use a drum type electrode containing a flat spiral coil, a small 'pancake coil' (Fig. 11.14).

The maximum instantaneous power, i.e. the power in watts of each pulse, can be large, 975 W, but the average power is, obviously, very low—it is about 38 W at maximum in the Diapulse. However, as pointed out by Barker *et al.* (1985) this is a significant fraction of the average adult basal metabolic rate.

Pain Relief and Other Effects of Pulsed High Frequency Energy

Experimental evidence

Artificially produced haematomas in rabbits' ears have been shown to heal faster under treatment (Fenn, 1969). Experimentally induced skin wounds showed less oedema when treated (Cameron, 1961). Experiments on the median-ulnar nerve of rats indicated that those treated for 15 min/day

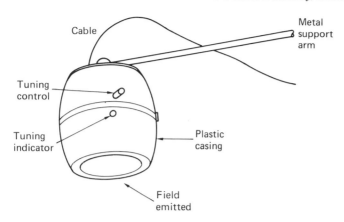

Fig. 11.14   Drum-type applicator for pulsed shortwave diathermy.

showed more rapid and more complete regeneration than the controls (Wilson and Jagadeesh, 1976). Carefully designed experiments involving the division and suture of the common peroneal nerve of rats demonstrated statistically significant benefits with pulsed energy treatment; degeneration, regeneration and maturation of myelinated nerve fibres were accelerated and fibrosis was reduced (Raji, 1984).

Clinical investigations

In a study on children after orchidopexy, less bruising and more rapid recovery was found in those treated with pulsed electromagnetic energy (Bentall and Eckstein, 1975). A double blind study on donor site healing after split skin graft removal showed significantly greater healing at 7 days in those treated compared with the controls (Goldin *et al.*, 1981). Ankle injuries have been used to assess the efficacy of pulsed energy; one study showed marked reduction of pain and disability (Wilson, 1972), while another (Pasila *et al.*, 1978) resulted in a less dramatic improvement. There have been several other clinical studies published. There is therefore good reason to expect that pulsed shortwave diathermy can accelerate the healing of soft tissue and, perhaps most important, regenerating nerve. In many of the clinical studies, comment was made on the pain relief experienced by the patients treated.

Therapeutic Uses of Pulsed High Frequency Energy

It is appropriate to treat all recent trauma both accidental and postoperative at an early stage, thus recent injuries, such as a sprained ankle, a crushed hand, muscle haematomas, local burns or acute synovitis can be treated immediately. Acute infections, such as paranasal sinusitis or pelvic inflammatory disease, may also benefit from treatment. As well as clinical impressions

151

(Wilson, 1981), the strong experimental evidence indicates that early treatment of peripheral nerve lesions would accelerate recovery. Treatment of all these may give pain relief, especially the relief of postoperative pain, but also some more chronic conditions, such as degenerative arthritis and pelvic inflammatory disease appear to become pain free, or have their pain reduced, after treatment with pulsed high frequency energy. Neurogenic pain—as in Sudeck's atrophy, phantom limb pains and osteoporotic pain— may also be helped (Wilson, 1981).

Application of Pulsed High Frequency Energy

There is some uncertainty concerning the dosage to be given, but the following provides a rough guide:

1. For acute conditions low average energy is used, 40 or 65 µs pulses with repetition rates of 400–600 pulses/s and either three 20 min treatments each day or, if that is impossible, a 1 h treatment each day.
2. If the intensity can be altered it is sensible to use higher intensities for more deeply placed targets. Where a drum-type applicator is used it is positioned as close to the affected area as possible but not touching the skin, leaving a space of a centimetre or so.
3. Chronic lesions seem to benefit from rather more average energy so that the longer pulses are used, again at 400–600 pulses/s.
4. For the relief of pain, moderate pulse lengths of 65 or 100 µs at 100 or 200 pulses/s for 10–20 min are used.

This does not entirely conform with other published opinions; Hayne (1984) recommends 200–300 pulses/s for pain relief and lower repetition rates (100–200 pulses/s) given two or three times a day in 15 min sessions for acute lesions. There is also a widely held opinion that short treatment times of 5–10 min are just as effective as the longer. Clearly, an open mind and more evidence on the matter are both needed. (It may be noted that the three quoted trials—Wilson, 1972; Bentall and Eckstein, 1975; Goldin *et al.*, 1981—used 600 pulses/s for 1 h, 500 pulses/s in three 20 min periods and 400 pulses/s in four 10 min periods respectively, for each day.)

Mode of Action of Pulsed High Frequency Energy

This is not clearly understood. There is disagreement about whether the effects are specific or simply due to the mild heating. Some, e.g. Lehmann and de Lateur (1982), maintain that all the proven effects can be accounted for by mild heating and consider there is no specific therapeutic indication for pulsed output. Others, pointing to the variety of effects, suggest that electrical changes may influence cellular membrane function. Cell damage is associated with depolarisation and it is suggested that recovery may be assisted by ionic movement provoked by the varying electric field. Cell division and other cellular activities may by aided by the vibrating charges. For some interesting further details see Hayne (1984). Another unresolved question concerns the pulsing parameters, pulse length, frequency and shape, and what influence they have on the effects. Almost all the research has been done with Diapulse so those parameters are often used and cited (Table 11.4).

Table 11.4   Some Pulsed High Frequency Energy Sources

| Function | Apparatus | | |
	Diapulse	Megapulse	Curapuls and Ultramed
Mode	Pulsed only	Pulsed only	Continuous and pulsed
Pulse width (μs)	65 only	Various from 20–400	400 only
Pulse repetition rates (pulses/s)	80–600	100–800 or 25–400	15–200
Intensity	6 settings	Not variable	10 settings
Maximum instantaneous power (peak power) (W)	975	approx. 500	1000
Average maximum power (W)	38	35	70

Potential Dangers with Pulsed High Frequency Energy

There have been no reported ill effects of this modality. In view of the supposed mode of action it would seem sensible to avoid rapidly dividing tissues, such as the fetus, or uncontrolled tissue growth, such as neoplasms. Similarly, tuberculous lesions should be avoided (because of the possibility of reactivating encapsulated lesions) and so should markedly hyperpyrexic patients.

Since there is no significant heating there is no risk of burns due to concentration of the field by metal on or in the tissues, or by water on the surface. However, it must be remembered that the treatment is relatively, not absolutely, athermic; the longer pulses at higher frequencies can cause heating and therefore some risk of overheating. Nonetheless, low intensity treatments are entirely safe and have been used in the presence of metal implants.

Like other high frequency sources they could affect cardiac pacemakers causing arrhythmias; less seriously, they can also affect hearing aids and other electronic equipment, such as modern telephones.

Low Power Pulsed High Frequency Energy

Machines are available which generate pulses similar to those described above but delivering only a tiny fraction of the power, e.g. the Therafield Beta. Claims made for their efficacy were not substantiated in a controlled trial (Barker *et al.*, 1985). Other studies, however, have found that these devices can aid wound healing; for example, Nicolle and Bentall (1982) found that oedema and bruising were diminished more often on the treated side in a controlled study of bilateral blepharoplasty.

HOW DISEASE PROCESSES ARE INFLUENCED BY EFFECTS OF HIGH FREQUENCY CURRENTS AND ULTRASOUND

Pain

Pain may be relieved by the modalities that have been discussed; in some instances due to resolution of the inflammatory processes, in others by their effects on the nervous system (see Chapter 5). Associated with the pain relief there is often a reduction in muscle spasm. Neurogenic pain, such as that of post-herpetic neuralgia, Sudeck's atrophy or phantom limb pain, seems to be successfully relieved by the pulsed modalities and sometimes by mild heating. It has been claimed that pain relief is achieved in some conditions by pulsed treatment directed to the autonomic nervous system. Pain relief is naturally a consequence of many of the beneficial effects discussed below. There is also a placebo effect associated with these therapies enhanced perhaps by the unfamiliar but impressive apparatus used. This may account for some of the immediate pain relief and, perhaps, other effects (Hashish *et al.*, 1986).

Acute Inflammation

Heating tends to increase the swelling and pain of acute inflammation although very mild heating can be helpful particularly if it assists drainage, as in acute paranasal sinusitis or pelvic inflammatory disease. In bacterial or viral infection it is important to avoid increasing the activity or dispersion of the micro-organisms by heating them directly, except those that are heat-sensitive like the gonococcus. Heating the adjacent tissues stimulates the defence processes such as leucocyte activity and increased blood flow; this treatment may have an important place in circumstances where antibiotics are inappropriate.

The beneficial effects of pulsed high frequency energy or pulsed ultrasonic energy on the inflammatory processes are clear. Some consider this to be a specific effect, others maintain it is due to the very mild heating. It would seem sensible to apply mild pulsed treatments to inflamed tissues leaving the area under treatment to be stimulated by the mechanical effects or mild heating, whichever it prefers!

Healing

The rate of healing of soft tissues, including skin, has been shown to be increased by mild pulsed ultrasonic and shortwave treatments (see e.g. Dyson and Suckling, 1978; Wilson, 1972; Goldin *et al.*, 1981). The mechanisms by which this occurs have been considered already.

Chronic Inflammation

The heating causes an increased blood flow and tissue metabolism which assists resolution. This is sometimes described as making the chronic processes more acute in character. Both degeneration and repair proceed simultaneously so that quite a small change may tip the balance in favour of resolution.

Fibrous Contractures and Scarring

Heat has been shown to allow collagenous structures to be more easily stretched. A significant temperature rise seems to be needed so vigorous heating is appropriate. The modality used will depend on the site and tissues involved. Any pain due to tension in these structures is therefore diminished.

Stiff Joints

Obviously, the effect of heat will depend on the cause of the stiffness. In normal joints the stiffness due to elasticity and viscosity of the periarticular tissues can be reduced by heat; shortwave treatment has been found to reduce stiffness by 20% for a short time (Wright, 1973). This is a reason for giving heat prior to exercise. It would also tend to diminish pain.

Calcification and Ectopic Bone Formation

Pulsed high frequency and pulsed ultrasonics have both been recommended and are used to encourage reabsorption.

Haematomas

During the first two days the haematoma must not be heated because bleeding may be increased. As resolution begins mild pulsed treatments with either shortwave or ultrasonics are applied, peripherally at first, but subsequently over the whole area. As reabsorption is encouraged so pain will diminish.

Ischaemia due to Peripheral Vascular Disease

Heating a proximal region, such as the thigh, to produce vasodilatation in the skin of the foot (sometimes called *reflex heating*) has been used as a treatment for peripheral vascular disease, but it is thought to cause only a redistribution of blood flow in the distal part, not an increase. This method of treatment can be very useful to produce mild vasodilatation in a distal region which cannot be directly treated due, e.g. to open infected wounds. It is usual to apply an inductothermy coil around the proximal part.

OTHER SUGGESTED EFFECTS OF ELECTROMAGNETIC ENERGY

Various pieces of evidence have been produced to show that very low strength electromagnetic fields, at various frequencies, can lead to changes in human and animal behaviour, changes in the nervous system, calcium metabolism, and other physiological mechanisms. The suggestion is that electromagnetic energy has a controlling and communicating influence on biological systems when applied at low levels which is lost with higher intensities, such as those used therapeutically. These interesting ideas are not generally accepted and their therapeutic significance has not been elucidated (Becker and Marino, 1982; Presman, 1970).

ELECTROMAGNETIC FIELDS AND SAFETY

With the rapidly increasing use of electromagnetic energy for communications and other purposes, some have wondered if it might pose a threat to health in the long term. No obvious link with any disease has been unequivocally proved to date, and studies are continuing.

INTERFERENTIAL STIMULATION

INTRODUCTION

Pain relief has been sought in many different therapies including interferential currents. This modality was originally devised about 40 years ago and is now being used more extensively than in the past. This interest is partly due to developments in electronic circuitry which has made more compact and relatively cheaper machines available.

THE EFFECTS OF PASSING ELECTRIC CURRENTS THROUGH THE TISSUES

There are three significant effects:

1. A unidirectional current (direct current, DC) leads to chemical changes and can be used for the introduction of therapeutic ions into the tissues or to promote healing; if excessive, it causes tissue damage (see Fig. 11.1).

2. A changing current intensity, either interrupted direct current or alternating current (low frequency current) can stimulate both nerve and muscle tissue with suitable intensities and rates of current change, e.g. faradism, sinusoidal current, or triangular pulses (see Fig. 11.1).

3. A high frequency oscillating current can cause tissue heating, e.g. shortwave diathermy, as considered in the earlier part of this chapter. Such currents have no chemical (polar) effects because any change is immediately and exactly reversed at the next alternation of current. They cannot stimulate nerve or muscle tissue because the change in ionic motion is too fast to cause significant change in cell membrane potential.

THE STIMULATION OF NERVE AND MUSCLE TISSUE BY LOW FREQUENCY CURRENTS

If an electrical disturbance, a movement of ions, is made to occur across a nerve or muscle membrane it may be sufficient to set off a nerve impulse or muscle fibre contraction. To do so it must alter the membrane potential beyond the 'threshold' value at which point the nerve impulse—or muscle fibre contraction—occurs completely, the 'all or none' effect. Increasing the electrical disturbance, the stimulating current, has no further effect on an individual nerve or muscle fibre, but stimulates a greater number of them leading to a stronger muscle contraction or more sensory effect. Thus, low frequency currents, such as faradism with, say, 0.5 ms pulses or sinusoidal with 10 ms pulses both at 50 Hz, will have a rate of change sufficient to stimulate nerve and muscle tissue at low current intensities. Using these currents, muscle contraction is a consequence of motor nerve stimulation. Slowly changing low frequency currents, e.g. triangular pulses, can stimulate muscle tissue directly since the motor nerves are able to accommodate to the slow rate of change while the muscle cannot.

Compared to the rest of the tissues the skin has a high resistance or impedance, measured in ohms. This leads to a high potential difference across the skin and superficial tissues resulting in maximum stimulation of tissues in this region, illustrated in Fig. 11.15a.

The impedance offered by the skin depends on the frequency of the current, the higher the frequency the less the impedance. (This occurs because the capacitance of the skin plays a greater part in transmitting the current at higher frequencies.) Whereas the impedance between a pair of 100 cm^2 electrodes on the skin was found to be about 1000 ohms for a 50 Hz current, it fell to about 50 ohms for a 4000 Hz (4 kHz) current (Ward, 1980). Currents of 4000 Hz and similar frequencies are known as medium frequency currents (see Fig. 11.1), and will obviously pass much more readily through the tissues than low frequency currents. They will not, in a simple regular form, stimulate nerve or other tissue. However, they can be modulated (surged) to give a low frequency current superimposed on the medium

157

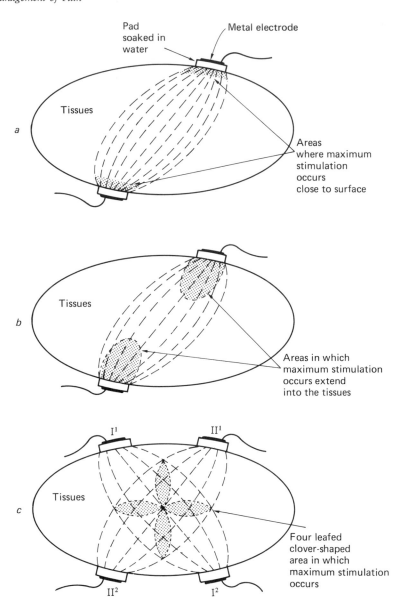

Fig. 11.15 The passage of currents through the tissues. *a*= Low frequency currents.
b= Low frequency modulation of medium frequency current. *c*= Interferential currents.

frequency (Fig. 11.16); this is similar in principle to the pulsing of high
frequency currents already described on p. 149 and in Fig. 11.13. The
resulting current will pass easily through the tissues because it is a medium
frequency current but will stimulate muscle and nerve because of the low
frequency variation.

This type of current is produced by some interferential machines and may
be called *electrokinesy*. Although the spread of medium frequency current is
more uniform than low frequency current it will still have a greater intensity

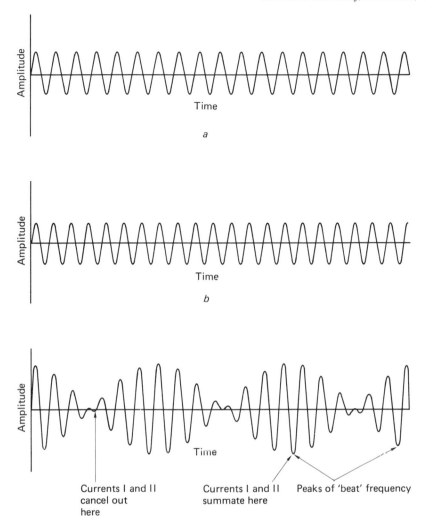

Fig. 11.16 Current frequency. *a* = Medium frequency current I. *b* = Medium frequency current II of slightly higher frequency than I. *c* = Result of combining medium frequency currents I and II.

close to the electrodes where maximum stimulation will occur; this is illustrated in Fig. 11.15*b*. Clearly it would be useful if the modulation, and hence nerve stimulation, could be made to occur in the deepest tissues; this is achieved by interferential currents.

INTERFERENTIAL CURRENTS

If two medium frequency currents of slightly different frequencies are passed through the tissues they will interfere with one another to produce a combined medium frequency current which varies in amplitude, i.e. it is *amplitude modulated*. This amplitude modulation is regular at a frequency determined by the difference in frequency of the two currents; it is called the 'beat' frequency. The idea is illustrated in Fig. 11.16. Thus an interferential machine could deliver one current at a constant 4000 Hz and the other a variable current between 3900 Hz and 3990 Hz which would allow a variable beat frequency of between 100 Hz and 10 Hz. This low frequency variation, the beat frequency, will stimulate nerve and muscle as already described. The great advantage of this method is that the stimulation is not produced close to the electrodes in the skin but near the centre of the four electrode arrangement as indicated in Fig. 11.15c.

It will be seen in Fig. 11.15c that the area of maximum stimulation is not square as might be expected, but of a four-leafed clover shape. It must be understood that this area merely shows the site of maximum current intensity in an homogeneous medium with small electrodes. The real interference field would pervade all the tissues between the electrodes and would be distorted by the different electrical properties of the various tissues, fat and muscle, etc. The reason for the four-leafed clover shaped area of maximum effect is that the two currents are summated not only in magnitude but also in direction, i.e. vector addition.

While the two medium frequencies remain constant so will the beat frequency, e.g. if the two frequencies differ by 50 Hz then the beat frequency will be a steady 50 Hz sinusoidal current. At suitable intensities, and applied appropriately, it could produce a steady, continuous muscle contraction—a *tetanic contraction*; similarly, it could cause a steady stimulation of sensory nerves. This may lead to a gradually diminished response due to habituation of the tissues to this particular current. It is also considered desirable to stimulate different nerve types and diameters during treatment. Both these deficiencies are corrected by continuously varying the beat frequency. This is called frequency swing or frequency sweep. The machine can be set to automatically change one of the medium frequency currents continuously to give a continuously varying beat frequency. The variation can be made to occur between specified upper and lower limits, e.g. 20–80 Hz; furthermore, the time taken by each of these swings or sweeps can be controlled on some machines. Thus it is possible to set the machine to swing repeatedly through a preset range of beat frequencies, say 20–80 Hz, during a preset period, say 6 s, followed by another 6 s period during which it swings back from 80 to 20 Hz.

Control of Interferential Output

The intensity of the currents, and hence of the beat frequency current, can be regulated to give more stimulation as required. There is an automatic timer to time the total treatment time, also separate controls for the timing and range of the frequency swing as indicated above. On some machines, provision is made to alter the pattern of the interference field regularly— called *rotating vector systems* or *dynamic interference field systems*. Essentially the four-leafed clover pattern of maximum stimulation shown in Fig. 11.15c is made to rotate to and fro through a small angle; this increases the area of effective treatment.

Application of Interferential Therapy

The currents are applied to the skin by means of electrodes which may be either malleable metal or of a special conducting rubber with a water soaked pad (spontex or lint) to pass the current to the skin. The wet pads serve to provide comfort and even current conduction; there is no danger of chemical or heat burns with interferential currents even if the electrode is placed directly on the skin. The electrodes and pads can be held in place either by bandaging or with rubber straps.

An alternative way of holding the electrodes in place is by means of a suction unit. Four flexible rubber cups are connected by tubes to a pump that can produce variable suction; metal electrodes are mounted inside the cups and connected by wires running inside the tubes to the interferential machine. Pieces of dampened spontex are placed inside the cups to provide good conduction to the skin. The suction is adjusted to be strong enough to keep the moist spontex in good contact with the skin without being uncomfortable. The suction pressure can be varied regularly during treatment which diminishes any risk of skin damage such as bruising. This is done automatically by the machine with cycles of a few seconds varying the force of the suction; the timing can be altered on some machines. The reasons for using suction are that it is a convenient way to apply the electrodes, it gives good even contact, and the varying suction has a gentle massaging action on the skin. This latter effect may cause mild vasodilatation which can lower the electrical resistance of the skin and may benefit the condition being treated due to the increased blood flow and mild mechanical stimulation of cutaneous sensory nerves.

Application and positioning of the electrodes

The relationship of the electrodes to the tissues is, literally, of crucial importance since the currents must be made to cross in the area being treated—the *target area*. The common arrangement is shown in cross-section in Fig. 11.15c in which the current of circuit I is carried by electrodes I^1 and I^2, while that of circuit II is carried by electrodes II^1 and II^2. For convenience the wires, or tubes, are usually colour coded. The electrodes can also be positioned in a coplanar arrangement (Fig. 11.17) for the treatment of a flat surface, such as the back. In order to ensure a large comfortable current throughout the area of treatment, the largest size of electrodes that can be conveniently applied are normally recommended (Savage, 1984).

The skin must be inspected and may be washed and left damp where the electrodes are to be placed to achieve the best conduction. The nature and

161

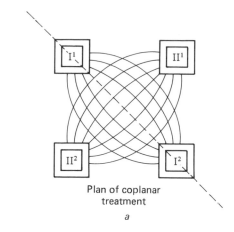

Plan of coplanar
treatment

a

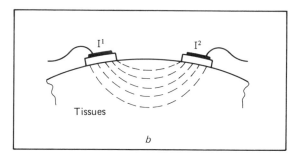

Fig. 11.17 A plan of coplanar treatment. *a* = Surface view. *b* = A cross-section along the line.

effects of the treatment should be explained to the patient and reassurance given that it is a harmless treatment producing no unpleasant sensations.

Effects of Interferential Currents

Different beat frequencies lead to different effects so that regular sweeps through a range of frequencies can lead to multiple effects. This explains why some physiotherapists propose different ranges of frequencies to achieve the same results. In general, the higher beat frequencies, around 100 Hz, are used for their analgesic effect whereas the lower beat frequencies, around 10 Hz, produce contraction of innervated muscle. All the effects appear to be due to stimulation of nerve tissue which leads to various secondary effects, such as muscle contraction and vasodilatation.

Pain relief

This is the most important effect and several mechanisms are thought to be implicated. These are as follows:

1. *Activation of the 'pain gate control' mechanism.* Stimulation of large-diameter afferent nerve fibres closes the 'gate' to nociceptive impulses in the substantia gelatinosa of the posterior horn of the spinal cord (see Chapter 5, Fig. 5.1, p. 30). Impulses of very short duration at a frequency of 100 Hz should selectively stimulate these large diameter nerve fibres and this could occur in interferential treatments (De Domenico, 1982).

2. *Activation of nociceptive fibres.* Activation of the nociceptive fibres themselves can diminish pain by means of the descending *pain suppressor system.* In this system nociceptive impulses passing up to regions in the mid-brain provoke impulses in neurons travelling back down the spinal cord to inhibit nociceptor neurons at the original level. Interferential currents could stimulate these fibres (see De Domenico, 1982).

3. *Physiological block.* It is possible, though not proven, that high frequency electrical stimuli—above 50 Hz—could cause a temporary physiological block in both finely myelinated and unmyelinated nociceptor nerve fibres (A-delta and C fibres).

   This appears to contradict section (2) above, but it is conceivable that both mechanisms could operate at different stages of the interferential current cycle. Both this effect and activation of the 'pain gate' would be expected to occur at a frequency sweep of 80–100 Hz, whereas the descending pain suppressor system is likely to be activated by frequencies in the 10–25 Hz region (De Domenico, 1982).

4. *Increased blood flow.* Pain suppression can also be due to an increased local blood flow and tissue fluid exchange; this may hasten the removal of chemical irritants acting on pain nerve endings and reduce pressure due to local exudate. Vasodilatation may occur as a result of stimulation of the autonomic nervous system (see below), and the regular mild muscle contraction has a pumping effect on vessels. (The varying suction pressure, when interferential current is applied by this method, may contribute to both the vasodilatation and the pumping effect.)

5. *The placebo effect.* Since the placebo effect occurs in all treatments it would be surprising if it did not contribute to pain relief with interferential treatment, especially since the machines are technically impressive and produce an unfamiliar, although not unpleasant, feeling.

In spite of widespread agreement amongst physiotherapists that interferential therapy has a marked pain relieving effect, there is a paucity of objective investigations into this analgesic effect. The time taken to elicit ischaemic pain at a range of pressures before and after interferential therapy was tested in one study (Pärtan *et al.*, 1953). The results showed that an increased pressure was needed to elicit pain after treatment indicating a rise in the pain threshold. The same study found a change in the strength/duration curves of muscle after interferential therapy. They used both square wave and triangular pulses and found a reduction in rheobase (the lowest voltage that will stimulate a nerve fibre given unlimited time) and chronaxie (the time for which current of twice rheobase must be applied to a nerve fibre to stimulate it); this effect was most marked immediately after treatment and returned to its initial state after 4 h or more. A study comparing the conduction velocities of nerves (median and ulnar) before and after interferential treatment showed no significant difference (Belcher, 1974). Further, a more recent study on jaw pain (Taylor *et al.*, 1987) concluded that there was no significant difference between three interferential and three placebo treatments. Thus the effects of interferential treatment on nerve action are neither fully quantified nor understood.

Muscle contraction

The lower beat frequencies stimulate motor nerves leading to the contraction of voluntary muscle (mainly at 10–50 Hz) and smooth muscle, via automatic nerves, extending to lower frequencies (Savage, 1984). Muscle contraction can be quite strong without any discomfort because, as already explained, there is little skin effect. When the beat frequency is varied, rhythmic muscle contraction will occur helping to reduce oedema or congestion by the pumping action on soft-walled vessels. It may also aid muscle control as in the treatment of incontinence.

Vasodilatation

Stimulation of the sympathetic ganglia with 100 Hz is claimed to produce reflex vasodilatation and be valuable for the treatment of causalgia (Wadsworth and Chanmugan, 1980). Skin temperature increases of 2–3°C were noted after interferential therapy by Pärtan *et al.* (1953). Other effects due to stimulation of the autonomic nervous system, such as increased rates of tissue healing, have been proposed.

Conditions Treated with Interferential Therapy

Pain

Interferential therapy is widely used for the relief of pain. It is considered to be particularly effective for the treatment of neurogenic pain such as postherpetic neuralgia, causalgia, phantom limb pain; it is also found to be of great value in the treatment of chronic pain both with and without oedema, but it is not considered as effective for the treatment of pain in the acute stage of post-traumatic injury (Wadsworth and Chanmugan, 1980). However, others use it and recommend it at this stage (Savage, 1984).

Muscle spasm

This would be diminished as a consequence of any reduction in pain; strong applications of electrokinesey, modulated medium frequency current through a single path (see Fig. 11.15*b*), have also been advocated for the reduction of muscle spasm (Wadsworth and Chanmugan, 1980).

Chronic ligamentous lesions, sprains and strains

Treatment of these lesions to relieve pain and accelerate healing is often recommended in conjunction with other treatments (Wadsworth and Chanmugan, 1980; Nikolova-Troeva, 1967a). Similarly a study on osteoarthrosis (arthrosis deformans), involving treatment with a number of electrotherapeutic agents, found a combination of microwave with interferential therapy to be most effective (Nikolova-Troeva, 1967b).

Gynaecological conditions

Interferential therapy has been applied to various gynaecological conditions, and one report of 300 cases claimed an average 90% improvement (Haag, 1979); swings of 0–100 Hz and 90–100 Hz were used with anterior and posterior electrodes so that the current crossed in the pelvis.

Stress incontinence

Since muscles can be stimulated by interferential currents with little skin effect, it might be expected that this would be a useful way to exercise weakened pelvic floor muscles and this has proved to be the case. Swings of 0–10 Hz or 0–100 Hz have been used, with the electrodes positioned anteriorly on the lower abdomen and posteriorly on the upper medial aspect of the thighs, and with the patient half lying. A study of 24 women treated with pelvic floor exercises and interferential therapy showed very convincing improvement (McQuire, 1975).

Chronic oedema

The muscle pumping and autonomic effects are useful in the treatment of postmastectomy or other chronic oedema.

Circulatory disturbances

The vasodilating effect is utilised, but vasoconstricting sympathetic stimulation by 0–5 Hz frequencies should be avoided, and the treatment should not be given if there is any risk of thrombosis (Savage, 1984).

Other conditions

Interferential treatment for asthma and migraine is sometimes given (Savage, 1984), again because of the effects on the autonomic nervous system.

Contraindications

1. Interferential therapy should not be used in the case of haemorrhage in a region, because the stimulation may cause further haemorrhaging. For the same reason, treatment of the pelvis during menstruation should be avoided.
2. Neoplastic tissue should not be treated directly in case the interferential treatment stimulates growth or encourages metastasis.
3. Acute infections should be avoided because the current may provoke the further spread of the infection.
4. Interferential therapy should not be used in cases of recent thrombosis, because there is a risk that the thrombus may be dislodged or disrupted forming an embolus and thus causing further damage.
5. Direct stimulation of the pregnant uterus should be avoided.
6. Cardiac pacemakers could be affected if the current were passed close to the heart or the implanted pacemaker itself. Interferential currents applied at a distance would be unlikely to cause any adverse effects.

A further important safety aspect is the recognition that unidirectional currents are produced by some interferential machines; various names are given for different types, e.g. 'Diadynamic currents' are a series of DC pulses of partial sine wave form. Skin damage can occur with such currents. Therefore the usual precautions taken when applying direct current should be followed.

It is clear that both the therapeutic and physiological effects of interferential currents require further research. On the evidence so far it seems to be a clinically valuable method of treatment which certainly warrants further investigation.

REFERENCES

Barker A. T. *et al.* (1985). A double-blind clinical trial of low power pulsed shortwave therapy in treatment of a soft tissue injury. *Physiotherapy*; **71(12):** 500–4.

Becker R. O., Marino A. A. (1982). *Electromagnetism and Life.* New York: State University of New York Press.

Belcher J. F. (1974). Interferential therapy. *N. Z. J. Physiother*; **Nov**; 29–34.

Bentall R. H. C., Eckstein H. B. (1975). A trial involving the use of pulsed electromagnetic therapy on children undergoing orchidopexy. *Kinderchirurgie*; **17(4):** 380–2.

Binder A., Hodge G., Greenwood A. M., Hazleman B. L., Page Thomas D. P. (1985). Is therapeutic ultrasound effective in treating soft tissue lesions? *Brit. Med. J*; **290:** 512–14.

Boyle A. C., Cook H. F., Buchanan T. J. (1950). The effects of microwaves: a preliminary investigation. *Brit. J. Phys. Med*; **13:** 2–8.

Brighton C. T. *et al.* (1981). A multicentre study of the treatment of non-union with constant direct current. *J. Bone Jt. Surg*; **163A(1):** 2–13.

Cameron B. (1961). Experimental acceleration of wound healing. *Amer. J. Orthopaed*; **53:** 336–43.

De Domenico G. (1982). Pain relief with interferential therapy. *Aust. J. Physiother;* **28(3):** 14–18.

DHSS Medical Scientific Services. (1980). Health equipment information, No. 88. London: HMSO.

Dyson M. (1985). Therapeutic applications of ultrasound. In *Clinics in Diagnostic Ultrasound,* Vol. 16 (*Biological Effects of Ultrasound*). (Nyborg W. L., Ziskin M. C., eds). New York: Churchill Livingstone.

Dyson M. (1987). Mechanisms involved in therapeutic ultrasound. *Physiotherapy;* **73(3):** 116–20.

Dyson M., Suckling J. (1978). Stimulation of tissue repair by ultrasound: a survey of the mechanism involved. *Physiotherapy;* **64(4):** 105–8.

Evans P. (1980). The healing process at cellular level: a review. *Physiotherapy;* **66(8):** 256–9.

Fenn J. E. (1969). Effect of pulsed electromagnetic energy (Diapulse) on experimental haematomas. *Can. Med. Assoc. J;* **100:** 251–4.

Fyfe M. C., Bullock M. I. (1985). Therapeutic ultrasound: some historical background and development in knowledge of its effects on healing. *Austral. J. Physiother;* **31(6):** 220–4.

Gammon G. D., Starr I. (1941). Studies on the relief of pain by counterirritation. *J. Clin. Invest;* **20:** 13–20.

Goldin J. H., Broadbent N. R. T., Nancarrow J. D., Marshall T. (1981). The effects of Diapulse on the healing of wounds: a double-blind randomised controlled trial in man. *Brit. J. Plastic Surg;* **14:** 267–70.

Haag W. (1979). Practical experience with interferential current therapy in gynaecology. *Der Frauenarzt;* **1(20):** 44–8.

Harris R. (1963). The effect of various forms of physical therapy on radio sodium clearance. *Ann. Phys. Med;* **7:** 1–10.

Harvey W., Dyson M., Pond J. B., Grahame R. (1975). The stimulation of protein synthesis in human fibroblasts by therapeutic ultrasound. *Rheumatol. Rehabil;* **14:** 237.

Hashish I., Harvey W., Harris H. (1986). Anti-inflammatory effects of ultrasound therapy: evidence for a major placebo effect. *Brit. J. Rheumatol;* **25:** 77–81.

Hayne C. R. (1984). Pulsed high frequency energy—its place in physiotherapy. *Physiotherapy;* **70(12):** 459–66.

Jones S. L. (1976). Electromagnetic field interference and cardiac pacemakers. *Phys. Ther;* **56(9):** 1013–18.

Kanui T. I. (1985). Thermal inhibition of nociceptor-driven spinal cord nerves in rats. *Pain;* **21:** 231–40.

Lehmann J. F., de Lateur B. J. (1982). Therapeutic heat. In *Therapeutic Heat and Cold,* 3rd edn. (Lehmann J. F., ed). Baltimore and London: Williams and Wilkins.

Lehmann J. F., Brunner G. D., Stow R. W. (1958). Pain threshold measurements after therapeutic application of ultrasound, microwaves and infrared. *Arch. Phys. Med. Rehabil;* **39:** 560–5.

Lehmann J. F., Masock A. J., Warren C. G., Koblanski J. N. (1970). Effect of therapeutic temperatures on tendon extensibility. *Arch. Phys. Med. Rehabil;* **51:** 481–7.

McQuire W. A. (1975). Electrotherapy and exercises for stress incontinence and urinary frequency. *Physiotherapy;* **61(10):** 305–7.

Millard J. B. (1961). Effect of high frequency current and infra-red rays on the circulation of the lower limb in man. *Ann. Phys. Med.;* **6:** 45–66.

Nicolle F. V., Bentall R. H. C. (1982). Use of radio-frequency pulsed energy in the control of post-operative reaction in blepharoplasty. *Aesthet. Plastic Surg;* **6:** 169–71.

Nikolova-Troeva L. (1967a). Interference-current therapy in distortions, contusions and luxations of the joints. *Münchener Med. Wochensch*; **109(11):** 579–82.

Nikolova-Troeva L. (1967b). Comparative studies on therapeutic results obtained by means of interference therapy and other methods in arthrosis deformans. *Phys. Med. Rehabil*; **8(3):** 239–61.

Pärtan J., Schmid J., Warum F. (1953). The treatment of inflammatory and degenerative joint conditions with interferential alternating currents of medium frequency. *Wiener Klin Wochensch*; **31:** 624–8.

Partridge C. J. (1987). Evaluation of the efficacy of ultrasound. *Physiotherapy*; **73(4):** 166–8.

Pasila M., Visuri T., Sundholm A. (1978). Pulsating shortwave diathermy: value in treatment of recent ankle and foot sprains. *Arch. Phys. Med. Rehabil*; **59:** 383–6.

Presman A. S. (1970). *Electromagnetic Fields and Life*. New York: Plenum Press.

Raji A. M. (1984). An experimental study of the effects of pulsed electromagnetic field (Diapulse) on nerve repair. *J. Hand Surg*; **9B(2):** 105–11.

Savage B. (1984). *Interferential Therapy*. London: Faber and Faber.

Scott B. O. (1957). *The Principles and Practice of Diathermy*. London: William Heinemann Medical Books.

Scowcroft A. T., Mason A. H. L., Hayne C. R. (1977). Safety with microwave diathermy. *Physiotherapy*; **63(11):** 359–61.

Taylor K., Newton R., Personius W., Bush F. (1987). Effect of interferential current stimulation for treatment of subjects with recurrent jaw pain. *Phys. Ther*; **67(3):** 346–50.

Wadsworth H., Chanmugam A. P. P. (1980). *Electrophysical Agents in Physiotherapy*. Marrickville, NSW Australia: Science Press.

Ward A. R. (1980). *Electricity Fields and Waves in Therapy*. Marrickville, NSW Australia: Science Press.

Wilson D. H. (1972). Treatment of soft tissue injuries by pulsed electrical energy. *Brit. Med. J*; **2:** 269.

Wilson D. H. (1981). PEME, the new beam for fractures. *World Med*; **Nov:** 97–8.

Wilson D. H., Jagadeesh P. (1976). Experimental regeneration in peripheral nerves and the spinal cord in laboratory animals exposed to a pulsed electromagnetic field. Proceedings of the Annual Scientific Meeting of the International Medical Society of Paraplegia 1975, Part III. *Paraplegia*; **14:** 12–20.

Wright V., Johns R. J. (1961). Quantitative and qualitative analysis of joint stiffness in normal subjects and in patients with connective tissue diseases. *Ann. Rheumat. Dis.*; **20:** 36–46.

Wright V. (1973). Stiffness: a review of its measurement and physiological importance. *Physiotherapy*; **59(4):** 107–11.

Chapter 12

Heat and Cold

NIGEL P. PALASTANGA

INTRODUCTION

The arguments concerning the relative merits of heat and cold in the management of pain are long and protracted. Each of these modalities has advocates who promote the advantages of their particular favourite, often without any comparative data. The net result of this situation is that the physiotherapist is faced with a conflicting mass of information regarding which form of treatment will be most effective in the modulation of pain. In this chapter an attempt will be made to rationalise the use of heat and cold for the reduction of pain, and to put into perspective the claims made for both. In the first part, various forms of therapeutic heat will be discussed, followed by a similar discussion on cold. Detail concerning the techniques of application is beyond the scope of this book, and the reader is referred to texts on electrotherapy (Forster and Palastanga, 1985; Wadsworth and Chanmugam, 1980) and cold therapy (Lee and Warren, 1974) for this information.

HEAT

The history of the use of heat to relieve aches and pains is as old as that of medicine itself. Therapeutic heat has been applied to the body by conduction from heated stones, sand, oils and water, or by radiant heat from sun or fire (Licht, 1984). Historically, heat has proven itself to be a very useful method of reducing pain, and although much of the evidence is empirical it cannot be ignored. Even when used today, some of the techniques of conductive heating or immersion in heated water must be very similar to those used by the Ancient Greeks and Romans. However, the advent of a more precise scientific and technological society has allowed the development of many different sources of therapeutic heat, the application of which can be accurately monitored in terms of depth of penetration and temperature rise achieved (Lehmann and de Lateur, 1984). The net effect however is a local or general rise in temperature, and it is this which is considered to produce the physiological effects responsible for a reduction in perceived pain.

Physiological Effects of Heat

This chapter is principally concerned with the modulation of pain utilising heat or cold. Other authors in this book have described in detail how pain is perceived, transmitted and modulated (see Section I). Consequently, only the mechanisms involved when heat is applied will be discussed here, and other more general considerations will be omitted.

To some extent the physiological effects produced by heat will depend upon the depth of penetration and level of temperature increase developed within the body. If excessive heat is produced, then the heat itself becomes a noxious stimulus which results in the perception of pain. This can be considered to be a warning of impending tissue damage, and as collagen starts to shrink and melt at temperatures above 50°C (Mason and Rigby, 1963), removal or reduction of the source of heat is essential to avoid a burn. Use of this mechanism has formed the basis for assessment of the level of heating which can be safely applied to patients, and requires the patient to have normal thermal sensation. When applying heat in any form, physiotherapists are required as a safety precaution to:

1. test the patient's thermal sensation;
2. warn the patient of the level of heating he should experience and to notify staff if the heat becomes uncomfortable.

It is interesting to note that the patient's subjective impression of the degree of warmth still forms the cornerstone of the use of heat, even when the technology used is highly complex.

Increased circulation

Heat is known to increase the circulation in superficial and deep tissues. A visible erythema is usually the result of applications of superficial heat, while conduction from superficial tissues or a deeper heating modality (e.g. microwave) can heat the deeper muscles. This increase in circulation is usually attributed to a vasodilatation of the walls of capillaries and arterioles produced by the direct effect of heat. Local axon reflexes may also operate, whereby sensory neurons have collaterals connected to the blood vessels, which again produce vasodilatation. The heat itself will produce an acceleration of metabolic rate (van't Hoff's rule) with a subsequent rise in the level of metabolites in the area. These metabolites can cause a vasodilatation of blood vessels by a direct action on their walls.

Overall, this increase in local circulation could well be responsible for reducing the level of nociceptive stimulation in a number of circumstances:

1. The pain associated with secondary muscle spasm or tension syndromes is attributed to a local ischaemia resulting from partial occlusion of blood vessels within the muscle. Heat produces a hyperaemia within the muscle which immediately resolves the ischaemia with a consequent reduction of pain.
2. Where pain is the result of nociceptor stimulation produced by chemicals as a result of trauma or inflammation, a gentle increase in the local circulation could well remove these chemicals and thus reduce the pain.
3. Where local pressure on nociceptive endings as a result of swelling is causing pain, gentle local heat could help reduce the swelling and therefore the level of pain perception. However, cold is probably a more effective modality in this circumstance, as heat can often aggravate the situation in the very acute stage.

Increased extensibility of collagen

Often, limitation of the range of movement is the result of the structures containing collagen shortening. These structures, e.g. ligaments, capsules, tendons and aponeuroses, cross joints. Heat has been shown to increase the extensibility of collagen (Gersten, 1955), and is thus very useful prior to physical movements aimed at stretching these structures. In terms of pain modulation, the fact that collagen is more extensible will allow it to be stretched further before the nociceptive endings are stimulated. This is an indirect, but useful effect as it is the pain of the stretching manoeuvre which limits this procedure.

The Gate Control Theory

The *gate control theory* (*see* Chapter 5, p. 30) of pain modulation was first proposed by Melzack and Wall in 1965, and then revised by them in 1982. Although it has its critics (Nathan, 1976) as a theory for the modulation of pain at a spinal level, it is still widely accepted. A detailed explanation of this theory is given in Chapter 5 (p. 30). Therefore only its relevance to heat (and later cold) will be given here. If it is accepted that the thermal sensation produced by local heat is carried to the posterior horn of the spinal cord in large diameter myelinated nerves, then it fulfils the criteria for 'closing' the pain gate to the predominantly small diameter nociceptive impulses. The synapses within the layers of the nucleus proprius and substantia gelatinosa will transmit the thermal sensation through to consciousness in preference to the nociceptive (pain) impulses.

Descending Pain Suppression System

This system involves areas of the brainstem releasing endogenous opiates within the nervous system (Basbaum and Fields, 1978) resulting in a reduction of the level of pain perception (*see* Chapter 5, p. 34). For this to operate, the level of heat applied has to be sufficiently powerful in order to produce a very strong (almost noxious) stimulus. As this is at the level which would produce a burn, the reduction of pain could only be achieved as a consequence of thermal injury. However, it is likely that endogenous opiates are produced as the result of a strong placebo effect which often operates when any form of physical therapy is applied.

Methods of Heating Tissues

The distribution of heat within tissues depends upon a number of factors, e.g.:

1. The amount of energy which is converted to heat.
2. The specific heat of the tissue will affect its thermal properties.
3. Biological systems, such as blood flow, will have a marked effect upon the level of heating produced.

Heat must be transferred to the tissues by some mechanism, and this may be by conduction or some other form of energy changing into heat within the body.

Conductive heating

This form of heating involves the transfer of thermal energy from a heated substance to the body tissues by conduction. Commonly, a number of methods of heat application are used as a treatment to modulate pain.

Immersion

Immersion in hot water or heated natural springs has been a popular treatment for multiple joint pains for thousands of years. Today, hydrotherapy is still widely used, patients are immersed in water heated to 37°C as part of their treatment for numerous conditions including the joint pain of rheumatoid arthritis and ankylosing spondylitis. This form of treatment has the added advantage that the physical forces which exist within the water can be used to assist or resist movements of the patient while they exercise in the water (see Chapter 15). Local immersion can be used for painful hands or feet.

Hot packs

Water heated to about 80°C can be used to heat special cloth packs filled with a silicon gel. The gel absorbs and retains the thermal energy, and is applied to the painful area wrapped in dry towels. The heat is conducted from the pack into the patient's tissues, and the degree of heat developed within the patient's tissues depends largely on the number of insulating towels used.

Electrically heated pads

These pads resemble a small electric blanket and utilise the thermal effect of an electric current to produce heat within the wires they contain. The whole pad is wrapped in layers of towelling and the heat conducted from the pad to the patient's tissues. Generally these flat pads are most easily applied to the back or neck, and the degree of heating is controlled by a simple switch.

Paraffin wax

Paraffin wax is heated into its molten state and kept at a temperature of about 44°C in a specially designed container. The patient has the molten wax applied to the painful area (usually the hands or feet) until a thick coat has solidified on the skin. As the wax changes state from liquid to solid, kinetic energy is released in the form of latent heat and this, combined with the original heat of the wax, is conducted to the patient. Consequently, a pleasant warmth is developed which is often very useful in conditions such as rheumatoid arthritis.

Absorption of electromagnetic waves

Infrared

Infrared rays are electromagnetic waves of radiation lying in a band between 750 and 400 000 nm in the electromagnetic spectrum. Any heated body emits infrared rays, but for therapeutic purposes specific infrared generators have been developed in order to apply the most appropriate spectrum of radiation to the patient. There is no contact between the patient and generator, the thermal effect being developed within the patient's tissues by conversion of electromagnetic energy into thermal energy once the infrared energy has been absorbed. In practice, two types of generator are available for the production of infrared rays:

1. *Non-luminous generators*. These utilise the principle of heating some material (e.g. fireclay or metal) via a wire carrying an electric current. Once heated, this material starts to emit electromagnetic radiation in the infrared range, with a peak production at a wavelength of 4000 nm. Most of this energy is absorbed and converted to heat in the epidermis and so must be conducted to deeper tissues to have any useful effect.
2. *Luminous generators*. Infrared is invisible to the human eye, so the generator is named because of the visible light which it also produces. The electromagnetic radiation is produced by an incandescent bulb and, in terms of the infrared wavelength, has a peak emission at a wavelength

of 1000 nm. This wavelength is absorbed and converted to heat in the dermis, and so penetrates more deeply than that produced by non-luminous generators. However, it is still relatively superficial and once again will require conduction to take place to affect the deeper tissues.

In terms of pain relief, infrared is a very superficial form of heat and the only advantage enjoyed over conductive heating is the non-contact application. The treatment of deep painful structures depends, as with conductive heating, on the conduction of heat down to them. In practice, the gentle application of infrared has proved a very useful means of reducing the level of pain by the mechanisms previously described, prior to using other forms of therapy, e.g. exercise.

Microwave

Microwaves are also a form of electromagnetic radiation which, when absorbed by the patient's tissues, are converted to heat. Two wavelengths are commonly used medically: 12.5 cm and 69 cm. The microwaves are produced by a generator and then projected via an emitter towards the patient. The microwaves penetrate the tissues quite deeply (see Chapter 11, p. 133), and they are absorbed by tissues high in water content, e.g. muscle. A penetration of at least 3 cm can be expected. Consequently, microwaves are useful when heat needs to be produced in deeper tissues. Useful therapeutic heating effects can be achieved within muscular tissue and so microwaves have been found of value in the management of soft tissue pain (see Chapter 11, p. 133).

Shortwave diathermy

Shortwave diathermy is used to produce heat deep within the tissues. The patient is positioned so that his tissues are influenced by either an electrostatic or electromagnetic field. Shortwave diathermy operates at a wavelength of 11 m with a frequency of 27.12 MHz (see Chapter 11, p. 116).

Capacitor heating is a method in which the patient's tissues are placed between two capacitor plates attached to the machine. A high frequency current oscillates between these two plates and so the patient's tissues are subjected to a strong electrostatic charge in one direction, and then in the reverse direction. Overall, this alternating electric field will exert an influence on charged particles within the field (the tissues) in such a way that heat is generated. The particles influenced are found in fluids (dipoles and ions) and in insulators (cell membranes and fat). Considerable heat is developed by the capacitor field method of applying shortwave diathermy by the oscillation of these charged particles, but unfortunately the greatest heat is produced in fat which limits the amount of energy that can be applied during the treatment.

In terms of depth of penetration shortwave diathermy should, in theory, produce heating right the way through as its name implies. In practice, this is rarely the case. The distribution of the field within the tissues and consequently the amount of heat developed will depend very much upon the arrangement of the tissues and positioning of the electrodes. Provided that an effective technique is chosen (Forster and Palastanga, 1985) then shortwave diathermy can form a useful method of applying heat to painful deep joints such as the hip. A number of important points of technique need to be observed in order to avoid concentration of the field with resultant damage to the patient's tissues (Forster and Palastanga, 1985). The mechanism of pain relief has been described earlier, but the effect of shortwave on the circulation throughout the area as well as its other thermal effects has made it a very popular method of managing painful joints associated with degenerative conditions such as osteoarthritis.

Inductive heating utilises the strong magnetic field which is generated around an inductothermy cable as a result of the high frequency current it is carrying within. The magnetic field is placed so that it passes through the patient. Eddy currents are produced relative to the magnetic lines of force in the patient's tissues which offer low impedance. The eddy currents themselves generate heat within tissues, such as muscle, and as such form a very useful method of fairly superficial heating.

One of the advantages of inductive heating, or inductothermy, is that the cable can be wound around a painful limb, or coiled to form a flat helix which can be placed on the back. This method of heating has been very popular for musculoskeletal pain.

Pulsed electromagnetic energy is a form of treatment where the danger of thermal damage which exists with ordinary shortwave diathermy has been removed by breaking up the applied energy into very short pulses (e.g. 65 µs) of very high energy (e.g. 975 W). No thermal effect is appreciated by the patient, but the influence of the electromagnetic energy on the electrical potential of damaged cells has shown itself to be of benefit in the management of repair, swelling and pain (Barclay, 1983). Although, strictly speaking, this is not a method of producing heat, it is necessary to consider this method of treatment alongside the more traditional form of thermal, continuous shortwave modalities. Most of the dangers associated with shortwave diathermy are removed if pulsed electromagnetic energy is used, and as a result its popularity as a method of treatment is increasing (see Chapter 11, p. 150ff).

Ultrasound

Therapeutic ultrasound is produced by the high frequency oscillation of a piece of piezoelectric material. The oscillation is the same as the frequency of the electric current producing it, and can be 0.75, 1, 1.5 or 3 MHz. Ultrasound used to be applied purely as a method of producing heat, as the acoustic energy absorbed by the tissues generated local thermal effects. Although the thermal effect of ultrasound is still recognised, other beneficial effects on the tissues have been reported (Dyson and Suckling, 1978). Even when a pulsed mode of application is used where short periods of ultrasound are interspersed with silences, a thermal effect is still produced.

The thermal effect of ultrasound, if sufficiently strong, could reduce pain perception by the mechanisms attributed to heat as described earlier (p. 170). In addition, it is probable that the mechanical stimulation of mechanoreceptors by ultrasound could have an effect on the transmission of nociceptive impulses at the posterior horn.

Ultrasound is applied via a couplant to the patient's tissues, but as the beam is transmitted into the tissues it undergoes marked attenuation as the result of: diffraction at tissue interfaces, absorption and scatter of the beam. The net result of these effects is that the useful intensity, and therefore the heat developed, reduces dramatically with depth. Consequently ultrasound is most useful when treating fairly superficial musculoskeletal conditions. As mentioned earlier there is much evidence relating to the usefulness of ultrasound in promoting repair and these effects are often required simultaneously with the relief of pain, e.g. sports injuries (see Chapter 11, p. 142).

COLD

Cold also has been used for the reduction of pain for thousands of years (Licht, 1984). Originally snow and ice were either stored in deep vaults or were transported from mountainous regions. As a result it was something of a 'luxury' treatment. Later, in the 19th century, cooling was achieved by the evaporation of spirits such as ether on the skin, a process that removes considerable heat from the tissues. Cold compresses have always been used for immediate pain relief, and the 'cold sponge' still plays an important part in the immediate management of painful sports injuries.

Today, ice forms the major source of cold application to the body. When placed on the skin, heat is conducted from the patient's body to the ice which then changes its state from solid to liquid, i.e. it melts. Simple as this process seems, it requires considerable thermal energy for the change of state from solid to liquid. As a simple example: 1 g ice at 0°C takes 491 J energy to form water at 37°C; 1 g water at 0°C takes 155 J energy to raise its temperature to 37°C.

This fact is of importance when using cold for therapeutic purposes, as greater cooling is achieved when ice is used. When ice is placed on the skin dramatic and immediate cooling occurs in the superficial tissues which experience a temperature drop of up to 15°C (30°C–15°C) within 2–5 min. Deeper muscular tissues are not cooled as much and usually only experience a temperature drop of 5°C (35°C–30°C) and this can take up to 20 min to develop at a depth of 2.5 cm, longer if the subcutaneous fat layer is thick. In a normal, intact physiological system this needs to be noted as by far the greatest degree of cooling has occurred in the subcutaneous tissues, with only a very small temperature reduction at a depth of 2.5 cm. Many of the effects of cooling are therefore achieved by the effect on the skin; this suggests that the physiological finding of a reduced velocity of conduction when axons are cooled has little significance but for the most superficial nerve fibres. Many of the older theories for reduction of pain and spasticity cite reduced velocity of conduction as the mechanism involved (Douglas and Malcomb, 1955), but laboratory investigations on exposed nerve tissue does not necessarily transfer to the intact physiological situation.

Physiological Effects of Cold

The two physiological effects of therapeutic cold which affect pain are that on the local circulation and that on the nervous system.

Circulatory effects

The initial response of the skin to the application of cold is a sudden local vasoconstriction which allows the skin to become very cold. Following this an attempt is made by the circulatory system to restore the body temperature to normal by a local vasodilatation to allow more warmed blood into the skin. There then follow short periods of alternating vasoconstriction and vasodilatation as the circulation 'hunts' for its normal level in order to prevent tissue damage. This gives rise to the so called *Lewis's hunting reaction* (Keatinge, 1961) whereby the circulation goes through periods of stasis and flushing.

In the management of recent injuries, use is made of the initial vasoconstriction which can last up to 10 min. The cold is applied immediately to the injured area in an attempt to limit the extravasation of blood from damaged vessels into the tissues. This vasoconstriction is attributed to reflex activity via sympathetic fibres and the direct effect of cooled blood on the vessel walls. Pain may be reduced, or prevented, by a reduction of swelling which itself stimulates nociceptors. Generally speaking, the cold application is followed by some form of compressive bandage.

The vasodilatation which occurs later, and then the alternate flushing effect, could usefully help reduce pain by removing substances which stimulate nociceptors as a result of trauma or inflammation. This effect is frequently utilised in the management of more chronic conditions where established swelling contributes considerably to the pain experienced. The circulatory effect of cold doubtless has a beneficial effect on the rate of repair.

Neural effects

When ice is applied to normally innervated skin it acts as an extremely powerful sensory stimulus. Use of this sensory experience can be beneficial in the treatment of hypertonic muscle states and pain.

When muscles are in spasm (the reversible condition of hypertonic muscles as a result of injury) or are spastic (as a result of an upper motor neuron lesion), pain is often a consequence of the result of an accumulation of metabolites within the muscle. Ice can have a marked and dramatic effect on muscle spasm, which allows a normal circulation to carry away the offending chemicals and thus reduce pain, so allowing normal use. In cases of spasticity, ice can reduce tone sufficiently for a similar effect on pain, but is far more important for its role of allowing the application of techniques to remedy the spastic patterns of movement.

In terms of pain modulation via its sensory effect, the sensation of cold would be carried to the posterior horn by large diameter, myelinated fibres and would consequently have a marked effect on the perception of pain. As described earlier and elsewhere in this book (see Chapter 5, p. 30) the pain gate would be closed (Melzack and Wall, 1965; 1982) to nociceptive impulses.

The application of ice itself can be considered a noxious stimulus, and as such the afferent impulses, generated by the application of cold could cause centres in the brainstem (notably the periaqueductal grey matter and raphe nucleus) to release endorphins at a spinal level and thus reduce pain.

In practice, this theory is borne out, and ice can often produce a dramatic reduction in the level of pain that patients perceive. Frequently, the severe pain of acute joint inflammation experienced by those with rheumatoid arthritis for example can be successfully reduced. Even the pain from relatively deep structures responds well to the application of cold and allows other useful procedures to take place. Cold can, in fact, be seen as a treatment in its own right, but is frequently used as part of a comprehensive treatment programme.

Cold can be applied in a number of ways to the body and the choice of packs, towels, immersion or ice cube massage depends on the area to be treated, and local facilities available. Gel packs are available which conductively cool the tissues and are cooled in the freezer compartment of a refrigerator. However, a study by McMaster *et al.* (1978) showed that a standardised technique using melting ice cooled more effectively than gel or chemical packs. Further details on techniques of application, contraindications and other effects should be sought in more basic texts (see e.g. Forster and Palastanga, 1985; Lee and Warren, 1974).

ALTERNATE HEAT AND COLD

Contrast baths, whereby both heat and cold can be applied alternately, are considered here.

The limb is placed first in hot water (40–50°C) and then into cold iced water (10–15°C). The time spent in each bath is usually until the greatest heating or cooling effect is felt, or a standard 4 min hot to 1 min cold for a total of 30 min.

Contrast baths are claimed to have a marked effect on the circulation, a fact supported by the vivid erythema produced. This circulatory effect could well modulate pain by mechanisms described earlier (p. 170). Secondly, each plunge into the iced water will act as a new sensory stimulus and so could modulate pain via the neuronal mechanisms described in the posterior horn and brainstem.

HEAT VERSUS COLD

In clinical practice, there are circumstances when one of these modalities is preferable to the other. For example, in the management of an acute sports injury cold is preferred as it limits the local extravasation of blood into the tissues and therefore limits the pain produced by swelling. It could be argued that the increase in circulation produced by the application of heat could well worsen the situation and so increase the pain. If, e.g. the offending injury were a haematoma in the quadriceps muscle, ice packs would usually be the treatment of choice initially, followed by compressive bandaging to maintain restriction on the size of the bleed. If, after a few weeks, the lesion had become chronic with fibrosis of the haematoma and associated binding down of adjacent muscle fibres, deep heat in the form of shortwave diathermy or ultrasound would then be the treatment of choice. In this latter situation, the heat is a preliminary to stretching and other manipulations of the fibrosed tissue which would follow.

Although cold has a dramatic effect in reduction of muscle spasm and pain, there are situations when the ice itself may make the spasm worse. For example, in the acute back or neck syndrome, the application of an ice pack or towel could increase local spasm. This is probably a combination of the irritative effect of the cold and the pressure of the towel on the neck or back. In this situation the gentle, comfortable warmth offered by conductive heating from a heat pad or the radiations of infrared or microwave may have a more effective place in the management of the spasm and pain of this condition, prior to the application of suitable physiotherapy techniques.

Occasionally the situation arises where the determined preference of the patient may influence the clinical judgement of the physiotherapist as to which agent to use. Frequently, in the management of recent injuries in the elderly, e.g. fractured surgical neck of humerus or dislocated shoulder, the idea of cold so terrifies the patient that its likely benefits are outweighed by the psychological trauma that its use might cause. In this situation the physiotherapist frequently has no choice but to use gentle heat to modulate pain prior to exercise, even though cold would be more appropriate.

Anatomical considerations may also enter into the equation when treating a deep joint such as the hip. The depth of this joint makes the only effective form of heat shortwave diathermy, as it is doubtful whether cold can affect

179

the joint at all, even if it were practical to apply ice in this region. The same arguments apply in part to the sacroiliac joint, however in this region the posterior soft tissues may respond well to cooling.

The eventual decision as to which modality to use should rest with the physiotherapist who will, as the result of her assessment, make a clinical diagnosis as to which tissues the modality should be applied to reduce the pain. Considerations, such as the relative acuteness, depth of tissues, anticipated effect, accessibility of the part, patient tolerance, relevant contraindications and so on will all have to be taken into account before the physiotherapist makes the decision as to whether heat or cold is to be used. Once a course of treatment is under way, frequent reassessment of the patient's progress will allow appropriate changes to be made in their programme if necessary.

REFERENCES

Barclay V. (1983). Treatment of various hand injuries by pulsed electromagnetic energy (Diapulse). *Physiotherapy;* **69(6)**: 186–8.

Basbaum A., Fields H.L. (1978). Endogenous pain control mechanisms: review and hypothesis. *Ann. Neurol:* **4**: 451–62.

Douglas W., Malcomb J. (1955). The effect of localised cooling on conduction in cat nerves. *J. Physiol;* **130**: 53–71.

Dyson M., Suckling J. (1978). Stimulation of tissue repair by ultrasound. *Physiotherapy,* **64(4)**: 105–8.

Forster A., Palastanga N. (1985). *Clayton's Electrotherapy, Theory and Practice,* 9th edn. London: Baillière Tindall.

Gersten J. (1955). Effect of ultrasound on tendon extensibility. *Amer. J. Phys. Med;* **34**: 362–9.

Keatinge W. (1961) Cold vasodilatation after adrenalin. *J. Physiol;* **159**: 101–10.

Lee J., Warren M. (1974). *Cold Therapy in Rehabilitation.* London: Bell and Hyman.

Lehmann J., de Lateur B. (1984). Therapeutic heat. In *Therapeutic Heat and Cold,* 3rd edn. (Lehmann J., ed.). Baltimore and London: Williams and Wilkins.

Licht S. (1984). History of therapeutic heat and cold. In *Therapeutic Heat and Cold,* 3rd edn. (Lehmann J., ed.). Baltimore and London: Williams and Wilkins.

McMaster W., Liddle S., Waugh T. (1978). Laboratory evaluation of various cold therapy modalities. *Amer. J. Sports Med;* **6**: 291–4.

Mason P., Rigby B. (1963). Thermal transitions in collagen. *Biochem. Biophys. Acta;* **66**: 448–50.

Melzack R., Wall P. (1965). Pain mechanisms: a new theory. *Science;* **150**: 971–9.

Melzack R., Wall P. (1982). *The Challenge of Pain.* Harmondsworth: Penguin.

Nathan P. (1976). The gate control theory of pain: a critical review. *Pain;* **99**: 123–58.

Wadsworth H., Chanmugam A. (1980). *Electrophysical Agents in Physiotherapy.* Marrickville, NSW Australia: Science Press.

Chapter 13

Manipulative Procedures

PETER E. WELLS

INTRODUCTION

The use of the hands for skilful and dextrous treatment is central to the practice of physiotherapy. Direct intervention by physiotherapists to alleviate pain is most clearly illustrated by those aspects of professional practice which involve various forms of handling and manipulative therapy. As the surgeon is typified by the cutting, repairing and replacing of tissues so is the physiotherapist by therapeutic handling and the various types of passive movement.

From the earliest part of their training physiotherapists begin to acquire the refined manual skills which make up the various manipulative procedures including massage and passive joint mobilisation. However, the so-called 'art' of manipulation is less a matter of acquiring ever more techniques, but more the skilful assessment of when and how they should be used. In this respect the selection, application and assessment of manipulative procedures for the treatment of pain is arguably the most 'skilful' aspect of manipulation.

Whatever the emphasis given in any particular case to the use of manipulative procedures, these are always considered alongside such things as the need for muscle re-education, relaxation, postural realignment and careful education of the patient. There is evidence that a combination of such treatment is more effective than the use of any one of them alone (Coxhead *et al.*, 1981).

GENERAL INDICATIONS

Manipulative procedures are applied to treating parts of the musculoskeletal system when pain and restricted movement, or occasionally excessive movement, have resulted from trauma, degenerative change and long-term postural stress. A large and varied range of ailments, the origins of which lie in some dysfunction or malfunction of musculoskeletal structures, respond to carefully selected and suitably modified manipulative treatment. The tissues of the spine, trunk, head and limbs are equally amenable to treatment by these methods.

The musculoskeletal structures include the joints with their ligaments and joint capsules, muscles and tendons including the tenoperiosteal junctions, the cartilaginous junctions between the vertebral bodies referred to as discs, and the fascia which commonly exists in dense sheets which envelop the muscular compartments of the body and forms the subcutaneous connective tissues (see also Chapter 14).

CLASSIFICATION OF MANIPULATIVE PROCEDURES

Since the subject of manipulation is bedevilled by semantics, it has come to mean different things to different people. For example, many of the general public and even the medically qualified associate manipulation with high velocity thrust techniques and little else, and many seem to believe that it involves very forceful and even aggressive procedures.

To those who regularly employ manual therapy in their day-to-day clinical work it covers a wide range of procedures from the very gentle to the more firm or vigorous.

Clearly there must be a framework within which can be defined the many procedures which are commonly employed across the wide spectrum known as manipulative therapy. Such a framework, now used by most physiotherapists, is as follows:

1. Soft tissue techniques (massage).
2. Regional mobilisation.
3. Localised mobilisation.
4. Regional manipulation.
5. Localised manipulation.

It should be made clear what is meant by each of these categories. Firstly, what is the difference between *mobilisation* and *manipulation*?

Mobilisation consists of passive movement techniques usually employing repetitive movement, which is under the patient's control. This means that if the patient for any reason communicates to the operator that he wishes the technique to be stopped then it can be. The patient is, of course, relaxed throughout and does not control the procedure by any active movement on his part. Repetitive oscillatory movements to relax muscles, relieve pain or carefully elongate tight structures come under the grouping of *mobilisation*.

A *manipulation*, on the other hand, consists of a single, high velocity thrust applied to a joint or series of joints and soft tissues. This procedure gaps or moves the joint very quickly and is carried out to create extra freedom of movement and to relieve pain. Because of its speed and the fact that it is only ever attempted while the patient is relaxed, the technique is not under the patient's control. It is over almost before he knows it has been done.

The categories that have been set down may now be defined and discussed.

Soft Tissue Techniques (Massage)

Whereas this range of procedures is sometimes grouped together as *'massage'* the tendency now is to use the expression *'soft tissue techniques'*, since the word massage has acquired a very general and non-medical connotation. This is unfortunate since skilled massage administered by the medically trained and experienced physiotherapist can give very beneficial effects in a number of conditions, especially orthopaedic and rheumatological ones.

The growth in the popularity of generalised and non-specific massage, administered by an assortment of non-medical masseuses and aimed at helping the individual relax, has been accompanied by a decline in the widespread use of massage by physiotherapists. One reason for the more restricted use of massage within physiotherapy is that recent decades have seen the growth in our knowledge of musculoskeletal biomechanics and neurology. As a result it is becoming clear that many problems previously thought to arise principally within soft tissues, such as muscles, do in fact owe more of their cause to joint disturbances. These problems then manifest themselves secondarily in muscles, fascia and so forth, e.g. fibrositis. In situations where patients complain of pain, tenderness and 'stiffness' of muscles, e.g. those of the neck and scapular area, more attention is now placed upon analysing very specifically the joint and movement abnormalities underlying the problem and less emphasis given to treating purely the soft tissue disturbances accompanying it.

Nevertheless, massage or soft tissue techniques maintain a rightful place in the field of natural medical alternatives to drug therapy and surgery. Their use is now restricted to very specific instances when they are judged to be particularly beneficial. In the treatment of painful musculoskeletal conditions and impaired function, massage is usually used in conjunction with other passive joint mobilising procedures. Where this is so, it goes without saying that each procedure is assessed independently, both for its inclusion in treatment and also its effects.

It is interesting to note the results of a recent investigation by Danneskiold-Samsøe *et al.* (1986) into the effects of massage. The reporting, by 21 patients out of 26 with myofascial pain, of a steady improvement in their symptoms during a course of 10 massage treatments (each of 30–45 min) was accompanied by a gradual decline in the increase (following each massage session) of plasma myoglobin concentration. A parallel gradual decline in muscle tension was also reported. It is clear from this investigation that the effects of massage are not all in the mind (important though that is) but that measurable biochemical changes may be observed as a result, and that these changes accompany the subjective reporting of improvement by patients with what is termed in this investigation *'myofascial pain syndrome'*.

While it is known that massage often produces a sense of well-being and may gain the confidence of the patient, its use by physiotherapists is perhaps best confined to those patients whose pain or other symptoms can be shown to arise from their muscles or other soft tissues. Those physiotherapists working in the field of psychiatry may take exception to this rule.

The principal massage techniques used for the relief of pain are:

1. Effleurage.
2. Stroking.
3. Kneading (petrissage).
4. Vibration.
5. Frictions.

Different techniques clearly have different effects and therefore reduction in pain during and following their use may be achieved by different mechanisms. It is easy to speculate upon some of these mechanisms but clearly it is not known for certain how the results observed are mediated. The selection of techniques will depend upon the cause as well as the intensity and reactivity (irritability) of the pain and other symptoms.

Effleurage

This technique consists of a stroking movement in the direction of the flow in the veins and lymphatics. The essential aspects of technique which will ensure the maximal effect are:

1. the relaxation of the hands which must mould to the shape of the part being treated;
2. the use of even pressure, the degree and rate of which must vary in order to be maximally effective but not aggravate the patient's symptoms. This pressure must be maintained throughout the movement;
3. each stroke must be carried to the nearest group of superficial lymphatic nodes. When small irregular areas are treated the technique is carried out using the fingers or thumb;

The effects of effleurage may be summarised as:

1. the hastening of the flow of blood towards the heart by mechanical pressure upon the superficial veins,
2. the acceleration of lymph flow in a similar manner;
3. the stretching of subcutaneous soft tissues;
4. the increase of circulation in the skin;
5. the stimulation of pressure and touch receptors in the skin.

The use of effleurage for the relief of pain is particularly justified when soft tissue oedema (especially that causing very high tissue pressure) and the resultant high concentration of metabolic by products such as histamine, bradykinin etc., appear to be contributing to the patient's discomfort or frank pain.

Part of the effect in modulating pain may occur as a result of the accentuation of the pain gate control mechanism (p. 30) in the central nervous system by the considerable sensory stimulation resulting from the technique.

Stroking

This technique is similar to effleurage but exerts less pressure and is performed in any direction on the body surface. When employed in the presence of pain, it is always slow, light and rhythmical. The whole palmar surface of the relaxed hand is used with even pressure, and care must be taken not to tickle or irritate the patient when lifting off the hands at the end of each stroke.

The effect of stroking is purely sensory. When carried out in a careful, rhythmical manner for a period of time its effect in calming and relaxing the tense and anxious patient may be considerable. Conversely, if there is any sign that the patient does not like being handled in this way and cannot accept the technique then it is, of course, abandoned. Any decrease in pain which results is probably due to sedative sensory effects and the effect upon the reduction of tension and the 'holding' effect of muscles.

Kneading (petrissage)

The various techniques of kneading are primarily directed at muscles and the connective tissue coverings which surround and divide them. The subcutaneous tissues are also affected. The tissues are either:

1. compressed and then released, as with circular kneading, a circular movement is carried out with one or both hands with pressure exerted inwards and upwards. Small areas are treated with the fingertips or thumbs.
2. grasped, lifted up, squeezed and then relaxed as with the technique of picking-up. Alternatively, the muscles may be grasped with both hands and lifted up, the hands then moving alternately backwards across the direction of the muscle fibres, as with wringing (Fig. 13.1).
3. rolled between the fingers and thumb with the hands lying flat on the surface, as with the technique of skin rolling. The tissues are rolled forwards by the thumbs and backwards by the fingers.

The effect of the kneading techniques are similar to those of effleurage as far as the circulation of the tissues being manipulated is concerned. In addition, muscle tissues are stretched by the slow deep technique and a mobilising effect may be achieved. The same occurs with the skin as a result of skin rolling. Slow, rhythmic kneading may also have a general sedative effect.

185

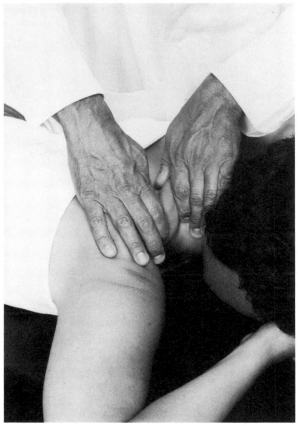

Fig. 13.1 *Wringing.* An example of a soft tissue technique to stretch and relax sore, tense muscles often found accompanying a chronic joint problem.

The use of kneading techniques for pain relief is mainly indicated in the more chronic situations where sore, tender, aching muscles frequently accompany underlying joint problems, e.g. in the paraspinal muscles and the other large muscles of the neck and trunk, particularly in the case of chronic recurrent cervical and lumbar spinal problems. In these situations, it is clearly vital to assess and treat any underlying joint problems as the first priority, thereafter employing soft tissue techniques, such as kneading when indicated. The same, of course, applies to muscle pain and tenderness in the upper and lower limbs and its relation to spinal or peripheral joint problems.

Where pain of a more severe nature and possibly a more recent onset is being treated, kneading techniques must be used with great care since any severe or irritable symptoms will be easily stirred, e.g. when treating a haematoma in a recently traumatised muscle. Both the rhythm and depth of the techniques must be adapted to the patient's response guided by a continuous assessment of the symptoms throughout the treatment session. Another example of this situation would be the early treatment of a cervical whiplash injury (i.e. within the first few weeks).

Vibration

This technique is a fine form of tremor conveyed through the hands or fingertips. It is a difficult technique to achieve. It is used in order to induce relaxation in muscles where soft tissue trauma, such as tears and haematomas are accompanied by severe muscle spasm. It is often the earliest and safest technique which may be given directly over a muscle haematoma for example.

The rationale for using vibrations in the treatment of acute soft tissue pain is two-fold: firstly, fine vibration appears to have a sedative effect. In situations where pressure and stretching of the soft tissues is not tolerated, vibrations may be the first step in establishing a manual approach and gaining some muscle relaxation. Secondly, the fine mechanical effect in and around the centre of the lesion may assist in hastening the resolution of inflammation.

It is interesting that many who suffer from chronic, recurrent muscular aches and pains find the use of a battery or electrically operated vibrator, directly applied to the affected muscles, gives considerable relief of their symptoms (see Chapter 5, p. 32).

Frictions

These are small penetrating movements, performed by the thumb or fingertips, in which the superficial tissues are moved on the deeper ones (Fig. 13.2). They may be done in a circular or transverse direction. The painful structure being treated must be located very accurately and deep friction transmitted by a gradually increasing pressure. Transverse frictions are the most commonly used, particularly with ligamentous injuries and tendon and tendon sheath disorders. Initially, full pressure and friction cannot be given because of the local pain response, but gradually as the friction continues a deeper penetration can be achieved as the tissues appear to become numbed. Cyriax (1984) emphasises that in order to be maximally effective, frictions must be very accurately localised, of sufficient depth and carried out for a sufficient length of time (up to approximately 20 min).

Frictions have a number of effects which may explain their usefulness in the treatment of certain types of painful soft tissue disorders such as muscular lesions, lesions of tendons (both with and without a sheath), ligamentous lesions and traumatic and other causes of pain and restriction in the capsule of the small joints such as the interphalangeal joints.

The effects of frictions are as follows:

1. They cause a local hyperaemia.
2. They aid in restoring mobility in various structures which, from their nature or position, tend to develop adhesions after injury or strain, e.g. in sprains of the medial collateral ligament of the knee and tears within muscles such as the hamstrings.

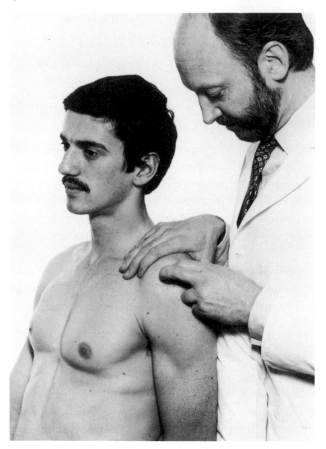

Fig. 13.2 *Friction.* Deep transverse frictions to the supraspinatus tendon. An unresolving tendinitis can be treated with this deep, localised stretching technique across the direction of the fibres of the tendon.

3. They assist in restoring the natural smooth gliding between a tendon and its sheath in tenosynovitis.

There are clear indications and contraindications for these important techniques (Cyriax, 1984). Using them in order to decrease pain and avoid the formation of dense scar tissue will facilitate the restoration of more normal movement. In doing so the natural repeated stretch of the soft tissues, without which scar tissue will always shorten (Evans, 1980), will be quickly restored.

Regional Mobilisation

Whereas trauma and degenerative changes frequently give rise to localised musculoskeletal disorders, in the spine it is common to find regional disturbances in movement and function associated with generalised stiffness and accompanied by varying degrees of pain.

It is in such situations that regional mobilisation techniques, which affect a group of joints and their soft tissues, are used. At the same time, by careful positioning, it is possible to direct the effects of regional mobilisation to a particular spinal level if this is considered necessary. As an example, regional rotation techniques are frequently employed for the cervical and lumbar spine to treat signs and symptoms arising from one vertebral level (Fig. 13.3). Similarly, with some peripheral joint complexes, e.g. the elbow and wrist, a technique may affect a group of articulations while aimed at the treatment of pain arising from one of them (Fig. 13.4).

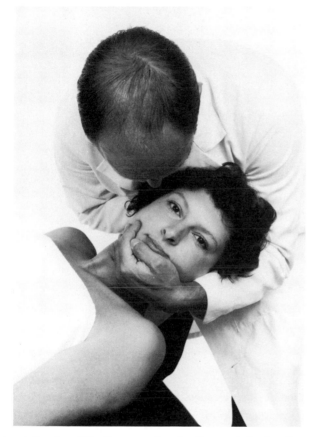

Fig. 13.3 A rotational mobilisation procedure for the cervical spine. By positioning the appropriate level of the neck midway between flexion and extension, this generalised technique can emphasise motion at that level. The movement is a repetitive oscillatory one, carried out through a prescribed arc of the available range of cervical rotation, invariably away from the painful side.

Included in this category of regional mobilisation is traction, a stretching force which is applied in general along the longitudinal axis of the tissues. The precise magnitude of the traction force, the position in which it is given and the time for which it is carried out may all bear upon its effect, and so it is important to administer traction in a very accurate and predetermined

189

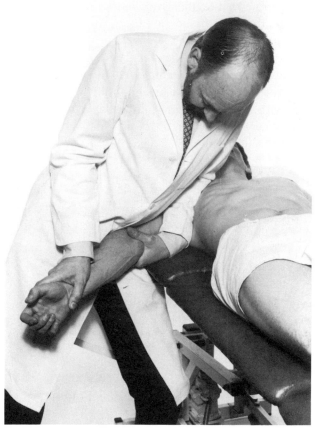

Fig. 13.4 A generalised mobilisation procedure for the elbow complex exploring both the pain response and movement characteristics towards the end of the extension range while an adduction stress is applied. Useful both as an examination technique, where necessary, and a treatment for certain types of elbow problem, this procedure does not determine which specific part of the elbow joint complex is at fault.

way. This is best carried out with specialised apparatus devised to do just that (Figs 13.5 and 13.6). However, this 'mechanical' traction is still clearly within the field of manipulation since the body tissues are passively moved, albeit in this case by a machine rather than by the operator's hands.

Spinal traction may also, of course, be administered by the hands, but it has the disadvantage that the physiotherapist can only sustain it for a short period of time.

Localised Mobilisation

In order to direct treatment in a specific way and assess it accurately, it is important to be able to locate the source of a pain precisely to a particular joint. For example, at the elbow differentiation must be made between the humeroradial, humeroulnar, superior radioulnar and even 'radioannular'

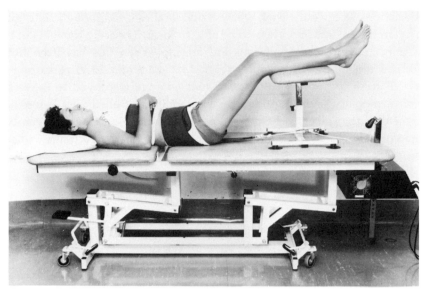

Fig. 13.5 *Lumbar traction.* An extremely effective passive technique for the relief of many types of lumbar pain and sciatic symptoms. The degree of hip flexion is used to determine the mid position of the relevant lumbar vertebral level being treated, and the legs are supported accordingly. Sustained or intermittent traction can be given as with the cervical spine. The lower thoracic levels can be treated with some modifications in positioning of the patient and the harness.

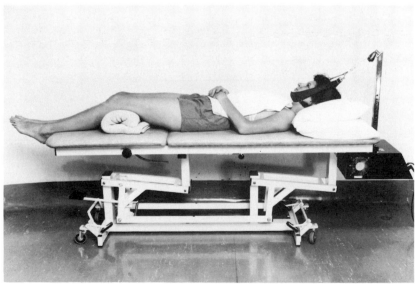

Fig. 13.6 *Cervical traction.* The level to which the tractive force is directed is determined by the degree of flexion of the head-upon-neck or neck-upon-trunk. In this instance, the cervicothoracic junctional region is being treated. Motorised traction such as this may be used to apply a sustained (not the same as constant) or intermittent force to take into account the degree of pain or stiffness to be treated. The upper thoracic levels can be treated with a similar arrangement.

articulations. In the same way, where a vertebral cause is giving rise to local or referred pain, it is important to be able to locate precisely the level of the spine from which the symptoms are arising. When this has been done, localised mobilisation procedures (Figs 13.7, 13.8 and 13.9) consisting of passive accessory or physiological movements are employed to move the joint or mobility segment at fault in a carefully controlled way (a mobility segment of the spine can be defined as the movable junction between two adjacent vertebrae, e.g. L5 and S1 including their associated joints and soft tissues).

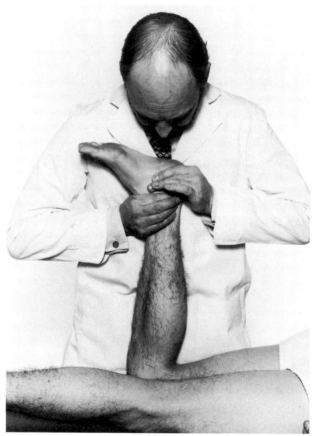

Fig. 13.7   A localised mobilisation technique for the subtalar joint, utilising the small degree of accessory rotational movement (rotational 'joint play') normally present.

While every attempt is made to localise forces with great care to the joint of the spinal level being treated, no manipulative procedure can ever be entirely localised since, especially in the vertebral column, the adjacent levels are bound to move somewhat also. Even so, it comes as a surprise to many observers to see how accurate such techniques can be in the hands of an experienced manipulative physiotherapist.

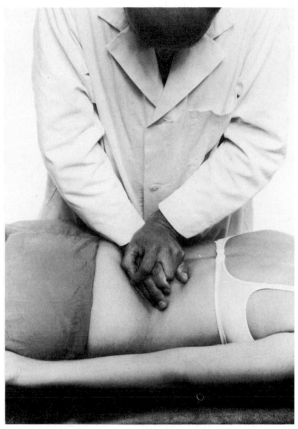

Fig. 13.8 A localised mobilisation procedure in a posteroanterior direction being performed at the 4th lumbar level. A small but definite range of accessory movement can be obtained, localised by a small area of the hypothenar eminence of the underneath hand. The movement may be a sustained or an oscillatory one.

Regional Manipulation

The majority of joint problems resolve with the use of regional or localised mobilisations and do not need a manipulative thrust technique. In the case of spinal dysfunction, about 15% of patients generally require one or more 'manipulations' to clear their symptoms and restore good functional movement.

If the restriction of movement affects a number of adjacent segments in the spine then a regional manipulation may be used (Fig. 13.10). By careful positioning and control fundamental to all manipulative procedures, these high velocity techniques of controlled amplitude can effectively regain movement simultaneously at a number of adjacent levels. However, such regional procedures are employed on far fewer occasions than the carefully localised ones.

193

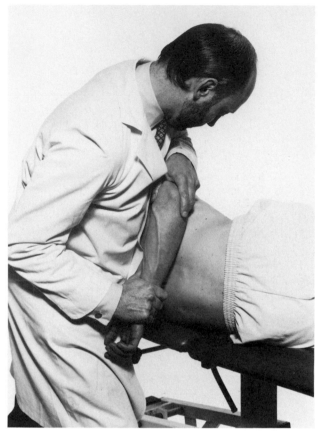

Fig. 13.9 A localised mobilisation procedure to the glenohumeral joint to improve the 'hand behind back' movement. The three components of this physiological movement— extension, adduction and internal rotation—can be mobilised separately in this position.

Localised Manipulation

When mobilisation has failed to gain completely the degree of joint mobility reasonably expected it may be necessary to carry out a localised manipulation (Fig. 13.11). By careful positioning and a very precise application of the force used, either with short or long leverage, a degree of movement can be obtained suddenly at a joint previously abnormally tight and restricted. The speed employed is crucial in most cases for a successful manipulation, both in the application of the force and in its release. The amplitude of the movement used is always small and very controlled, as part of the built-in safety of each manoeuvre. Considerable skill is required to carry out localised manipulation successfully and such skill takes much time and practice to acquire.

It is doubtful whether any localised manipulation is ever as entirely localised as the title suggests. Even with the most careful positioning and force application adjacent joints and tissues invariably receive some of the stress imparted by the technique. The point is that this is minimal when

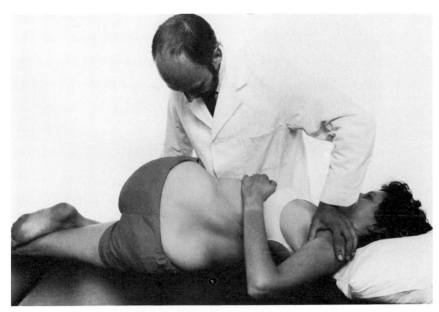

Fig. 13.10 A generalised rotational manipulation for the mid to lower lumbar spine. Such a procedure is usually performed to improve the local signs and symptoms arising from regional stiffness in the low back. Even though the force and amplitude are carefully controlled, such a procedure would not be used in the presence of segmental hypermobility within the area.

expertly carried out and, of course, far more localised than a generalised manipulation seeks to be.

Localised manipulation is mainly used in the treatment of spinal problems. However, it is occasionally used in the treatment of peripheral joints, e.g. the glenohumeral joint, sacroiliac joint and the small joints of the hand or foot.

MANIPULATION UNDER ANAESTHETIC (MUA)

There may come a point in treatment when mobilisation and manipulation cease to improve the situation further, or progress is exceedingly slow. At this stage, the surgeon or physician in overall charge of the patient may decide that a manipulation of the spinal level or peripheral joint concerned should be carried out under an anaesthetic. While that decision is the doctor's alone, it will usually be made after consultation with the physiotherapist who has been carrying out the treatment. Obviously a procedure that can be achieved while the patient is conscious and able to respond is preferable to that performed while the individual is anaesthetised and cannot react. The subjective and objective responses to any manoeuvre are what guides treatment and the degree of gentleness or vigour used. The conscious subject can report changes in their symptoms immediately and objective testing likewise will give essential information quickly. However, if fibrosis in the soft tissues of the joint is so dense that a firm manoeuvre is required which would be too uncomfortable for the unanaesthetised patient, or if they

195

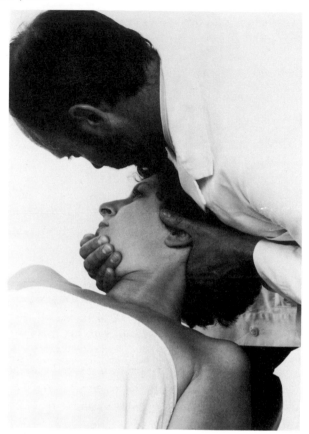

Fig. 13.11   A localised posteroanterior thrust technique to mobilise the left atlanto-occipital joint. The cervical spine is well short of full rotation and a small direct thrust with the left hand directed through the plane of the joint achieves the movement.

are unable to relax or are of a body build which prevents the procedure from being carried out, then the use of an anaesthetic may provide a way forward.

The use of this technique has been criticised on the grounds that it is like taking a sledgehammer to crack a nut. However, when used sparingly and for specific indications the results may be seen to justify the means.

Maitland (1986) has pointed out that 'follow-up' physiotherapy is only indicated if the symptoms have not responded sufficiently to MUA. If complete relief of symptoms is gained then follow-up treatment is unnecessary. He also makes the following important observation:

'Where manipulation of the conscious patient has failed, MUA may be successful. The converse is also true. Sometimes . . . patients may require a balance of both'.

THE EFFECTS OF MANIPULATIVE PROCEDURES

When the effects upon the body of the various passive movement procedures are discussed, there is a danger of confusing observations of what results with how results are thought to be achieved. To guide thoughts on this matter Maitland (1986) has proposed a 'two-compartment' approach to rationalise the information obtained. Firstly, there is the compartment in which information concerning anatomy, biomechanics, pathology and diagnosis is accumulated. The second compartment contains the history, signs and symptoms of any particular patient that has been examined.

It is natural when discussing manipulative procedures to want to rationalise what happens during and after treatment by relating any changes in the second compartment directly to alterations in the first. However, while the effects of manipulation upon the patient's symptoms and signs can be observed and can be reported by the patient, it is speculative to attempt to describe how exactly those effects have been achieved. In other words, it cannot be said precisely in any given case how improvement in the signs and symptoms has been achieved but only that it has.

Therefore, the short answer to the question: 'How and why does manipulation work?' must, in all honesty, be that it is not known for certain. However, it is possible to hypothesise mechanisms using the considerable volume of information now available and growing steadily relating to joint and soft tissue neurology, pathology, biomechanics and pain studies. The effects and uses of soft tissue or massage techniques have been discussed earlier in this chapter (pp. 183–8). Manipulative procedures directed primarily to the spinal or peripheral joints require some further consideration. Firstly, it should be stated that the basic effects we wish to achieve in terms of the signs and symptoms are as follows:

1. To decrease pain and other symptoms.
2. To decrease muscle spasm.
3. To improve mobility of the joints and soft tissues.

The mechanism whereby these effects are achieved by treatment would probably be by one or more of the following:

1. An alteration in the bias of sensory input from the joints and soft tissues by an increase in the stimulation of the mechanoreceptors located within them.
2. Reflex effects upon spasm.
3. The prevention or limitation of the formation of inelastic scar tissue and the restoration of extensibility to the soft tissues.
4. The improvement of tissue–fluid exchange.
5. The psychological effects of being carefully assessed and treated sympathetically.

These two lists summarise the two-compartment way of thinking mentioned earlier.

It is useful when discussing the possible ways that manipulation achieves its effects to keep in mind the cycle of events, aptly named a 'vicious circle', invariably encountered when the patient is taken for treatment (Fig. 13.12).

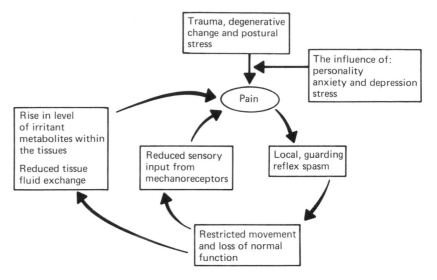

Fig. 13.12   The vicious circle of pain.

Stimulation of Articular Mechanoreceptors and its Effects upon Pain

It is only since the mid 1960s, that details of the morphology and precise function of the articular receptors have been known (Wyke, 1967). It represented an exciting breakthrough in knowledge for those concerned with the treatment of musculoskeletal pain and dysfunction, and in particular for physiotherapists, since it provided evidence to demonstrate conclusively the mode of response of specific receptors (types I, II, III and IV) in joint structures to a wide spectrum of mechanical and nociceptive stimuli.

Types I, II and III are mechanoreceptors. Type III receptors are· absent from the spinal joints (Wyke, 1981) but are present in the ligaments of peripheral joints. Type I articular receptors are located in the fibrous capsules of the spinal apophyseal joints, whereas type II receptors can be found in the deeper layers of the capsules and in the articular fat pads. Type IV are nociceptive receptors found in the ligaments and fibrous capsules of the spinal joints, in the walls of articular blood vessels and in articular fat pads. Unlike the mechanoreceptor system, the articular nociceptive system is, under normal circumstances, completely inactive, and only becomes active when levels of mechanical stress become excessive or when chemical irritants accumulate in the tissues.

Coincidentally, there was about the same time that these receptors were described the publication of a new theory on pain mechanisms by Melzack and Wall (1965). It took as one of its central themes the modulation of nociceptive afferent input in the spinal cord by continual afferent barrage from mechanoreceptors. In spite of the criticism of the theory (Nathan, 1976) and its modification over the last two decades, this central idea held firm and is of fundamental importance in any account seeking to show how manipulation achieves its effects. Stated briefly, one function of the mechano-receptor system is pain suppression. When the nociceptive system is activated for any reason, the transmission of these impulses through the central nervous system will vary according to the degree of mechanorecep-tor stimulation and impulse transmission occurring at the same time. The greater the level of mechanoreceptor activity, the greater the effect of pain suppression.

Consequently, as suggested by Wyke (1979, 1985) the passive manipula-tion of, or the application of traction through, limb and spinal joints has many reflex and perceptual consequences. These include the relief of pain as a result of the presynaptic inhibition of pain impulses through the synapses in the basal spinal nucleus via the mechanoreceptor stimulation that is inevitably associated with all manipulative procedures. The well-trained manipulative physiotherapist can operate this neurological mechanism with a high degree of refinement.

In other words, a large part of the total effect of manipulation is achieved by modulating nociceptive and sensory input from the periphery by gaining maximal inhibitory effects from the stimulation of the mechanoreceptors located in skin fascia, muscle, tendons, ligaments, joints capsules, etc. By this mechanism it is possible to break into, and thereby begin to break down, the 'vicious circle' of pain and restricted movement.

Reflex Effects upon Spasm

The local reflex protective spasm, which accompanies so many painful musculoskeletal conditions, often diminishes progressively as pain relief is gained. On the other hand, such spasm, as the clinician knows well, may persist and become a major obstacle 'protecting' the damaged structures well beyond the point in time where the restoration of movement is desirable. The judicious use of suitable manipulative procedures can reduce this persistent and counterproductive spasm. This in itself will hasten the return of normal movement and thus enhance a more 'normal' sensory barrage from the periphery into the central nervous system. Movement, then, begets movement provided that excessive pain is not produced.

Prevention of the Formation of Disorganised and Inelastic Scar Tissue and the Loss of Extensibility in the Soft Tissues

It is a fact of pathology that either by a slow process of degenerative change or as a result of sudden or repeated trauma, fibrous scar tissue is laid down within the musculoskeletal tissues. While little can be done in practice to prevent this natural healing reaction from occurring, a knowledge of the events and their time-scale helps prevent or minimise the less desirable effects of the process. The major undesirable effect of scarring within the soft tissues, including those of the joints, is that if it is not subjected to repeated stress at the right time, the fibres which give it strength will organise themselves haphazardly into a disorganised meshwork (Evans, 1980). Such an arrangement produces a weak and inextensible scar which, in turn, produces pain when stretched. In contrast, scar tissue which is stressed to an appropriate degree at the right stage will form fibres running parallel to the normal stress lines of the tissue and, with repeated movement, a mobile scar will be formed which does not restrict movement. One way of achieving some of the healthy stress upon such tissue is by manipulative techniques which utilise repeated careful stretching movements (Mealy *et al.*, 1986), though, of course, such procedures will only achieve maximal benefit if followed up by appropriate and repeated movement by the patient. There are exceptions to this rule, such as the early treatment of a tenosynovitis arising from overuse of the affected part. In this case, rest is more appropriate between treatments.

The same rationale applies to the use of stretch in the case of a spinal nerve root which is in the process of becoming adherent to the surrounding

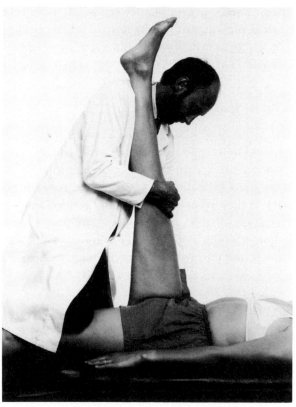

Fig. 13.13 Straight leg raising technique to mobilise the pain-sensitive structures in the intervertebral canal. This procedure is carefully graded and only ever used in the presence of chronic non-irritable symptoms when it has been estimated that some or all of the symptoms are arising from a lack of mobility between the nerve root and surrounding structures.

tissues within or beyond the intervertebral foramen. Inflammation and degenerative change occurring in these tissues diminish the mobility of the nerve, which normally moves to a limited but appreciable extent during trunk and limb movements (Breig and Marions, 1963). A traumatised nerve which has become adherent in this way may be the source of chronic referred limb pain (Fahrni, 1966), and quite apart from joint manipulation, there remains the effect in such cases of 'mobilising' the nerve and its coverings within the intervertebral foramen. Particular techniques are used to achieve this effect (Fig. 13.13) and can be applied in treating the cervical as well as the lumbar spine.

Improvement of Tissue–Fluid Exchange

The repeated functional movement of joints and their associated tissues and the contraction and relaxation of the muscles which move them during everyday activities promote the normal flow of blood and lymph by a pumping and 'milking' effect. The normal nutrition and health of tissues, such as cartilage and muscle as well as collagenous structures are probably, in part, due to such regular movements (Lowther, 1985). The action of stretching, which occurs naturally throughout the spine and the peripheral joints as part of the individual's normal activities maintains the extensibility of the musculoskeletal structures, especially the collagenous tissues.

When pain and joint restriction reduce such movement, often in a very masked way and for a considerable period of time, normal healthy tissue–fluid interchange is impaired (Grieve, 1981). Muscles maintained in a state of chronic guarding spasm become weak from disuse. The regular rhythmic pumping action around the affected joints is lost. The normal sensory barrage from the joint and its soft tissues is depleted. This will be the case whether it is spinal or peripheral joints or soft tissues which are affected. Manipulative techniques, by helping to restore movement, restore normal biomechanical forces to the muscles, collagenous tissues and local blood vessels and the lymphatics. By these measures some part of the effects upon pain and mobility may be mediated.

Psychological Effects

All manipulative therapy by definition involves close physical contact between the patient and operator, and the skilful and sympathetic handling of tense, painful and aching tissues. Apart from the neurophysiological effects related to manipulative therapy, the psychological benefit which may be derived from this form of treatment may be considerable. The value of 'therapeutic handling' is demonstrated every day by patients who register enormous relief when the source of their problem is found, discussed and handled very specifically and with due care. The remark 'I've longed for someone to find that spot and do something about it', is satisfying to both

201

patient and manipulator alike and when it is followed up with a demonstrable change in the patient's signs and symptoms, it helps establish a bond of trust and a spur to recovery.

How much of this effect can be ascribed to a 'placebo response' is not possible to say. It is generally believed that some 20–30% of the improvement noted in any trial is due to the placebo effect, and presumably manipulation is no exception. It is still not known what the mechanisms are which underlie this aspect of the total response to treatment.

On occasions, a patient may appear to be developing a psychological dependence upon being manipulated. If treatment is merely reinforcing ideas of physical dysfunction when the valid testing of signs and symptoms does not bear this out, then such treatment should be reconsidered and the patient referred back to his doctor. It should always be borne in mind that what a patient's pain and disability means to him may differ greatly from what it means to the physiotherapist. However, the limitations of manipulative procedures must be acknowledged.

DIAGNOSIS, PATHOLOGY AND MANIPULATIVE PROCEDURES

Dr James Cyriax and Mr Geoffrey Maitland, two great pioneers in the development of the treatment of musculoskeletal disorders, emphasise the paramount importance of a comprehensive and systematic examination and assessment of the moving parts of the body in order to make a precise diagnosis. Diagnosis is the *sine qua non* of manipulation (Cyriax, 1984; Maitland, 1986).

However, the exact cause may be unclear even though it is recognised as a benign, mechanical one. In these cases the referral may simply state for example 'low back pain', 'backache and sciatica', 'painful, stiff shoulder' or 'retropatellar pain' and so on. It may be that the diagnosis and the pathology implied by it come within the category which requires extra care and caution, and this will be observed in these cases. Certain diagnoses, as seen, contraindicate the use of high velocity thrust techniques but do not preclude the use of carefully controlled mobilisation techniques or certain soft tissue techniques. A few diagnoses actually dictate precisely what specific techniques should be used. As an example, nerve root irritation or compression arising from the cervical spine and giving severe and highly reactive symptoms into the upper limb should only ever be treated initially by gentle sustained cervical traction. Similarly, the patient suffering from a locking incident of the knee due to a meniscal tear will sometimes require a very specific manipulative procedure to free the mechanical block to movement arising from this internal derangement. The number of such instances when the diagnosis and pathology specifically dictate what technique must be used initially is small, however, when considered alongside the majority of musculoskeletal problems where the precise mechanisms causing the signs and symptoms may not be absolutely clear.

The case of the painful stiff neck is a good example. Many such patients are x-rayed and seen to have cervical spondylosis (i.e. cervical disc degeneration), a condition which is, of course, frequently asymptomatic. They may also have cervical arthrosis affecting the synovial apophyseal joints and the upper cervical articulations, particularly between the axis and the atlas. Disc degeneration is a normal process of ageing and one that eventually overtakes everybody's spine to some extent. That is not so in the case of apophyseal arthrosis which seems to occur less commonly. However, the fact remains that the ubiquitous cervical spondylosis or spondylarthrosis may clinically present in a whole variety of ways ranging from a patient with a mildly aching and slightly stiff neck to someone with a truly agonising and unpleasant pain radiating from the neck to the shoulders, arm and hand, accompanied by pins and needles, numbness and other neurological signs. Both may be diagnosed as due to 'cervical spondylosis'. The treatment approach in these two cases is entirely different. The diagnosis as such gives no indication of the precise treatment techniques to be used. It is the particular combination of signs and symptoms, in addition to certain other factors, that guides the treatment in such situations and not the diagnosis. Obviously an understanding of the nature of the problem conveyed by the diagnostic label 'spondylosis' is essential but this more clearly defines certain boundaries within which the manipulator works rather than indicating precisely what must be done. It is certainly feasible that a number of different manipulators employing differing techniques may each provide relief to the patient with a particular type of painful stiff neck. They each achieve this in their own way for a variety of reasons obviously, but the principal one is likely to be that they understand how to handle joint problems with the appropriate degree and type of movement. Each manipulator skilfully does what is required to restore function to the painful stiff joints so that they move painlessly, even though they achieve this employing differing techniques.

Localisation of the Sources of Symptoms

The most common fault in using manipulative procedures is in not directing the treatment specifically to the source of the problem, be it a specific structure or tissue, a specific joint or a specific level of the spine. Cases may be quoted where treatment by physical means has failed to achieve the relief of symptoms which is sought because it has not been directed accurately to the source of the symptoms. Obvious examples can be drawn from those cases where pain and other symptoms arise from the spinal structures, but closely resemble the clinical presentation of local disorders. Even some localised soft tissue tests such as palpation, stretch and, on occasions, isometric muscle contraction may give rise to pain where a long-standing spinal disorder is eventually implicated as the source of the symptoms. Some commonly encountered situations are quoted below as examples.

Tennis elbow

Frequently the 'classic' signs and symptoms in a patient with this condition may be altered by treatment directed to their cervical spine. Alternatively, or in addition, definite joint signs may be elicited by localised accessory movement testing directed to the humeroradial or superior radioulnar joints. It is not to deny that the soft tissue changes associated with this condition do exist and even on occasions require surgical intervention. But in at least some cases, the tennis elbow results from complex cervicobrachial mechanisms (Gunn and Milbrandt, 1976) and does not respond to techniques directed solely to the soft tissues of the extensor region of the forearm. If the condition does respond to local techniques, such as frictions and injection, but arises from an underlying joint problem or a spinal disorder it is likely to recur.

Shoulder pain

Conditions as classic as supraspinatus tendinitis and capsulitis, frequently have their origin totally or in part in the cervical or uppermost thoracic spine. A specific shoulder action or activity may be the precipitating or triggering factor and not the causative factor in the onset of symptoms in these cases.

Anterior knee pain

This commonly arises from the vertebral region somewhere between the thoracolumbar and 3rd lumbar levels (Chadwick, personal communication, CSP Congress Lecture, 1986). Much valuable time may be wasted applying a variety of locally directed treatments if the true source of the patient's pain is not revealed by careful spinal testing, especially palpation. Again, this does not deny the fact that anterior knee pain may be related to a purely local cause and respond to specific methods directed to the knee.

Hand symptoms

Not uncommonly the symptoms usually associated with *carpal tunnel syndrome* may be linked with vertebral dysfunction, in particular stiffness and pain elicited with passive accessory and physiological movement testing at the 4th thoracic vertebral level. Pins and needles, puffiness and dusky bluish discoloration of the hands may accompany this condition, and these may all be relieved by mobilisation or manipulation directed to the relevant vertebral level. This condition may coexist with carpal tunnel syndrome and should particularly be suspected where local measures to relieve the patient's symptoms and signs have had limited effect.

In any situation such as these, where the physiotherapist suspects a source other than that quoted by the referring doctor, the doctor should be consulted and the findings discussed prior to any course of treatment being undertaken. It is unacceptable that where a local cause was suspected at initial examination a different source, if suspected by the physiotherapist, is treated without discussion with the referring medical practitioner.

A rather different situation exists where the source of a patient's problem does lie within a local structure, e.g. a muscle, tendon, ligament or joint. Again a common fault in treatment when using manipulative procedures is a failure to be sufficiently specific. For example, a patient who has sustained an inversion sprain of the ankle frequently suffers from symptoms (and has signs) which have arisen from trauma sustained by the calcaneocuboid joint. If treatment is directed only to the lateral ligament of the ankle in this situation then symptoms in the region of the sprain may well persist. Similarly, e.g. a pain at the point of the shoulder may lead to treatment being directed to the glenohumeral joint or the acromiohumeral soft tissues when, by careful differential testing, the acromioclavicular joint may be found to be at fault.

The pitfalls of attempting to relate treatment by manipulative procedures or other physical measures to a 'diagnostic label' without the essential tools of meticulous differential testing are clear. Precise diagnosis should implicate the structures which are the primary source of the patient's problem.

EXAMINATION AND ASSESSMENT

No treatment, and particularly that in which manipulative techniques are to be included, should ever be commenced without an appropriate and sufficient examination having first been carried out by the person undertaking that treatment. Such an examination can never supplant that of the referring doctor, but is meant to supplement it. Indeed no logical treatment can ever be planned nor the response to it assessed until a thorough picture of the presenting signs and symptoms has been elicited, following the familiar format of 'listening', 'looking', 'testing' and 'feeling'.

One expert, writing of the examination preceding spinal manipulation, made the following point (Grieve, 1975):

'... the vitally important therapist's examination is less of a diagnostic sorting procedure than an 'indications' examination concerned solely with the manner in which a joint problem is manifesting itself, and with localisation of the vertebral segment(s) involved'.

Exactly the same could, of course, be said of the examination of the non-spinal joints and soft tissues. But since manipulative procedures are associated in many people's minds with spinal problems and must take into account particular considerations of the vascularity and neurology of those regions, the points made will relate in the main to examination and assessment of the cervical, thoracic or lumbar spine. The relevance of most of the points to other musculoskeletal problems should be clear.

The **subjective section** of the examination will elicit the following:

1. The problem complained of, i.e. pain, stiffness, locking, giving way, weakness and unable to work, unable to play sport, etc.
2. The precise areas and depth of the pain and its severity, any paraesthesia and any reduced or absent sensation.
3. The type of pain, e.g. burning, throbbing, shooting, stabbing.
4. The behaviour of the different areas of pain over a 24 h period related to activities, e.g. walking, running, lifting, carrying, and postures, e.g. sitting, lying, standing; particular attention must be paid to severe night pain.
5. The history of the onset, e.g. related to a particular trauma or slow and insidious.
6. The past history, to elicit previous episodes, any pattern of development and previous treatments and their effect.
7. Points which alert the physiotherapist to the possibility of a condition having developed for which the patient should be referred back to the doctor. For example, with lumbar problems the development of retention and/or 'saddle' anaesthesia as a result of involvement of the cauda equina or the presence of symptoms of spinal cord involvement at the cervical or thoracic levels or sudden unexplained weight loss.
8. Details of relevant medical history and medication, e.g. diabetes, anti-coagulant therapy, steroid therapy.

Before the objective part of the examination is undertaken, literally before one places hands on the patient, it is vital to pause and consider the information elicited so far. This process of assessment, trying to resolve the meaning of information gathered, will direct the remainder of the examination. While examination and assessment are two words often used interchangeably, they do not mean the same thing. It is one thing to be able to examine well, but another to interpret what all the information means. As already stated, the physiotherapist's examination is not the primary diagnostic sorting procedure but more an 'indications' examination and, therefore, it is the following aspects which need particularly to be decided at this point:

1. *Which structures must be tested as possibly contributing to the problem?*
   For example, a patient sent with a diagnosis of 'cervical spondylosis' may simply have localised unilateral neck pain with a slight restriction of movement and little else. On the other hand, the patient may present with more severe pain, a gross restriction of movement, weakness of the muscles of the shoulder or arm, neurological deficit from nerve root irritation or compression and a tight sore shoulder joint, apparently

related to their chronic cervical problem. Tests which will incriminate or exclude structures over which the symptoms spread will need to be used. If muscle weakness and shoulder joint restriction are found to be contributing to the problem they will need to be included for treatment at some point.

2. *Are the symptoms severe?*

Severity is conveyed by the degree to which the problem restricts the individual's activities. For example, a severely stiff and painful lumbar spine may seriously affect the ability to continue with a particular occupation or may interfere markedly with sleep. Likewise, a severely sprained ankle may markedly limit walking. Severe symptoms will need to be examined with great care, particularly when dealing with a stoical patient.

3. *Is the condition irritable?*

Irritability is defined by three factors: the ease with which symptoms are provoked, the intensity of those symptoms, and the time taken for them to settle following the provoking activity. Irritability must be determined before any active or passive procedures or treatments are undertaken, lest the patient's pain is unnecessarily stirred.

4. *What is the nature of the problem?*

The nature of the problem has a number of aspects upon which not only the detail of the objective examination will depend, but also to some extent the treatment. Two aspects may be mentioned:

(a) *Serious pathology*. While it is assumed that the serious disease processes which are referred to under contraindications (p. 208) have been excluded at the time of the doctor's examination, the possibility that such pathology may begin to manifest itself during the time the patient is seen by the physiotherapist is always kept in mind.

(b) *The source of symptoms*. Special consideration needs to be given to whether, for example, a spinal problem is primarily arising from the disc or the apophyseal structures and whether the nerve root is involved and how. The latter may manifest itself as a chronic nerve root ache or alternatively an acute and highly irritable pain. The handling of the patient's tissues and the extent to which they are encouraged, for example to move further during movement testing will pay due regard to all these factors. As another example, if dizziness is complained of, then the objective examination must explore this symptom in some detail, so that its source (particularly if seeming to come from vertebral artery problems) can be clarified with the doctor.

The **objective section** of the examination will elicit the following:

1. The presence of factors which may possibly be contributing to the present problem. Examples in the case of spinal problems include a short leg, poor posture, weakness of the abdominal muscles.

2. The movements that are limited and by how much and what limits them —pain, spasm or resistance.

3. Details of postural deformities and whether they relate to the present episode. An example might be a lumbar scoliosis shifting the upper trunk away from or towards the painful side. Alternatively a joint such as the elbow or the knee may be seen to be held in a degree of flexion, e.g. when compared with the other side. An attempt must always be made to carefully reduce such a deformity, noting its relation to pain and range of movement in order to determine whether or not it is related to the present problem.

4. The presence of neurological deficit. Power, sensation and reflexes will all be tested as a routine part of a spinal examination particularly where pain radiates beyond the proximal joint, i.e. shoulder or hip.

5. Involvement of the pain-sensitive structures of the intervertebral canal. For example, the straight leg raising, prone knee flexion and slump test (Maitland, 1986) will demonstrate abnormalities of dural tension and these will influence treatment and may be used to assess the efficacy of that treatment.

6. Factors which aggravate dizziness (if this is complained of by the patient with a cervical problem).

7. Palpable differences in the texture of soft tissues and in passive physiological and passive accessory intervertebral movements. This last section of the examination, palpation, is arguably the most informative. Provided no other part of the examination is omitted, skilful and meticulous palpation will help tie together all the other examination findings.

The overall aim of the objective examination is to reproduce the patient's symptoms or to aggravate them *provided the severity, irritability and the nature of the problem permit this to be done*. The specific tests and palpation details which do this are highlighted in the examination by an asterisk (*) so that significant objective as well as subjective findings are assessed continuously to guide the treatment. When symptoms are severe, and particularly if irritable, all testing thought likely to exacerbate them is avoided, in exactly the same way as manipulative techniques judged likely to aggravate the signs and symptoms are not used.

CONTRAINDICATIONS

Disease processes and injuries which affect bone and joint structures as well as other soft tissues and weaken them, making them especially vulnerable to stress, are contraindications to all forceful manipulative procedures. In addition, the use of certain drugs such as steroids and anticoagulants precludes any vigorous passive treatment.

The well trained manipulative physiotherapist who works with the full knowledge of the patient's medical condition knows clearly those situations in which, for example, manipulative thrust techniques are absolutely contraindicated and those where even mobilisation is barred. The physiotherapist is also aware of conditions in which care must be exercised regarding the choice of specific techniques used and the degree of vigour which may or may not be employed. The first rule of manipulative treatment (as with all therapy) is *do no harm* and the responsible operator always errs on the side of caution. When there is any doubt regarding the suitability of any procedure in a given situation it is not employed.

It is the responsibility solely of the patient's doctor to diagnose his medical condition referring the patient, as seen fit, for assessment and treatment by another properly trained professional. The referring doctor will have identified any pathology which is an absolute bar to manipulative treatment and any which requires caution. Such absolute contraindications are more usually related to certain vertebral or spinal conditions.

The cases in which spinal manipulation (i.e. the techniques using rapid, short amplitude thrust) is completely contraindicated are as follows:

1. malignant disease of the bone or soft tissues;
2. bone disease such as osteomyelitis, osteoporosis, (of whatever cause) and tuberculosis;
3. spinal cord compression;
4. cauda equina compression;
5. recent fractures;
6. vertebrobasilar insufficiency;
7. inflammatory arthritis such as rheumatoid arthritis and ankylosing spondylitis;
8. bony or ligamentous instability of whatever cause, e.g. spondylolisthesis, fractures, craniocervical and lumbosacral anomalies;
9. severe degenerative changes and long-standing spinal deformity;
10. severe nerve root irritation or compression;
11. pregnancy; generally all vigorous procedures to the lower thoracic and lumbar spine are to be avoided after the 3rd month;
12. pain of unknown origin;
13. recent whiplash trauma to the neck;
14. anticoagulant therapy and current or recent steroid therapy;
15. certain psychological states where there is clear evidence that the patient has developed an obsessional dependence on 'having his spine clicked back'.

A number of these conditions also preclude the use of mobilisation techniques.

Furthermore there are situations in which particular care needs to be exercised, as with the following:

1. severe pain, particularly if it is easily stirred and takes some time to settle;
2. acute nerve root pain;

3. if spinal movements and/or palpation reproduces distally referred symptoms;

4. worsening signs and symptoms, such as those due to increasing nerve root compression.

Of the conditions listed as contraindications to manipulation, a number may safely be treated with mobilisation techniques and soft tissue procedures provided that specific safeguards are observed. For example, the patient with known vertebral artery disease may gain great relief from pain arising from coexistent cervical problems if treated by carefully graded mobilisation techniques and soft tissue procedures. Obviously rotational movements which reproduce their dizziness will be totally avoided. But gentle traction, localised accessory movements and attention to the cervical soft tissues are usually safe and acceptable provided they do not aggravate the dizziness.

TREATMENT

The use of manipulative techniques is related directly to the examination findings and the assessment of those findings. Moreover, mobilisation, manipulation and soft tissue techniques are chosen from a variety of different treatment modalities which the physiotherapist may choose to employ. Eventually, following due assessment, they may be used in combination with: corrective exercise to enhance mobility or restore good muscle tone; postural correction and advice; or temporary splinting and supports such as a cervical collar, a lumbar corset, a sacroiliac belt or a wrist splint.

Manipulative therapy is not a panacea for every mechanical musculoskeletal ailment. Skilfully used, however, it may play a valuable part and is often most important in the overall management of the condition. Sometimes manipulative therapy has quite a dramatic effect, as with certain spinal problems. It is the communication of these sudden 'cures' by one patient to another or to their doctor or by one physiotherapist to another which has generated the myth that a certain type of manipulation is a 'hole in one' curative procedure. Like most myths it is powerful and, in this instance, may do considerable harm in misleading patients and doctors as to what they should expect, and in making the less experienced practitioners of the art feel a failure if they do not regularly come up with such rapid successes. Every able manipulative physiotherapist has these successes but invariably they can be predicted. Most spinal and peripheral joint problems can be divided into those which will give a quick response and those which will take longer, and even perhaps require protracted treatment. This will apply irrespective of how good the physiotherapist is. It is related to the nature of the problem and that involves the type, extent and the stage of the pathology at the time the patient is seen.

Treatment is also related not only to the relief of symptoms and signs but advising the patient how best he may avoid further episodes of pain and disablement. A knowledge of the prognosis related to various syndromes is essential therefore in order that the manipulative physiotherapist can give the patient realistic advice. For example, lumbar discogenic problems are prone to recur if the patient does not regain and maintain a good painless range of lumbar extension and flexion, habitually sits in chairs and cars with a sagging flexed posture of the lumbar spine, spends prolonged periods in sustained flexion either while seated (as when driving) or standing, and lifts incorrectly.

In the case of treatment of a joint and its immediate supporting structures one of the principal guiding factors is whether that treatment is initially to be for pain or for inert tissue resistance and stiffness. Passive mobilisation procedures to treat pain which is severe and limits movement are carefully controlled so that they are carried out without provoking symptoms. They therefore are applied in the early part of the available range of movement whether it be accessory or passive physiological movement. With peripheral joint problems, pain which is severe and limits movement early in range is treated with small amplitude accessory movements. The use of movements of too great an amplitude or the employment of passive physiological movements at this stage would provoke and aggravate the symptoms rather than settle them. When pain is not severe nor irritable and does not limit movement markedly the techniques used may be applied further into the range. Eventually it may be necessary to work into the pain, when this is permissible, to clear the symptoms and signs. If, on the other hand, restriction of movement is due to the resistance imposed by changes in the various inert soft tissues then the techniques used will generally be applied up to and at the point of restriction, assuming that pain and muscle spasm are minimal.

A number of other factors guide the choice of technique and how it is performed. For example, in the cervical spine, if rotation is to be used it is carried out towards the painless direction. If an acute joint-locking is manipulated, a procedure is used which safely and painlessly opens the joint with great speed.

Where a manipulative thrust technique is judged necessary, it is because it has been preceded by gentler techniques which have failed to achieve the degree of progress expected. In spite of having been applied with suitable vigour at the limit of the reduced range of joint movement, mobilisations in this case will cease to have further effect; a manipulation may achieve the final improvement. On the other hand, mobilisation procedures may be continued after manipulation and frequently in these circumstances then achieve further improvement and progress. The same is true of the use of various soft tissue techniques.

A manipulative thrust technique is used when the pain felt by the patient is a local one and only spreads locally. This is invariably related to an abnormally tight vertebral mobility segment which has been localised by passive testing. A hypermobile joint or a case of spinal mobility is never manipulated nor does a manipulation ever push through spasm.

There are then factors which guide the manipulative physiotherapist in selecting techniques and there is an order of efficacy to further guide the order in which they are employed. One important guiding principle is that the force used is the minimal possible to achieve a reasonable result. That force is carefully controlled and graded at all times, irrespective of what type of manipulative technique is being used.

It is the ability to monitor and interpret changes (sometimes subtle) in the many aspects of the signs and symptoms that make up one particular patient's problem, which is the key to successful treatment by manipulative therapy. Finely tuned assessement is the secret of the effective manipulator, and not an ever increasing store of techniques. The precise level of the spine or the specific joint to be treated, the type of technique used and its gentleness or vigour, the modifications, additions and subtractions to what is done are all aspects of assessment upon which the degree of success will depend. In turn, all of these aspects hinge upon the abilities of the physiotherapist as a communicator. Details of the subtle and involved process that goes to make up that skill would require another chapter!

The Use of Orthoses

The management of a painful musculoskeletal problem may involve the use of an orthotic device to support and rest the part. The prescription for a permanent support, such as a rigid collar for a patient with a painful and unstable rheumatoid neck, is clearly the responsibility of the doctor. Many orthotic devices, however, are used as a temporary measure to protect the part and control pain, mainly between physiotherapy treatments, especially when the patient is required to carry out activities or take up postures which are known to exacerbate their symptoms.

Examples of orthoses include the following:

1. Lumbar support (belt or 'corset').
2. Sacroiliac belt, especially for painful, hypermobile joints.
3. Lumbar–sacroiliac support for pregnancy.
4. Cervical collar.
5. Wrist splint.
6. Elbow splint (for tennis elbow).
7. Thumb splint (carpometacarpal or metacarpophalangeal).
8. Sorbo rubber insoles/shock pads for various ankle and foot problems, osteoarthritis of the hip.

The following points should be considered prior to providing a patient with any orthosis:

1. Do not provide any orthotic device unless it is *specifically* indicated, i.e. it

can be shown to be advantageous to the patient and fulfils a specific aim. For example, of the large number of patients with painful neck problems referred for physiotherapy, only some benefit from the use of a cervical collar. Those who may do fall, in the main, into the spondylotic as opposed to the arthrotic group (Table 13.1).

Table 13.1   The Features of Spondylosis and Arthrosis Compared (after Stoddard, 1969)

Spondylosis	*Arthrosis*
Common	Less common
Acute episodes; may be complete freedom between bouts of symptoms; may be asymptomatic and not need treatment	Never completely free of symptoms, which should be treated
Nerve root pressure common; spinal cord pressure may occur	Nerve root pressure is uncommon, but root irritation may occur on certain movements
Stiffness in acute episodes spread over weeks or months	Daily variability of stiffness, easing with movement
Commonly affects: lower cervical mid thoracic lower lumbar	Commonly affects: upper cervical upper and lowest thoracic lower lumbar
Routine x-rays commonly show changes	Routine x-rays frequently reported as normal
Pain aggravated by some positions, eased by others	Posture or position makes little difference in general

Providing a collar for a patient with predominantly arthrotic cervical problems may well worsen his symptoms, since the 'stiffness' associated with such degenerative change is usually in great need of graduated mobilisation and frequent specific exercise by the patients themselves. Furthermore only *certain* spondylotic problems benefit significantly from a cervical support. This would be firstly when the symptoms are severe, particularly those referred into the upper limb; secondly when cervical movement is markedly restricted by pain and spasm, and thirdly when sleep is interrupted because of pain. The symptoms must be shown to be improved in these aspects by the use of the collar.

2. Fit the orthosis *personally* (i.e. do not hand over the task to a colleague to do if you are busy), making sure it is the correct size and shape, comfortable and supports, stabilises or immobilises as required. Make certain the patient or his helper can apply the device correctly and knows how to remove it if it becomes uncomfortable.

3. Explain when it is given that it is a *temporary measure* and will soon be discarded as treatment settles the symptoms and painless movement is

regained. Start to decrease the amount of time that the patient wears the device as soon as possible. For the patient who complains of night pain, which is relieved by use of a soft collar, the abandonment of its use at night should only be advised once the daytime pain is under control without the use of the collar. There is some evidence (Mealy *et al.*, 1986) that initial immobilisation (for 2 weeks in this study) with rest in a soft collar following whiplash injury gives rise to prolonged symptoms compared with early active management.

4. Where the patient's history is of a chronic, recurring problem and his work or hobbies include activities which may provoke the pain, advice to wear the support while undertaking these activities may help prevent an attack.

   An example is the wearing of a lumbar support during prolonged periods of gardening for an individual with a degenerative low back problem. It should be stressed, in such cases, that the wearing of the support or splint is only necessary as a temporary measure and a period of regular specific movements to maintain the ranges of movement of the affected area should always be undertaken daily as a priority, while the orthosis should for most of the time be kept stored away.

RECURRENCE OF SYMPTOMS

The nature of many joint problems, particularly those of the spine, is that they are liable to recur and even grow worse. If patients are not careful about their lifestyles, they will continue, perhaps unwittingly, to predispose themselves to further painful episodes.

Manipulative treatment aids recovery, but the maintenance of the improvement gained is the responsibility of the individual patient himself. The most important points of prophylaxis are the maintenance of a full range of movement in all directions for the joint, and the avoidance of postures and activities which give rise to symptoms. Every patient should expect and receive careful instruction as how best to avoid further problems and how to maintain full range painless movement. Manipulation may be an important factor in the patient's recovery but it is never the only one. It is often the case, e.g. with low back pain, that the eventual answer to a particular patient's problem in the long term is a regular regime of specific mobility exercises and meticulous attention to seated posture. The manipulative physiotherapist is failing in her duty if this is not made very clear to the patient and pursued with sufficient emphasis.

RESEARCH

The effectiveness of manipulative techniques is not an easy aspect to research, particularly in the case of spinal pain. Many investigations have been undertaken, particularly with regard to low back pain, to compare manipulation with other forms of treatment, but a large proportion of these trials have proved very unsatisfactory for various reasons. The main reasons are outlined below.

The Selection of Patients

For example, in the case of low back pain a variety of mechanical causes are included. So far there is no universally accepted categorisation of the causes and mechanisms of low back pain and therefore a heterogeneous mix of pathologies and syndromes are invariably admitted into a trial. It may be that it will eventually be shown that manipulative therapy is highly effective for some conditions, less so for others or, more likely, that it achieves rapid results in certain clinical situations and slower results in others.

A useful analogy can be drawn from the use of ergotamine for migraine where it has been stated that if this drug were used in a trial for headaches of a wide variety of causes it should be shown to be ineffective. However, it is, as we know, a highly effective treatment for migraine headache.

Measures for Improvement

The criteria chosen to assess progress during a trial of manipulative techniques ultimately depend upon the patient's interpretation of pain, a subjective and highly personal experience. Even the attempts to make objective observations, such as measuring movements and the straight leg raising test used in the assessment of certain lumbar problems, rely to a great extent on the way that pain affects the individual. The criteria of when a patient returns to work is again not a very reliable measure of real progress because individuals may or may not return to work for a variety of reasons. Often these reasons are not known to those treating them. Financial and social pressures may persuade some patients to return to work even though they still have considerable pain, while others may not return to work even though their symptoms appear minimal.

One experienced researcher in the field stated (O'Donaghue, 1983):

'More sensitive measures of progress need to be established along with the criteria which would allow the early identification of those patients who are likely to respond to manipulation'.

Personal Skills of the Manipulator

If it is believed that skills of assessment and of the choice of techniques and the way in which they are carried out have a bearing upon the outcome of treatment, then the danger of measuring the individual skills of the operator and not 'manipulation' *per se* becomes obvious. In a trial which uses many manipulators (and it must to obtain sufficient patient numbers in the specified time), great attempts need to be made to describe exactly what is being done under the umbrella of 'manipulation'. This is not easy and when the choice is made too constricting, e.g. with 'one rotational manipulation each week for 3 weeks', the criticism is immediately advanced that it is not a treatment that any other manipulator would have chosen to do anyway and if it was to fail nobody would be surprised.

The Double Blind and Single Blind Trial

The classic double blind trial, devised to test the efficacy of drugs, requires that both the patient and the doctor assessing him are unaware which treatment has been received. Clearly the patients are always aware whether they have or have not received 'manipulation'.

The single blind trial, when only the assessing doctor is unaware of the treatment, is possible but it is not easy to always guarantee that the doctor remains unaware of the type of treatment given.

A more comprehensive discussion of manipulation trials can be found in Grieve (1986).

REFERENCES

Breig A., Marions D. (1963). Biomechanics of the lumbo-sacral nerve roots. *Acta Radiolog. (Diag.)*; **1**: 1141–60.

Coxhead C.E., Inskip H., Meade T.W., North W.R.S., Troup J.D.G. (1981). Multicentre trial of physiotherapy in the management of sciatic symptoms. *Lancet*; **1**: 1065–8.

Cyriax J. (1984). *Textbook of Orthopaedic Medicine*, Vol. 2, 11th edn. London: Baillière Tindall.

Danneskiold-Samsøe B., Christiansen E., Andersen R.B. (1986). Myofascial pain and the role of myoglobin. *Scand. J. Rheumatol*; **15**: 174–8.

Evans P. (1980). The healing process at cellular level: a review. *Physiotherapy*; **66(8)**: 256–9.

Fahrni W.H. (1966). Observations on straight leg raising with special reference to nerve root adhesions. *Can. J. Surg*; **9**: 44–8.

Grieve G. (1975). Manipulation. *Physiotherapy*; **61(1)**: 11–18.

Grieve G. (1981). *Common Vertebral Joint Problems*. Edinburgh: Churchill Livingstone.

Grieve G. (1986). *Modern Manual Therapy of the Vertebral Column*. Edinburgh: Churchill Livingstone.

Gunn C.C., Milbrandt W.E. (1976). Tennis elbow and the cervical spine. *Can. Med. Ass. J.*; **May 8, 114**: 803–7.

Lowther D.A. (1985). The effect of compression and tension on the behaviour of connective tissues. In *Aspects of Manipulative Therapy*, 2nd edn. (Glasgow E. F., Twomey L. T., Scull E.R., Kleynhans A.M., eds) pp. 16–22. Edinburgh: Churchill Livingstone.

Maitland G.D. (1986). *Vertebral Manipulation*, 5th edn. London: Butterworths.

Mealy K., Brennan H., Fenelon G.C.C. (1986). Early mobilisation of acute whiplash injuries. *Brit. Med. J*; **292**: 656–7.

Melzack R., Wall P.D. (1965). Pain mechanisms: a new theory. *Science*; **150**: 971–9.

Nathan P. (1976). The gate-control theory of pain: a critical review. *Brain;* **99**: 123–58.

O'Donaghue C.E. (1983). Controlled trials of manipulation. *The Manipulation Association of Chartered Physiotherapists Newsletter;* **14**: 1–6.

Stoddard A. (1969). *Manual of Osteopathic Practice.* London: Hutchinson.

Wyke B.D. (1967). The neurology of joints. *Ann. Roy. Col. Surg;* **41**: 25–50.

Wyke B.D. (1979). Neurology of the cervical spinal joints. *Physiotherapy;* **65(3)**: 72–6.

Wyke B.D. (1981). The neurology of joints: a review of general principles. In Biology of the Joint. *Clin. Rheumat. Dis;* **7(1)**: 223–39.

Wyke B.D. (1985). Articular neurology and manipulative therapy. In *Aspects of Manipulative Therapy,* 2nd edn. (Glasgow E.F., Twomey L.T., Scull E.R., Kleynhans A.M., eds) pp. 72–7. Edinburgh: Churchill Livingstone.

Chapter 14

Connective Tissue Massage

JEAN and LOUIS GIFFORD

INTRODUCTION

The discovery and development of connective tissue massage (CTM) can largely be attributed to the observations and insight of Elizabeth Dicke, a German physiotherapist, who in 1929 suffered a severe postinfection circulatory disturbance in her right lower limb. The severity of the condition was such that amputation of her lower leg was advised. While bedridden during the illness, she experienced severe back pain, and her leg, as well as being painful, was cold, bluish and the dorsalis pedis pulse was absent to palpation. She attempted to relieve the back pain by applying pulling strokes on the skin over the painful areas of the back and sacrum. She discovered that the inelastic, hypersensitive and fixed tissues on the painful side were loosened by these strokes, and the tension of the skin was lowered to the level of the uninvolved side. Simultaneously, the pain in the back eased and an acceptable sensation of warmth took its place.

While persisting on successive days with the stroking, pins and needles were gradually felt in the affected leg, followed by an agreeable sensation of warmth. In further treatments, she incorporated areas around the greater trochanter and along the iliotibial tract. Gradually the superficial venous circulation reappeared in the thigh and leg, and within 3 months a satisfactory reduction in her symptoms was established.

After recovering she systematically observed her patients, and was soon able to pinpoint areas of tension consistently related to known pathological states in the viscera and extremities. She found the regions of increased tension or resistance, generally visible as retracted areas (Fig. 14.1), by stroking the patient's back with her finger.

Unknown to Elizabeth Dicke, Head (1893) and Mackenzie (1909) had previously published works relating surface changes to internal disorders. Henry Head, an English neurologist, was the first to show that in diseases of the internal organs, certain skin areas innervated by the same cord segments became hypersensitive to touch, pressure and temperature. These areas,

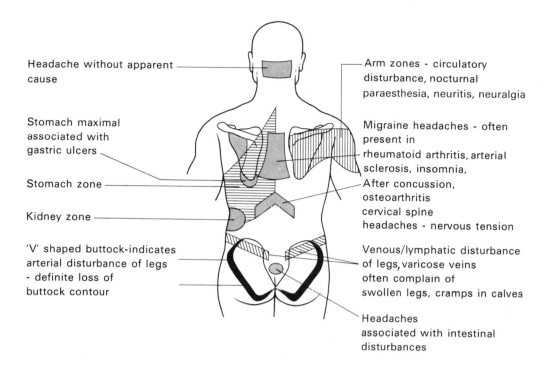

Headache without apparent cause

Stomach maximal associated with gastric ulcers

Stomach zone

Kidney zone

'V' shaped buttock-indicates arterial disturbance of legs - definite loss of buttock contour

Arm zones - circulatory disturbance, nocturnal paraesthesia, neuritis, neuralgia

Migraine headaches - often present in rheumatoid arthritis, arterial sclerosis, insomnia,

After concussion, osteoarthritis cervical spine headaches - nervous tension

Venous/lymphatic disturbance of legs, varicose veins often complain of swollen legs, cramps in calves

Headaches associated with intestinal disturbances

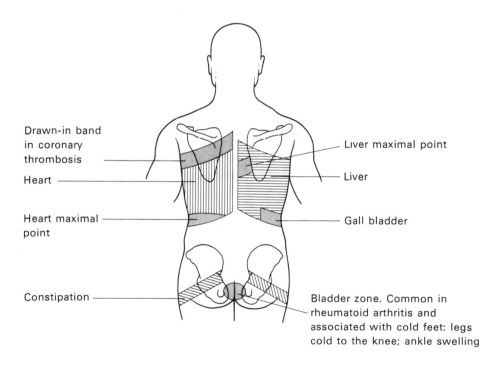

Drawn-in band in coronary thrombosis

Heart

Heart maximal point

Constipation

Liver maximal point

Liver

Gall bladder

Bladder zone. Common in rheumatoid arthritis and associated with cold feet: legs cold to the knee; ankle swelling

Fig. 14.1   The connective tissue zones—with some practical notes (adapted from Ebner, 1975).

which appear during the acute phase of disease and disappear with its recovery, are commonly known as *Head's zones*. For example, in pathology of the gall-bladder, hyperalgesia is found in the segments T6 to T10.

Later, Mackenzie (1909) observed hypertonic alterations and hypersensitivity in muscles belonging to the same segment as diseased organs. Dicke had independently stumbled upon and described visible and palpable changes in the tension of the skin, subcutaneous and other connective tissues that were segmentally related to visceral pathology in a similar way to the observations of Head and Mackenzie.

It seems likely (Ebner, 1972) and reasonable to assume that all tissues of the same segment, including the circulation, are subject to changes in the presence of organ pathology. The connective tissue areas observed by Dicke have remained relatively unchanged over the years, and are referred to as *connective tissue zones* or *reflex zones* in the most recent literature (Luedecke 1969; Ebner, 1975). They are generally located homolaterally in the segment of the affected organ, and, as a rule, do not occupy the segment uniformly. Thus certain *maximal points* of tension within the reflex zones are especially noticeable. An example is the zone affected by liver and gall-bladder malfunction (Fig. 14.2). Tension is particularly increased between the right scapula and the vertebral column at the level of T4 to T6 and over the inferior angle of the right scapula. The inferior costal margin on the right frequently appears to be drawn in, and there is increased tension over the lateral margin of the right latissimus dorsi. Maximal points also occur in the liver and gall-bladder zones anteriorly on the chest and laterally over the right shoulder (Fig. 14.2).

Head's zones of hypersensitivity (Fig. 14.3*b*) and Mackenzie's zones of

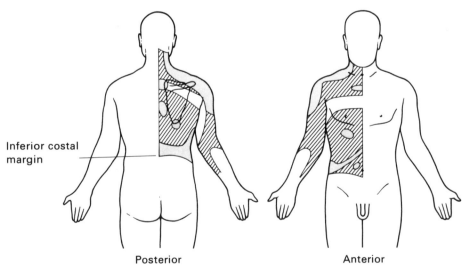

Inferior costal margin

Posterior   Anterior

Fig. 14.2 Liver and gall-bladder connective tissue zones. The shaded area represents maximal points (adapted from Ebner, 1975).

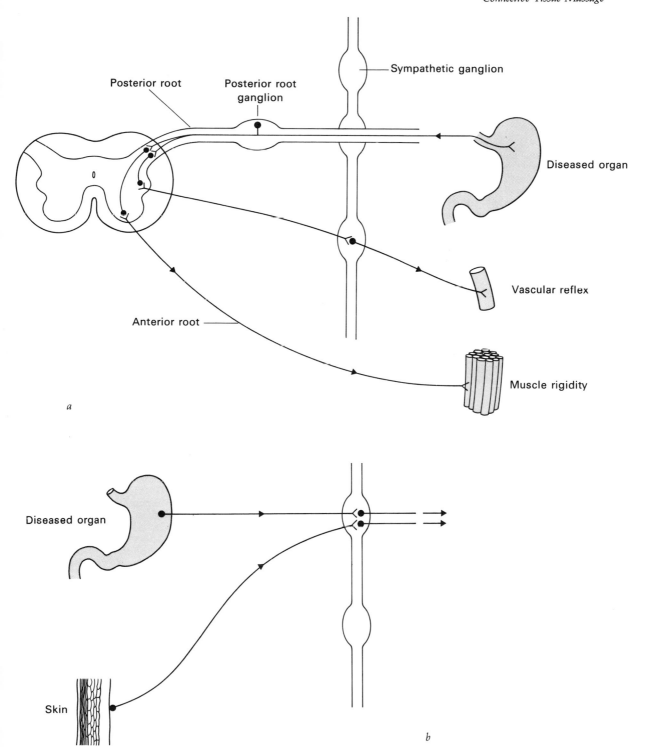

Fig. 14.3 *a* = Reflex arc at the spinal level. The impulse from a diseased organ is referred to muscle and blood vessels. *b* = Impulses arising from the diseased organ associated with cutaneous hyperalgesia.

221

increased muscle tone (Fig. 14.3*a*) are commonly viewed as being mediated via the viscerocutaneous reflex mechanism (Luedecke, 1969; Hall, 1979).

The development of the connective tissue zones are also considered to be via similar pathways (Bischof and Elmiger, 1963), although the more widespread and sometimes remote zones are yet to be convincingly explained. Ebner (personal communication) views the expansive and inter-connecting nature of the body's connective tissue as a possible mediator of tension to regions beyond those embryologically related to the diseased organ. Her theory is simply explained if one imagines a tight cotton sheet being pinched between finger and thumb at any chosen point. Widespread folds of tension are seen to radiate surprisingly far from the small area held by the fingers (Fig. 14.4). Ebner (1975) further emphasises that since all structures function *inter*dependently, a disorder in any one part of the body can have far reaching effects, even to the extent that it may interfere with the function of the whole organism.

Fig. 14.4   A tight sheet to illustrate tension radiation.

Both Mackenzie and Head limited the use of their observations purely to diagnosis. Kohlrausch in 1937 (Kohlrausch and Leube, 1953) was the first to try to influence internal organs through treatment of the body surface using 'fine vibrations' and 'loosening frictions'. In the following year he began his collaboration with Elizabeth Dicke, and together with Leube (Luedecke, 1969), they defined CTM as it is practised today. They discovered that the application of CTM led to the reappearance of normal tension in the connective tissue zones and the simultaneous recovery of the internal complaint.

For many years man has tried empirically to influence morbidity in organs by treatment of the body surface. Nearly everyone has at some stage experienced the soothing warmth of a simple hot water bottle when suffering from some minor disturbance. It is impossible that heat reaches the internal organ, yet comforting responses are received. It is well known that segmental irritation of the skin can produce impulses which are received by the organ of the same segmental innervation level (Sato *et al.*, 1975). The responsible neural pathway is known as the *cutaneovisceral reflex*, knowledge of which has helped explain and lead to the development of many successful therapeutic procedures directed at apparent deeper tissue dysfunction (Travell and Rinzler, 1946; Stoddard, 1962, 1969).

The mechanism of the effectiveness of CTM has not been explored or clarified completely. Bischof and Elmiger (1963) take the view that the specific stimulation of the 'pull' on connective tissue provides sufficient stimulus to elicit the cutaneovisceral reflex, and that this is solely responsible for the effects of the massage. Luedecke (1969) more openly felt that its mode of action could not be explained purely as a result of this reflex, as the treatment often influences tissues not segmentally related to the regions treated. Most authors (Luedecke, 1969; Ebner, 1978) are of the opinion that autonomic reflex pathways, widespread circulatory changes and endocrine release are involved in the production of the frequently powerful reactions to CTM.

THE STROKE

CTM involves the special stroking manoeuvre first described by Dicke (1954). The stroke consists of a tangential pull on the skin and subcutaneous tissues away from the underlying fascia. The deft, deceptively easy manipulation is carried out by the middle finger assisted and supported by the ring finger. The proper stroke of CTM is *always* a pull on the tissue, *never* a push or a pressure. Three stages are recognised that may help in understanding the procedure (Figs 14.5 and 14.6). These are:

1. to touch firmly,
2. 'take up the slack' by flexing the distal interphalangeal joints, and then
3. 'pull'.

Stage (2) is produced by the long finger flexor muscles, and stage (3) by flexion of the elbow which makes it incumbent so that the *radial aspect of the wrist* always leads the stroke (see Fig. 14.6).

Two types of stroke are performed:

1. The short stroke just described, where no movement of the fingers on the skin occurs.

a

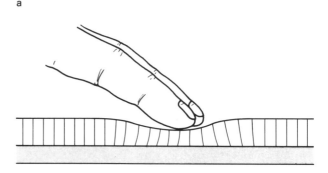

b

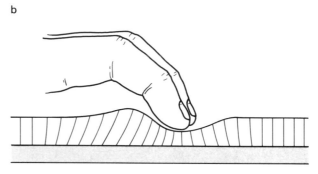

Fig. 14.5   The stroke. Stage 1 = 'Touch'. Stage 2 = 'Take up the slack'.

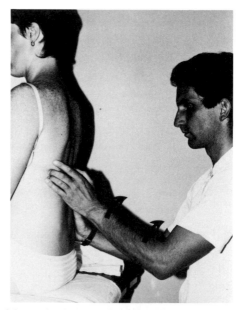

Fig. 14.6   Stage 3 of the stroke showing elbow flexion and radial aspect of the wrist 'leading the stroke'.

2. The long stroke in which the fingers, maintaining tension from stages (1) and (2), are allowed to run through the tissues. With this stroke, healthy tissue passes as a fluent fold in front of the moving finger. When resistance is encountered in faulty connective tissues, the stroke must never be forced through them. The physiotherapist should then alter her technique and may choose either to (a) substitute the long with short strokes; (b) to slow the stroke, or (c) to reduce the strength of the stroke by slightly extending the distal interphalangeal joints of the manipulating fingers (Fig. 14.7).

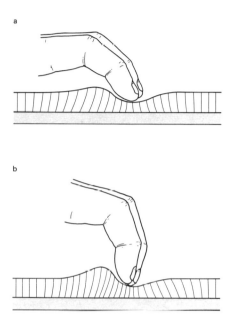

Fig. 14.7 Diagram to show how the strength of the stroke can be altered by changing the angle of the terminal phalanx to the skin.

RESPONSES TO CTM

Subjective

Normal sensation

When the fingers stroke normal tissues, relatively little resistance is felt and the patient reports only a mild scratching sensation, which is indicative of correct application of the technique. If more tense tissues are stroked, the patient may feel a sensation resembling cutting or scratching, as if the pull were with the finger nails instead of the finger tips. Leube and Dicke (1944) consider the cutting sensation as pathognomonic for recognising the proper nervous reflex. As tension decreases with use of the technique, so the intensity of the cutting sensation also decreases. The cutting sensation should cease simultaneously with the end of the stroke, and it should not persist after treatment ends.

Abnormal responses and undesirable reactions

Feelings of diffuse, dull pressure locally or in remote regions; cardiac oppression; shortness of breath; abdominal discomfort; dull pressure in the bladder; signs suggestive of shock and itching are all undesirable reactions that may be encountered. These are indicative of poorly executed and sometimes excessive use of the technique, or that CTM was an inappropriate treatment. Bischof and Elmiger (1963) view these reactions as being 'expressions of increased disturbance of the autonomic nervous system'. They are generally seen during the early use of CTM in autonomically labile patients, and imply initial caution and strict attention to technique.

Objective

When the strokes are performed in abnormally tense connective tissue zones, or even normal tissues if the technique is executed vigorously, the three stages of the triple response occur. Firstly a red line confined to the area of the stroke appears; this is later followed by a 'flush' of spreading redness and finally, if the tissues are particularly tense or the stroke vigorous, an area of superficial swelling emerges. The strength and duration of the skin reaction is directly proportional to the tension of the surface connective tissues. In some conditions, where chronically tense tissues are encountered, the skin reaction may still be visible for up to 36 h. Again, as tension is relieved, so the intensity of the reaction subsides.

In contrast, in most peripheral vascular conditions such as Raynaud's disease, the expected cutting sensation and skin reactions can only be obtained very faintly, if at all, even though tension in appropriate zones is found to be very high. In a similar, but reciprocal way to most other conditions, as tension is relieved, so normal sensory and skin responses concomitantly *increase* to normal in parallel with the improvement of the condition.

Profuse sweating is frequently seen following or during CTM, even in those who do not usually visibly perspire, suggesting parasympathetic stimulation (Ebner, 1968). If CTM is performed on one side only, it is possible to observe homolateral perspiration. Other 'autonomic' reactions that are frequently encountered include the appearance of gooseflesh and the enlargement of the pupils, both of which may present when only the caudal portion of the sacrum is treated.

Ebner (1975) reports that Volker and Rostovsky (1949) measured skin temperature of the foot in patients with circulatory disturbances of the leg and showed that dilatation occurred following CTM administered to the sacral and lumbar areas. Hall (1979) noted a 6.5°C increase in the temperature of the big toe of a normal subject following similar proximal treatment. It appears that CTM has a powerful effect on the vascular system. Bischof and Elmiger (1963) have pointed out that the vasodilatory effect of CTM was greater than that obtained with pharmacological agents, and as good as that seen following a sympathetic block. It is also noteworthy that dilatation of upper extremity vessels has been shown to occur when the pelvis is treated (Ebner, 1975), and that maximum skin temperature increase occurs 30 min after CTM, and can persist for up to 1 h. These observations tend to deny the role of the segmental reflex mechanism, and it has been suggested that humoral mechanisms are more likely to account for these effects (Ebner, 1975). However, some autonomic nervous system reactions are seen from 1 to 2 h following CTM in the form of fatigue, a pleasant desire to sleep, bowel movement and diuresis. It is probably upon these findings that Terich-Leube (1957) bases his postulation that the massage slightly emphasises the general state of the autonomic nervous system on the parasympathetic side.

The following is a summary of the effects of CTM outlined by Ebner (1975):

1. CTM helps harmonise the relationship between the sympathetic and parasympathetic part of the autonomic nervous system.
2. Within the segments treated, it helps 'normalise the circulation between organs and organ systems and other tissues belonging to that segment'.
3. Locally it improves the blood supply of the surface tissues in the area under treatment, and in particular the connective tissue element.

The treatment stroke provides a stimulus that bears *little result* if it is too weak, *harmonises* if it is adequate, and *overemphasises* the sympathetic side of the autonomic nervous system if it is too strong. It is this overemphasis which produces the rather unpleasant and occasionally dramatic side-effects alluded to earlier.

EXAMINATION

The haphazard application of CTM in an undisciplined and unsystematic way and without prior examination can only enhance criticism of this convincingly effective procedure. In addition to any standard examination required, the patient must also be inspected for the presence of connective tissue zones before CTM is instituted.

Generally, the patient is examined and treated in the sitting position with back straight, hips and knees at right angles, feet comfortably supported and the hands resting on the thighs. The trunk and buttocks should be adequately exposed (Fig. 14.8). The slight postural contraction necessary to maintain this position allows freer movement of the skin on the subcutaneous tissues. If the patient's condition makes it necessary, both investigation and treatment positions can be adjusted accordingly.

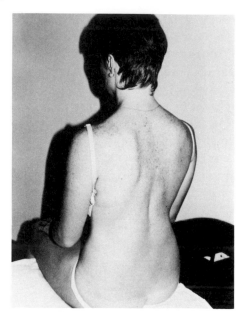

Fig. 14.8 Patient position.

Visible Investigation

Visible connective tissue zones are not always apparent to the untrained eye, and only become obvious when changes have taken place in the deeper layers between subcutis and fascia. Visible zones typically appear as band-like drawn-in areas, or flattened planes of tissue over the back and buttocks (see Fig. 14.1). Thus in venous/lymphatic disturbances of the legs, a drawn-in band can be observed passing from the middle third of the sacrum, parallel to the iliac crest laterally and forwards over the gluteus medius. The patient may report frequent swelling of the legs and feet when hot, cramps in the calf, varicose veins or even a past history of phlebitis. If the tendency is present in both legs, the zones are present on both sides, otherwise they are present only on the affected side. The severity of the drawn-in area indicates the more severely affected side (Ebner, 1975).

Manual Investigation

Three techniques of palpation are used to confirm the presence of zones. Zones not sufficiently developed to become visible are often detected while palpating. The more superficial skin layers are palpated using both hands applied simultaneously on either side of the back. The physiotherapist's slightly flexed fingers of both hands gently engage the body surface using just sufficient pressure to obtain adherence between the finger tips and the patient's skin (Fig. 14.9). Small to and fro pushes are then used to displace the subcutaneous tissues against the fascia. These are performed sequentially over the connective tissue zones so as to obtain information about them.

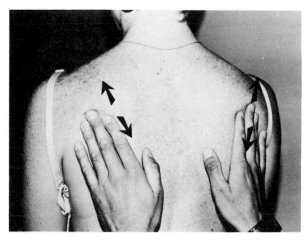

Fig. 14.9 Palpation of the superficial layers. The arrows indicate the direction of the small pushes (see text).

Palpation generally begins in the buttock and sacral regions moving upwards over the low back towards the zones between and over the scapulae.

The examiner should also bear in mind that areas of hypersensitivity (*Head's zones*) and increased muscle tone (*Mackenzie's zones*), if found to be present are informative, and can add further weight to any conclusions already drawn. It is thus vital for the operator to be conversant with the segmental supply of the various organ systems.

The deeper layers are palpated by pulling away a skin fold from the fascia (Fig. 14.10). The technique is carried out beginning at the lower costal margin and progressing upwards to the shoulder region, always comparing right and left sides and relating significant tightness to the known connective tissue zones. Suspicions aroused on examination are frequently confirmed when strong resistance to the CTM stroke is met during treatment.

Details of the visible and palpable connective tissue zones should be adequately recorded for 'diagnostic' and later comparative purposes.

Finally, the so-called *diagnostic stroke* (Bischof and Elmiger, 1963) reveals the vascular skin reaction, the tissue tension, tissue density and tissue sensitivity over the immediate paravertebral area on the right and left from L5 to C7 (Fig. 14.11). This stroke is, in effect, a *long stroke* passing the length of the back, and therefore through many of the connective tissue zones. While the physiotherapist performs the diagnostic stroke, the patient is asked to report the sensation he feels. Proportional changes in sensation, tissue resistance and vascular response can be equated to provide ever-increasing support for a confident assessment of zonal tension. Appropriate, but carefully worded questioning, should be undertaken to ascertain the patient's condition with regard to the suspected organ malfunction. For example, in a patient with obvious buttock contour changes suggestive of

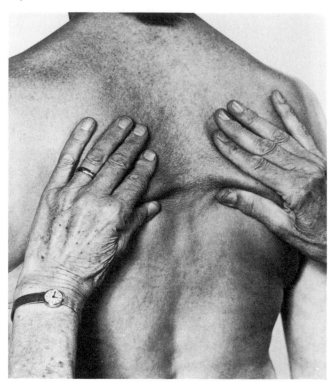

Fig. 14.10 Picking up the deeper layers.

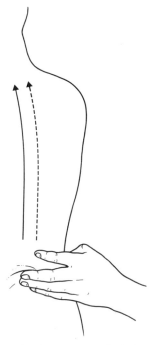

Fig. 14.11 Diagram to illustrate the diagnostic stroke (adapted from Bischof and Elmiger, 1963).

'arterial leg disturbance' (see Fig. 14.1), the physiotherapist might casually ask if he has any difficulties walking. A typical picture of gradually worsening intermittent claudication may emerge. Details of walking distance before onset of pain, what he does to relieve it, how long it takes to subside, and how far or long he can continue walking is vital information on which the future effect of treatment may be gauged. In such a patient, assessment of the peripheral pulse strength provides a further means of monitoring progress.

The temptation to enthusiastically overemphasise examination findings should be avoided, as it may unduly worry a patient who has not been referred for the problem revealed.

Zones frequently present without any 'pathological background' (Bischof and Elmiger, 1963). The patient may have suffered the indicated disturbances earlier in life, or he may have a tendency to suffer them under conditions of stress. These zones are referred to as *mute* or *silent zones*, and attention to them in treatment is seen as of vital importance to the overall success of the massage (Terich-Leube, 1957).

TREATMENT

It is known empirically (Luedecke, 1969) that the connective tissue zones have connections with each other, thereby setting up feedback circuits. The therapeutic influences of the stroke may reach the organ, nerves and vessels innervated from the same segmental level, but also be received by other connective tissue zones, and affect other zones via these. For example, paraesthesia of the hands often disappears while treating caudal areas, and frozen shoulders frequently show dramatic increases in range of movement following similar caudal treatment. It may help the understanding of this effect if the reader recalls the 'tight sheet' explanation used on p. 222.

The observation that these intersegmental connections existed and that only after tension in the caudal section had been removed was it possible to work successfully elsewhere, was found at an early stage of CTM development.

As a general rule, nearly all treatments should start in the sacral area of the back and work slowly and systematically towards the area of the complaint. Ultimately, all regions which show positive zonal signs must be included if the final aim of CTM treatment specified by Ebner (1975) is to be upheld. That is:

'To normalise within the limit of still functioning vascular pathways the tension over the whole body surface'.

The treatment areas on the trunk are divided into *sections*. These, and strokes performed over the limbs, head and anterior trunk have been described in detail elsewhere (Ebner, 1975). The importance of the caudal or *basic section* (Fig. 14.12) cannot be overstressed, as it is clear from exper-

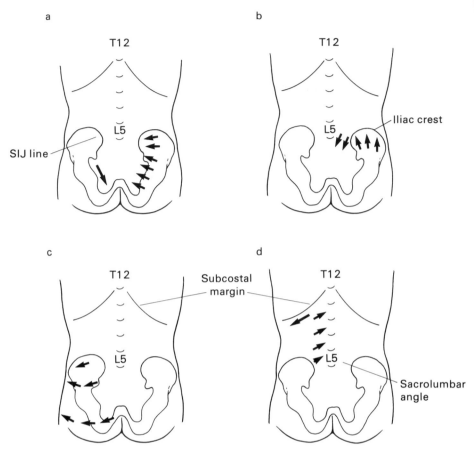

Fig. 14.12 Basic section (adapted from Ebner, 1975). ***a***= 1st set of strokes. ***b***= 2nd set of strokes. ***c***= 3rd set of strokes. ***d***= 4th set of strokes.

ienced workers in Europe and in the English-speaking countries of the world that:

1. a degree of success can often be obtained from treatment of this area alone;
2. normal tension and normal responses (subjective and objective) in the basic section must be achieved if any degree of success in other regions of the body is to occur;
3. if any undesirable reactions appear during treatment, it is likely that insufficient attention has been given to the basic section, and that the physiotherapist should immediately return to it to overcome the reaction.

It is important that the CTM strokes are not performed in a haphazard way over the body surface. Strokes tend to follow dermatomes, direction of muscle fibres and muscle fascia, tendons, and at right angles to intermuscular septa and fascial borders. Special 'stretching manipulations' (Ebner, 1975) are used in the axilla, elbow, palm and foot, which provide a final stretch to the connective tissue when tension has already been relieved by the stroking technique.

During treatment, comforting flat-handed *release strokes* are performed routinely at the termination of the basic and thoracic sections.

As treatment progresses away from the basic section, it is not uncommon to encounter areas where local and general responses occur that are inappropriate and cannot be altered, even with strict attention to the basic section and operator technique. General patient discomfort, local tickling combined with a lack of the normal scratching sensation, or visible circulatory response while treating the thoracic region is a typical example. The use of rapid, and consequently very sharp, stimulatory strokes to appropriate 'trigger points' (Ebner, 1975) usually provides the correct response when treatment is resumed. Trigger point strokes are thought to provide a strong 'circulatory stimulus' (Ebner, 1975), and are found:

1. in a triangle formed by the external abdominal oblique, latissimus dorsi and the superior border of the iliac crest;
2. on the posterior aspect of the greater trochanter;
3. at the angle between the lateral end of the clavicle and the spine of the scapula;
4. in the adductor hiatus of the thigh;
5. in the popliteal space behind the knee.

The reader should note that these are not related to the well known myofascial trigger points described by Travell and Simons (1983).

Application and Treatment of Pain

The role of CTM in the treatment of pain may be difficult to visualise in the light of the foregoing discussion. It will be recalled that CTM started as a therapeutic procedure, attempting to influence deep-seated pathology. The early German physiotherapists enjoyed a unique relationship with their medical colleagues, who referred patients with pathologically affected organs in order to observe the results. They noted beneficial effects in the following: heart diseases; respiratory conditions; disorders of the digestive system (stomach, intestinal tract, liver and gall-bladder); diseases of the urinary system; gynaecological and obstetric conditions; many neurological conditions and in particular, circulatory disorders of the extremities. It is unlikely that many physiotherapists encounter such relationships with medical practitioners today. However, it was only through treatment of patients with disorders classically amenable to physiotherapy (who coincidentally had some of the above conditions) that the beneficial results of CTM on organ pathology have been verified, and the pleasing effect on the referred condition was discovered. Thus, spinal and peripheral joint problems (whether benign or of traumatic origin), sciatica, neuralgia, nerve root pain, osteoarthritis and rheumatoid arthritis are a few examples that have been found to respond well. The rationale underlying the successful application of CTM in musculoskeletal disorders is based on the assumption that increases in local circulation to pathologically tense connective tissues helps to rebalance their depressed fluid content, and thereby increase extensibility. Additionally, in conditions where circulatory stasis has resulted in abnormally high concentrations of unwanted metabolic by-products, the benefits of increasing local blood flow are self-evident. This may be a mechanism by which CTM has a direct effect in the alleviation of pain. There is some evidence that CTM is as effective as epidural injection, and more effective than pethidine in the treatment of persistent post-sympathectomy pain (Frazer, 1978).

A large proportion of patients seeking help from physiotherapists for painful disorders of the musculoskeletal system also endure minor and sometimes major disturbances of other body systems. The relationship of

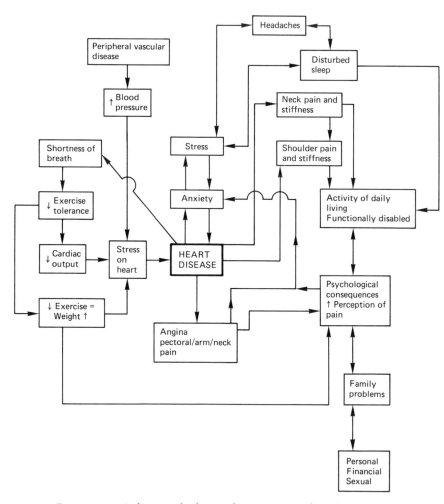

Fig. 14.13 A theoretical scheme of events issuing from heart pathology.

'organ' pathology and musculoskeletal pain has perhaps been underestimated. CTM, in conjunction with standard examination procedures, provides a unique opportunity for the evaluation of such relationships, as well as providing a successful physical alternative to traditional management.

The commonly held aetiological association between heart disease and frozen shoulder (DePalma, 1973) serves as a useful example of the type of 'thinking processes' involved when tackling a patient's problem with CTM. Figure 14.13 illustrates a theoretical, but none the less plausible scheme of events issuing from a pathological heart disorder. Examination of this patient would reveal typical patterns of pain and restriction associated with the neck and shoulder problems for which he had been referred. The inclusion of an examination for connective tissue zones may reveal relevant heart, peripheral arterial, headache zones and perhaps silent zones. Figure 14.14 illustrates the way in which CTM is thought to influence this patient's problem.

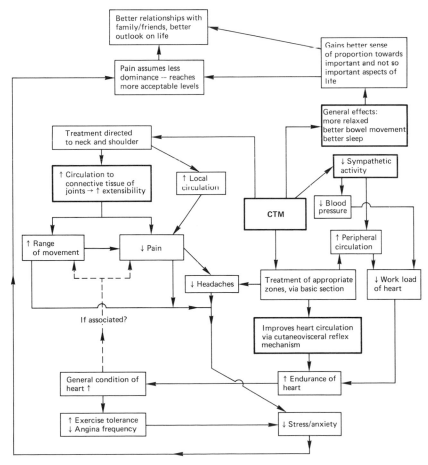

Fig. 14.14 Postulated mechanism of how CTM benefits a patient with neck, shoulder and heart problems.

There are many clinical presentations which can be fitted into this broad scheme and to which CTM can be usefully applied. Thus, in middle-aged and elderly patients with low back pain, the physiotherapist may encounter such problems as intermittent claudication or migraine headaches. Women during the menopause frequently suffer musculoskeletal problems and are often found, via CTM, to suffer a wide variety of bizarre physical, mental and personal complaints that they had been understandably anxious about revealing. It is the authors' experience that these patients receive considerable help through the physical pathway of CTM combined with sympathetic and confident consideration of their stressful state.

In attempting to answer the following questions, it might help the reader, who may be thinking of a particular presentation, in deciding whether CTM would be an appropriate avenue of treatment.

1. *Would an improvement in circulation to the symptomatic region be beneficial?*
   All disorders involving the circulation benefit from CTM, provided the pathology has not reached an irreversible situation. The authors have achieved success in the alleviation of Raynaud's disease, intermittent claudication, varicose ulcers and gangrene. The latter two conditions should be treated without entering the affected areas, as the skin is excessively fragile.
2. *Does the physiotherapist think that the general condition of the patient, both physical and mental, may be contributing to the presentation?*
   If so, CTM examination is likely to be revealing and treatment beneficial.
3. *Will the patient find this form of treatment acceptable?*
   It is not easy to explain to a patient that treatment of his neck should begin over his buttocks! The patient must be taught that treatment areas, and areas which cause discomfort and show pathological symptoms, are not always the same. It may help if the patient understands that for treatment to be effective, the buttock and low back regions must be treated first. Patients easily accept the confidence and skill of an experienced physiotherapist.

CONTRAINDICATIONS

Although possibly self-evident, it should still be stated that CTM is contraindicated in conditions where any increase in circulation is likely to be detrimental. Of particular note are: malignancy; acute inflammatory conditions; closed abscesses; during menstruation and the final trimester of pregnancy. In patients with notably low blood pressure, a degree of caution should be exercised as the massage can produce quite dramatic peripheral dilatation. The operator should progress treatment slowly and be vigilant for early signs of shock.

It is hoped that this short chapter has provided some interest and new thoughts for those who have already discovered CTM, as well as for those to whom it is unfamiliar. CTM has a fascinating history, and differs quite markedly from trends in manual therapy today.

Over the years quite significant numbers of physiotherapists have been taught the technique, yet most have done little more than experiment enthusiastically with it for a few weeks during post-course euphoria! Others have simply been unable to approach their patients with CTM. This is not meant to be a criticism of these physiotherapists, as their difficulties and evaluation of CTM are understandable. However, it does serve to highlight several points that are vital for the future survival of CTM (see below). It also underlines the loopholes that these clinicians have found, and which need to be overcome before more widespread use of the technique is likely to occur. Thus:

1. It is paramount that a physiotherapist understands the nature and background of a technique before being able to apply it confidently and effectively to patients. CTM has a dated and questionable scientific foundation which badly needs re-evaluating and researching.
2. It is only an effective modality if undertaken in the logical and carefully controlled way described. The emphasis must be on scrupulous examination and reassessment, precision of technique, and informed observation of the patient and his tissues. Just as manipulative therapy has gained attention via its widespread use and excellent results, so must CTM. Once it becomes more widely recognised as a valuable clinical tool, CTM may attract the scientific attention it so desperately needs.
3. Attention can be focused on CTM via:
   (a) the favourable results of treatment;
   (b) the more widespread teaching of the technique, which in the authors' opinion, should extend to undergraduates;
   (c) the recognition of its value by referring medical colleagues.

REFERENCES

Bischof I., Elmiger G. (1963). Connective tissue massage. In *Massage, Manipulation and Traction* (Licht S. ed.). Baltimore: Waverly Press, pp. 57–83.

DePalma A.F. (1973). *Surgery of the Shoulder*, 2nd edn. Philadelphia: J.B. Lippincott Co.

Dicke E. (1954). *Meine Bindegewebsmassage*. Stuttgart: Marquardt. (Cited by Bischof and Elmiger, 1963).

Ebner M. (1968). Connective tissue massage: therapeutic application. *N. Z. J. Physiother*; **3(14)**: 18–12.

Ebner, M. (1972). *Connective Tissue Massage, Uses and Contraindications in Obstetrics and Gynaecology*. Newsletter No. 32. London: The Obstetric Association of Chartered Physiotherapists.

Ebner M. (1975). *Connective Tissue Massage. Theory and Therapeutic Application*. New York: R.E. Krieger.

Ebner M. (1978). Connective tissue massage. *Physiotherapy*; **64(7)**: 208–10.

Frazer F.W. (1978). Persistent post-sympathetic pain treated by connective tissue massage. *Physiotherapy*; **64(7)**: 211–12.

Hall J.M. (1979). An analysis of connective tissue massage. In *Aspects of Manipulative Therapy* (Idczak R.M., ed.). Proceedings of a multidisciplinary international conference on manipulative therapy, Melbourne, Australia.

Head H. (1893). On disturbances of sensation with especial reference to the pain of visceral disease. *Brain;* **16**: 1–133.

Kohlrausch W., Leube H. (1953). *Hochergymnastik.* Jena: Fischer. (Cited by Bischof and Elmiger, (1963).

Leube H., Dicke E. (1944). *Massage Reflektorischer Zonen im Bindegewebe bei Rheumatischen und Inneren Erkrankungen.* **Jena**: Fischer. (Cited by Bischof and Elmiger, 1963).

Luedecke U. (1969). History, basis and technique of connective tissue massage. *Aust. J. Physiother;* **15(4)**: 141–8.

Mackenzie J. (1909). *Symptoms and their Interpretation.* London: Shaw and Sons.

Sato A., Sato Y., Shimado F., Torigata Y. (1975). Changes in gastric motility produced by neuceptive stimulation of the skin in rats. *Brain Res;* **87**: 151–9.

Stoddard A. (1962). *Manual of Osteopathic Technique,* 2nd edn. London: Hutchinson.

Stoddard A. (1969). *Manual of Osteopathic Practice.* London: Hutchinson.

Terich-Leube H. (1957). *Grundriss der Beindegewebsmassage.* Stuttgart: Fischer. (Cited by Bischof and Elmiger, 1963).

Travell J., Rinzler G.H. (1946). Relief of cardiac pain by local block of somatic trigger areas. *Proc. Soc. Exp. Biol. Med;* **63**: 480–7.

Travell J.G., Simons D.G. (1983). *Myofascial Pain and Dysfunction: The Trigger Point Manual.* Baltimore: Williams and Wilkins.

Volker R., Rostovsky E. (1949). Ueber den therapeutischen wert der BGM bei gefaess-stroerunger der gliedmassen. *Z. Rheumaforsch;* **8**: 192. (Cited by Ebner, 1975.)

Chapter 15

Hydrotherapy

ALISON T. SKINNER and ANN M. THOMSON

INTRODUCTION

The term hydrotherapy is derived from the Greek *hydor* meaning water and *therapeiu* meaning to heal. Hydrotherapy was first used by the Greeks in the time of Hippocrates (460–375 BC), who treated disease with hot and cold water, diet, rest and as few drugs as possible. Following the Greek influence, the Romans began building baths (1st century AD) for both recreational and curative purposes. During the Dark Ages there was little use of therapeutic baths, but in the reign of Elizabeth I they came back into fashion. Then, in 1697, Sir John Flayer published a paper entitled *An enquiry into the right use and abuse of hot, cold and temperate baths in England*. His views, however, were not well supported in England, but in Germany tepid baths were used extensively for the relief of muscle spasm and in the treatment of hyperexcitable patients. During the late 19th and early 20th centuries, mineral baths and spas increased in popularity throughout Europe and the United States.

Gradually, hydrotherapy has become a widely accepted therapeutic modality used by physiotherapists in the treatment of a variety of patients with many different diseases or disorders.

THE PHYSICAL PROPERTIES OF WATER AND PAIN RELIEF

Water has certain physical properties which have a direct bearing on pain relief. These are: *buoyancy, hydrostatic pressure, turbulence* and *temperature*.

Buoyancy

This is a force acting in the opposite direction to the force of gravity and is experienced as an upthrust. The force of buoyancy can thus provide weight relief, the extent of which is dependent on the proportion of the body below water level. If the body is immersed to waist level, the weight relief is approximately 50% of the body weight. If the water is at shoulder level,

239

weight relief is approximately 90% of the body weight. Pain due to weight-bearing can thus be relieved in a hydrotherapy pool. The patient, having been relieved of this pain, can be re-educated in standing up, sitting down, or standing on one leg. The normality of movement restored is a factor in the maintenance of pain relief after the patient has left the pool. Buoyancy, with or without floats, can provide complete support for the body in supine floating. This position enables the patient to relax, thus easing muscle tension or spasm with the consequent relief of pain. There is no localised pressure on the patient's bony prominences when floating, and this is very comfortable for patients who have lost body tissue after a debilitating disease.

When the body is supported by buoyancy, the arms, legs and trunk may be moved just under the surface of the water and parallel with it. This freedom of movement can help to regain a full range of movement in joints with the result that synovial fluid may sweep across the cartilage bringing nutrition and lubrication back to the joint surfaces. The movement also facilitates fluid movement through the tissue and fascial planes helping to drain the metabolic products which have accumulated and which act as a noxious stimulus.

Hydrostatic Pressure

This property of water provides an even pressure on all surfaces of an immersed limb or body at any one given depth. However, the pressure is greater deeper in the water and less nearer the surface (Fig. 15.1).

The pressure gradient therefore aids the flow of venous blood and lymph in an antigravitational direction when the patient is standing in the pool, and this may help reduce oedema in the foot and lower leg. Thus where oedematous fluid creates tensions and distortion within the tissues with consequent pain, the effects of the hydrostatic pressure may be utilised for pain relief.

Turbulence

This is an irregular movement of water molecules. Within a hydrotherapy pool, turbulence may be created by an underwater douche, which is a jet of water from a hose pipe. The douche is used to apply a pressure on the tissues and may be moved around a painful area. It is, therefore, like a deep soft tissue manipulative technique without contact between the physiotherapist's hand and patient's skin. Patients report dramatic pain relief from this modality, and it is interesting to postulate that this may be due to pressure and the stretching of tight tissues and movement of fluid through the various fascial planes as well as the stimulation of mechanoreceptors. Turbulence may also be created by the physiotherapist moving through the water. When the patient is lying in the floating position (float lying), and

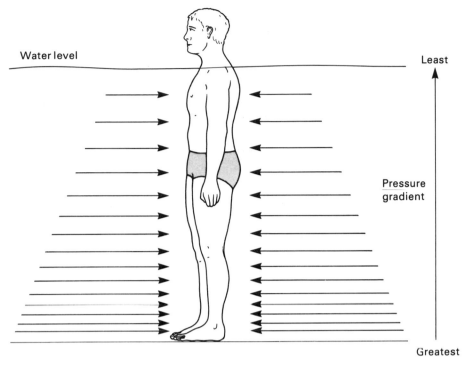

Water level

Least

Pressure
gradient

Greatest

Fig. 15.1   The effects of hydrostatic pressure when the patient is standing in the water.

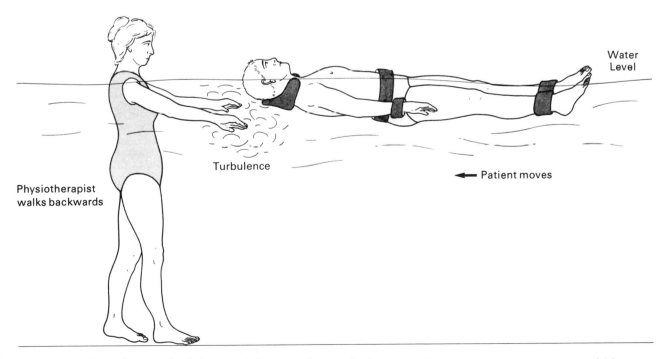

Water
Level

Turbulence

Patient moves

Physiotherapist
walks backwards

Fig. 15.2   The application of turbulence with the patient lying in the floating position.

turbulence is created just beyond the patient's head, the effect is that the patient moves through the water (Fig. 15.2). This has a relaxing effect and may be used to ease muscle tension or spasm especially in the neck and shoulder girdle area.

If a patient has difficulty in walking through the resistance of the water and this causes discomfort, the physiotherapist may walk in front of the patient so that a wake is created for the patient to walk in (Fig. 15.3). This makes walking easier and therefore reduces the discomfort.

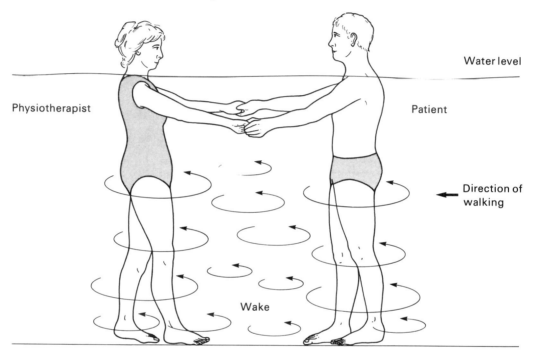

Fig. 15.3   The application of turbulence with the physiotherapist and the patient walking through the water.

Temperature

The water in a hydrotherapy pool is generally maintained at a temperature of between 35°C and 36°C. Therefore during the time a patient is being treated, the whole body is warmed. This induces relaxation of muscle spasm, promotes increased flow of circulation and facilitates movement of joints. The effects of heat in pain relief have been discussed in Chapter 12 (p. 170–1).

TECHNIQUES ASSOCIATED WITH PAIN RELIEF IN THE
HYDROTHERAPY POOL

Relaxation Techniques

Conscious relaxation

The patient is in float lying and is encouraged to feel that the floats and water are supporting the body totally. The suggestion of floating and 'letting go' encourages the patient to relax.

Contrast relaxation

The patient is again in float lying (Fig. 15.4). Instructions are given so that the patient tightens the muscles which increase in tone, then relaxes with a consequent lengthening effect on the muscles. For example, where the back extensors are to be relaxed, the patient is instructed to lift the pelvis up out of the pelvic float, hold and then relax. Where the knee flexors are to be treated the patient is instructed to push the foot down against the float into the water, hold and then let go. The knee is then straightened by buoyancy and the flexors relax.

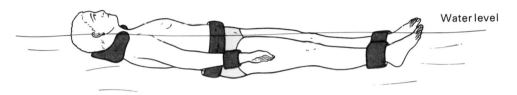

Water level

Fig. 15.4 Float lying.

Passive movements and relaxation

With the patient supported in floats, the physiotherapist stands behind the patient's head and places a hand on either side of the chest wall, to straighten and support the upper trunk. The patient's upper trunk is then moved rhythmically from side to side so that the pelvis and legs move reciprocally in an easy and relaxed manner. The pelvis can also be held by the physiotherapist and the trunk, head and arms moved in a similar way. The physiotherapist may hold the patient's feet together and produce a side-to-side or figure-of-eight movement, which produces a rhythmical reciprocal movement of the whole body.

Hold relax technique (see also Chapter 8)

This technique is used to increase range of movement at a joint where increased muscle tension caused by pain is the limiting factor. The muscle group limiting the movement is made to contract strongly against the resistance of the physiotherapist and this is followed by a relaxation phase where there is a lengthening effect on the muscle.

Generally, the patient's position is chosen so that buoyancy assists movement into the new range. This helps to break up the pain–spasm–pain cycle.

243

Repeated contractions (see also Chapter 8)

This technique involves applying maximal resistance to the agonist muscles involved in a movement making the muscles work isotonically, then isometrically, then isotonically with consequent lengthening due to reciprocal inhibition of the antagonists. In the pool, the resistance can be applied by turbulence, with or without buoyancy. As with hold relax, there is breaking up of the pain—spasm—pain cycle with the added benefit of strengthening the agonist muscles.

Exercises

Exercises are directed towards improving coordination, increasing joint range, strengthening muscles and improving function. Buoyancy may be counterbalanced, assisting or resisting with the added effect of floats, bats, or flippers. While these exercises may not be of direct obvious benefit in relieving pain, the restoration of normal function is usually associated with pain relief.

Breathing exercises

The patient lies in the water on a half-stretcher with the legs moved to one side, which stretches the chest wall muscles and trunk side flexors of the opposite side. The physiotherapist gives the instruction to the patient to breathe in deeply on the stretched side and then to breathe out. Just prior to the inspiratory phase, the physiotherapist applies slight stretch to the patient's legs and pelvis which stretches the intercostal muscles and at the same time applies manual pressure on the thorax to encourage inspiration. This technique is of value in the treatment of patients who have had a thoracotomy or have ankylosing spondylitis. Patients appear to find deep breathing and trunk mobility exercises easier after this technique of breathing exercises and these are thus of value in pain control.

DISEASES OR DISORDERS WHICH ARE APPROPRIATE FOR PAIN CONTROL OR RELIEF BY POOL THERAPY

Rheumatic Disorders

Rheumatoid arthritis

Patients with this disease benefit from the effects of weight relief particularly on the joints which are recovering following an active stage in the disease. In the warmth and support of the water, patients are able to exercise in a pain reduced state increasing muscle strength, maintaining or increasing joint movement and improving stamina and general fitness.

Osteoarthritis

Patients with osteoarthritis of the spine, hips, knees or shoulders benefit from hydrotherapy. Where there is bilateral osteoarthritis of the hips or knees, the weight relief allows for muscle strengthening and re-education of gait in the presence of pain relief with resultant functional improvement. With the patient on a half-stretcher, longitudinal oscillatory passive movements applied in the long axis of the femur help to control pain in patients with advanced osteoarthritis of the hip. The hold relax technique is of particular benefit for relaxing spasm in the hip adductors and flexors and in the knee flexors where appropriate. The spasm of the lumbar spine extensors associated with osteoarthritis of the spine also responds to relaxation techniques. Mobility and pain relief in the lumbar spine may be obtained by treating the patient in float lying. The physiotherapist places her hands under the patient's lumbar spine and performs an oscillatory movement in a posteroanterior direction, thereby encouraging relaxation of the lumbar spine extensors.

Ankylosing spondylitis

The nature of this condition results in pain being present in many joints at one time. The buoyancy and warmth of the water therefore help to reduce this widespread pain. Relaxation techniques and breathing exercises, together with spinal mobility and extension exercises, are all important for the control of pain in patients with this condition. There appears to be some indication that hydrotherapy has a prophylactic effect in ankylosing spondylitis. In this instance, patients attend for hydrotherapy at 6 monthly intervals to ensure that the joints are kept mobile, muscle strength is maintained and good posture is practised. Thus the pain associated with joint stiffness and soft tissue contractures can be prevented or lessened.

Spondylosis

Patients with cervical spondylosis report benefit from relaxation techniques where the pelvis is moved by the physiotherapist and the trunk, head and arms swing reciprocally. This helps to ease the tension in the neck and shoulder muscles which is associated with this condition. The neck extensors may be strengthened by the patient pushing against the neck float with the chin tucked in. This also stretches tightness of the upper cervical spine extensors, which is so often associated with spondylosis. The pain of lumbar spondylosis responds to relaxation and to repeated trunk rotation exercises, especially when the upper trunk is fixed and the pelvis rotates.

Patients with these conditions tend to have exacerbations and remissions of pain. Hydrotherapy is indicated after the initial acuteness has settled, because it affords relief of severe pain. This then allows for the restoration of mobility and progress towards the restoration of function.

Orthopaedics and Trauma

Fractures of the lower limb

Fractured neck of femur

Elderly patients who have sustained fractured neck of femur are usually treated by internal fixation and early mobilisation. Walking on land is painful because these patients find it difficult to keep weight off the limb even with a frame or crutches. The weight relief afforded by buoyancy restores the patient's confidence in an otherwise painful walking pattern. Rising from a chair is also difficult, and this movement can be practised in the pool with the assistance of buoyancy. Thus hydrotherapy helps to accelerate the rehabilitation of these elderly patients.

Fractures of the femoral and tibial shafts

Patients with these fractures often have pain and stiffness in the knee. Hold relax technique, repeated contractions and progressive exercises for strengthening the muscles that control the knee given in the warmth of the water enable these patients to recover mobility and function.

Fractures of the upper limb

Fractured neck of the humerus with or without a dislocated shoulder

Patients with these injuries are often elderly and are afraid to move the arm because of the pain. The patient sits on a stool or stands in the pool with the shoulders under the water and is encouraged to relax so that buoyancy may raise the arm and flex the shoulder joint. The warmth of the water reduces the pain, and the patient regains confidence in moving the arm. This approach facilitates the re-education of reversed humeroscapular rhythm. If there is spasm of the adductors, hold relax technique may be used to regain abduction. Once the patient is confident in moving the arm up to 90° from the chest wall, the starting position is changed to float lying, in which position the arm can be assisted into full elevation.

Back pain following trauma or operation

Following operations such as laminectomy or fenestration patients may begin pool therapy approximately 10–12 days after the operation. Following trauma to the back, the patient is often given a period of bed rest immediately after which pool therapy may begin. In these patients, the back extensors are often in spasm and it is important to break the pain–spasm–pain cycle. Relaxation techniques, general at first and then localised to the area of greatest spasm, relieve the pain and enable the patient to feel freedom of movement within the spine. Where the patient is afraid of pain on spinal movement, encouragement is given in moving the arms and legs. These activities make the muscles controlling the trunk act as fixators which helps to accelerate the circulatory flow through spinal structures removing inflammatory exudate and relieving pain.

Knee surgery

Patients who have reparative surgery for a knee injury often have a history of long-standing knee pain. These patients benefit from pool therapy by the weight relief, by techniques such as oscillatory distraction, which reduces intra-articular friction and by having the strength of the quadriceps increased with progressive exercises. These patients have a daily programme of part hydrotherapy and part dry-land rehabilitation. Where pool therapy is given first, patients report relief of pain which improves their performance and function in dry-land rehabilitation.

Amputation

Patients with lower limb amputations sometimes develop painful contractures over the flexor aspects of the hip and/or knee. Passive stretching is applied to the tight structures with the patient lying on a half-stretcher in the water. The discomfort of the stretching is reduced by the warmth of the water and therefore the effect is more quickly obtained than on land. Buoyancy may be used to assist the stretching, e.g. if the patient is lying prone on a half-stretcher buoyancy will assist hip extension and help stretch the tight flexors and associated soft tissue contractures.

The patients enjoy swimming, and the freedom of movement afforded by the water contributes to the overall sense of well-being.

Neurological Conditions

Multiple sclerosis

Patients with this condition often suffer back pain, which is relieved in water due to a combination of warmth and support. It is worth trying passive movements and relaxation to reduce spasticity, which will further relieve pain and this may then be followed by passive stretching of structures contracted due to prolonged sitting in the later stages of the condition.

While hydrotherapy may not have any effect on the course of the disorder, patients report several days of comfort and easier movement following pool treatment. The management of these patients should employ 6 to 8 treatment sessions at approximately 6 monthly intervals. A careful watch should be kept for the occasional patient with multiple sclerosis who does not like the humidity and warmth of the pool and becomes very tired as a result. Such a patient may not be suitable for this type of treatment.

Hemiplegia

The painful shoulder associated with hemiplegia can be treated with some success. The patient sits on a stool with buoyancy assisting the affected arm up to 90° flexion. If the physiotherapist then supports the patient's arm with one hand, and helps to protract the patient's shoulder girdle with the other hand, tightness of the retractors is eased and the patient finds shoulder movement easier. If flexion and extension of the shoulder are then encouraged in the horizontal plane just under the water surface, there is reduction of pain which has a carry-over into functional activities on land.

Polyneuropathies

In the early stages of recovery from these conditions, the comfortable handling of the patient is difficult because of hypersensitivity of the patient's skin. Treatment in the pool with relaxation in float lying reduces the hypersensitivity so that re-education techniques for the recovering muscle groups is more comfortable for the patient. Initially, the patient needs to be lowered into the water and taken out again in a sheet to avoid handling of the skin.

Respiratory Disorders

Thoracotomy

Following thoracotomy, patients may have a combination of pool treatment and dry-land exercises. The humidity in the pool room is high, therefore when the patient breathes in there is water vapour in the inspired air. This helps to loosen secretions and makes coughing less painful. The warmth of the water surrounding the chest wall also reduces pain and thoracic mobility improves. This effect carries over from one day to the next so that the patient finds arm movements and breathing exercises on land more comfortable. Patients may be treated in the pool 2 days after the operation with the wound covered by a plastic dressing. According to Boyd (1976) patients benefit from daily treatment in the pool and may participate in a group programme. A patient who had this regime following a second thoracotomy had a more speedy recovery than after the first thoracotomy, the postoperative management of which did not include pool therapy.

Haemophilia

Pain in this condition arises from a bleed into joints or muscles, which if untreated, results in contractures and loss of functional movement patterns. Passive stretching exercises given to the tight muscles are much more comfortable with the patient in a pool rather than on dry land. Joints are treated with mobilising exercises and selective muscle strengthening designed to restore muscle balance. Osteotomy of the femoral or tibial bones is often necessary where repeated bleeding has caused loss of joint cartilage with consequent deformity. Patients have pool treatment when the stitches have been taken out after 10 days, and although full joint range may not return, there is restoration of pain-free function.

SUMMARY

That pain relief is a therapeutic entity of hydrotherapy is undisputed in terms of patients' reports. It is interesting to consider why there may be this pain relief. The water is at 35–36°C, therefore the whole body is immersed in a medium, the temperature of which is above that of the skin (33.5°C); this, therefore, affords relaxation which in turn reduces muscle tension and the pain–spasm–pain cycle is broken. The warmth of the medium also produces a redistribution of circulation so that there is an increase of blood flow through the superficial tissues. The activity of sweat glands is increased following pool therapy because the body loses heat gained during treatment by evaporation of sweat. There is also an increased rate of circulation through the vessels of the working muscles during exercises performed in the pool. These effects may produce chemical changes within neurons and result in pain relief which lasts longer than the pool therapy.

There is no doubt that patients find movements easier in the warm pool than on dry land and are therefore able to perform activities through a greater range of movement. Muscles are therefore shortening and lengthening and joint surfaces are moved through a greater range than on land. This must move synovial fluid across articular cartilage, and tissue fluid through tissue spaces which improves nutrition and may restore chemical balance within the tissues with consequent pain relief.

Patients who are unable to move well on land derive great pleasure from the freedom of movement in the pool. This applies particularly to patients with rheumatoid arthritis, ankylosing spondylitis, multiple sclerosis and acute pain associated with degenerative disorders of the joints both peripheral and spinal. These patients leave the pool room with a sense of well-being and achievement. It is probable therefore, that some of the pain relief reported by patients is due to a raising of the pain tolerance level which enables the patient to manage the pain although it may well be still present.

Overall, therefore, pool therapy has a place in the number of skills available to the physiotherapist in the relief or control of pain in patients.

REFERENCE

Boyd J.M. (1976). A new program for thoracotomy patients. *Physiotherapy (Can)*; **28(5)**: 274–6.

FURTHER READING

Farrell R.J. (1976). A hydrotherapy program for high cervical cord lesions. *Physiotherapy (Can)*; **28(1)**: 8–12.

Golland A. (1981). Basic hydrotherapy. *Physiotherapy*; **67(9)**: 258–62.

Reid Campion M.J. (1985). *Hydrotherapy in Paediatrics*. London: William Heinemann Medical Books.

Skinner A.T., Thomson A.M. (1983). *Duffield's Exercise in Water*, 3rd edn. London: Baillière Tindall.

Section III

Special Areas of Intervention

Chapter 16

The Management of Postoperative Pain

ELIZABETH S. CHANEY

INTRODUCTION

Postoperative pain, in the majority of cases, is inevitable, and without effective management it exaggerates the complications associated with surgery. This book is concerned with a variety of methods of pain relief, many of which should be effective in controlling postoperative pain, although some of these techniques may not be practicable in the immediate postoperative situation.

The methods commonly used for controlling postoperative pain are: *drugs* (administered by a variety of routes), *cryoanalgesia, inhalation therapy* (entonox), *transcutaneous electrical nerve stimulation* and *acupuncture.* However, although it is rare for the physiotherapist to be directly responsible for the control of postoperative pain, she does have an important part to play in assessing a patient's ability or limitations as a result of an ineffective analgesic regime. Furthermore, the physiotherapist is necessarily involved postoperatively in a variety of ways in the management of the patient, who even with prescribed analgesia, will experience discomfort or frank pain with certain postures, movements and activities.

THE EFFECTS OF POSTOPERATIVE PAIN

The Effects of Pain on Lung Function

The postoperative complications associated with general anaesthesia are well documented. As a direct result of the administration of premedication, anaesthetic agents, and immobility during surgery, there is a marked reduction in lung function, the effects of which are as follows:

1. Respiration is depressed due to a reduced response of chemoreceptors to hypercapnia, hypoxia and acidosis.

253

2. Problems of gas exchange arise due to long periods of immobility with ventilation/perfusion mismatching, although there are other factors to be considered, e.g. obesity, age, pre-existing lung disease and the effects of cigarette smoking.

3. Inhaled anaesthetic agents make bronchial secretions thicker and more tenacious.

4. Lung volume is reduced, particularly in upper abdominal and thoracic operations. This may be as a result of diaphragm 'splinting', paralytic ileus or regional atelectasis.

5. The cough reflex is diminished or lost altogether as a result of a reduction in the response of the bronchial cilia.

The consequences of these changes are hypoxaemia, sputum retention and pulmonary collapse. In conjunction with a prolonged period of sedation on the patient's return to the ward, the situation is self-perpetuating. Postoperative pain will also have detrimental effects on lung function (particularly after abdominal or thoracic surgery), the patient being unable to breathe deeply and cough. Thus the problem of sputum retention and pulmonary collapse is compounded.

One role of the physiotherapist, postoperatively, is to assist the patient in regaining preoperative lung function. This can be done by deep-breathing exercises and the elimination of secretions, preferably by effective coughing. Postural drainage may well be necessary, both to aid the drainage of retained secretions and to improve ventilation/perfusion matching. Obviously, the control of pain during these procedures is of prime importance.

Effects of Pain on General Mobility

Mobilisation is a shared responsibility for the physiotherapist in most areas, but in some units, e.g. orthopaedics, neurosurgery, the physiotherapist has the major responsibility of mobilising a patient. Pain inhibits mobility, and general mobility is extremely important because not only does it prevent problems of weakness and joint stiffness with the consequent delayed return to full functional independence, but it will also help to improve lung function. Exercise increases the demand for oxygen by the body, and thus the rate and depth of respiration will increase.

For maximum benefit to be gained from physiotherapy postoperatively, full patient cooperation is necessary. The majority of patients are very willing to comply with treatment, but find they are unable to do so because of pain. Thus it is to the advantage of both patient and physiotherapist that the physiotherapist shows an interest in and is concerned with the management of postoperative pain.

Before looking at pain control and its management it is valuable to consider why pain occurs, what influences its perception and to ascertain whether any of these factors are particularly relevant in the case of the postoperative patient.

FACTORS INFLUENCING POSTOPERATIVE PAIN

Pain occurs as a result of stimulation of nociceptors which have been demonstrated to be present in all body tissues except nervous tissue (though they are present in the meninges and epidural tissues), and particularly in the skin. These stimuli pass to the brain where they are perceived and evoke a response (see Chapters 2–5).

With regard to surgery, all incisions will create activation of these receptors and it could be anticipated that the larger the incision, with the inclusion of more structures, the greater the stimulation and hence the greater the pain will be. For example, a patient having undergone thoractomy will experience more postoperative pain than a patient having undergone an inguinal hernia repair. Similarly, it could be anticipated that two patients having undergone the same operation would experience the same amount of pain. However, from experience we know this is not the case, the reason being that pain perception is influenced by other factors, e.g. anxiety, expectation of pain, previous experience of pain, understanding of pain, and the patient's culture and background. While patients who are admitted to hospital for planned surgery or investigations which may result in surgery vary in their attitudes to this situation, undoubtedly the majority of them are anxious. Such anxiety will, of course, influence their perception of pain postoperatively. The expectation of postoperative pain is yet another problem to add to the list. The majority of patients expect pain and their response is often directly related to their expectations (Wallace, 1985). Additionally, a patient has problems to cope with other than that of the surgery and its outcome, e.g. the new surroundings, unfamiliar professional staff (of whom there are many) and so on.

Although, in healthy subjects, pain can be measured by various methods, such as visual analogue scales (see Chapter 2, p. 15) and electrical stimuli, there seems to be no general assessment that can be applied in the clinical situation to determine the amount of pain a patient will experience. In cases of minor surgery, some patients do not consider pain to be serious enough to warrant analgesia (McQuay *et al.*, 1982). However, every patient who undergoes some surgical procedure will have individual expectations and responses, and thus any individual's precise response to postoperative pain cannot be assumed.

PREOPERATIVE PHYSIOTHERAPY

Physiotherapy treatment begins preoperatively. In view of the complications that are known to arise following major surgery, it is valuable for the physiotherapist to see the patient prior to surgery for several reasons (obviously in cases of emergency this is not possible):

1. introduction of the physiotherapist to the patient;
2. assessment of usual lung function and general mobility;

3. preoperative treatment for any existing pulmonary complaint or functional disability;
4. discussion.

The 'discussion' should be a two-way conversation with the patient, covering many topics including the need and nature of postoperative physiotherapy. At this time, the patient can relate any fears and anxieties regarding surgery to the physiotherapist. Hopefully the physiotherapist will be able to allay most, if not all, of these fears and anxieties, but if not she is in a position to direct the patient to the person who can. It is at this point that postoperative pain and its management can be discussed in general terms, the physiotherapist getting to know the expectations of an individual perhaps in the light of past experiences.

Without dwelling on the subject too much, the physiotherapist can reassure the patient that analgesia will be prescribed and administered by the medical staff, but that its effectiveness is very much dependent on the patient relating back to all staff, so that an optimum regime may be maintained.

It has been shown that the knowledge of a relaxation technique does help to reduce postoperative distress, although not necessarily pain, and if thought to be suitable the physiotherapist might wish to teach the patient such a technique at this time (Morgan *et al.*, 1985).

THE MANAGEMENT OF POSTOPERATIVE PAIN

The following aspects will be considered:

1. Physiotherapy
2. Medication
3. Cryoanalgesia
4. Inhalation therapy (entonox)
5. TENS
6. Acupuncture

Physiotherapy

Although some patients do not suffer from postoperative pain following minor surgery, some do. Although this possibility should not be ignored, the majority of patients undergoing larger operations will experience enough pain to warrant treatment, particularly as more physiotherapy will be required; the larger, longer operations predispose to more complications as described earlier (p. 255). In such circumstances, it is vital that analgesia be well controlled.

Who is responsible for the management of postoperative analgesia?

It is difficult to identify one particular professional as the individual solely responsible for the management of postoperative analgesia. Medication is prescribed by the medical staff and administered by the nursing staff, but if the regime is not adequate this must be noted by the physiotherapist, as effective treatment cannot be carried out until the patient's pain is controlled.

Although observations of the patient, both at rest and during activity, by all staff can indicate that analgesia has been ineffective only the patient can say whether his pain is well under control. It may take some pertinent questioning of the patient by staff, on noticing any difficulty, to ascertain the exact nature and degree of the discomfort. All professionals caring for the patient are involved with the management of pain, and in order to ensure optimal analgesia, good communication between all staff and the patient is essential.

All staff concerned with the postoperative care of a patient are able to observe the patient for signs of discomfort and distress resulting from ineffective analgesia. Such signs would include shallow respirations and reluctance to move. The physiotherapist has more opportunity than most to monitor these limitations.

The physiotherapist is a frequent and regular visitor to the patient's bedside and unlike some members of 'the team', expects and needs sustained effort and cooperation from the patient in order that maximum benefit is achieved from treatment.

With a knowledge of the preoperative status of both lung function and mobility, the physiotherapist can easily recognise any reduction in these parameters. On discussion with the patient, the reason for such problems can be identified. With explanation and reassurance the patient might relax somewhat and thus any pain can be reduced to such a level that the patient finds it tolerable to continue with treatment. However, should this not be so then the physiotherapist is able to communicate to the medical staff that a change in analgesic prescription might be advantageous.

Physiotherapy should not be continued while pain is still a problem, because the patient's trust in the physiotherapist will be reduced, replacing trust with fear, which does not help to promote good physiotherapy at a later time. In the meantime, while awaiting further analgesia, instruction in how to cope with the pain can be given to the patient. Such instruction would include relaxation with gentle diaphragmatic breathing and relieving the tension on an incision.

Account should be taken of the patient's position and the degree of mobility that is expected, so that the patient who is comfortable while still will also be able to move without discomfort. A patient experiencing pain will adopt a posture that will either relieve or reduce the pain. In most cases this involves reducing the length of the muscles in the region of the discomfort (Table 16.1). The physiotherapist is well-qualified to educate the patient (as well as other staff) in comfortable positioning, the most effective way to breathe deeply and to cough, as well as supervising mobility.

In most cases, early mobilisation is in the best interest of the patient,

Table 16.1   Postures Adopted by Patients to Relieve or Reduce Pain Following Surgery

Operation	Posture Adopted
Thoracotomy	Side flexion to side of incision
	Rotation to side of incision
	Elevation of shoulder and shoulder girdle on opposite side
	Reduction in abduction and elevation of shoulder on side of incision
Midline, vertical abdominal incision	Forward flexion of trunk
	Bilateral hip and knee flexion
Sternotomy	Thoracic flexion
	Protraction of shoulder girdle
High lateral, oblique abdominal incision	Side flexion of trunk to side of incision
Low abdominal incision	Hip and knee flexion
Orthopaedic fixation	Flexion of joints in proximity of incision

although following all surgery there will be a period of bed rest. This may be as short as a few hours or as long as several weeks. In either case, it is important for the physiotherapist to consider lung function as well as comfort, for the longer the period of bed rest, the more important this matter becomes. It is vital to ensure that the position chosen is not detrimental to lung function, e.g. a well-supported high sitting position is ideal for patients who have undergone abdominal surgery. In this position the lungs ventilate well and the action of the diaphragm is not compromised by the abdominal contents as the abdominal muscles are not stretched, but relaxed. This is also important when considering comfort. The knees may or may not be supported by a pillow depending on the patient's individual needs.

In the case of thoracotomy, high-sitting or half-lying may not be very comfortable for a patient due to pressure on the wound posteriorly and the 'dragging' of intercostal drains if they are present. Thus, side-lying or high-side lying (on the opposite side from the incision) might be the position of choice, with support from a pillow for the drains (see Fig. 16.1g).

As well as being comfortable for the patient, this position will facilitate good alveolar ventilation, and the pulmonary ventilation/perfusion ratio will be well-matched in both lungs. The physiotherapist should make sure that the patient is turned far enough onto the side so that there is no restriction to diaphragmatic movement from the abdominal contents. The patient's uppermost leg should be supported on a pillow. In both these positions, the physiotherapist can assist the patient in deep-breathing exercises. Should pain constitute a major problem in achieving good lung expansion, then it may be necessary for the patient to be taught the use of intermittent positive pressure breathing apparatus (e.g. Bird respirator) which will, with a limited amount of effort from the patient, achieve greater expansion.

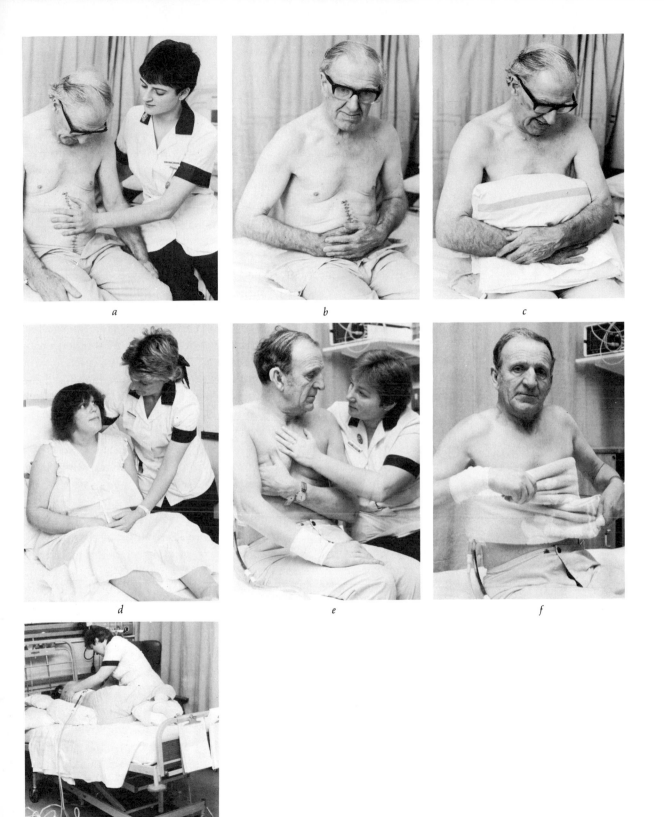

Fig. 16.1a–g Methods of support during coughing.

It is essential for the physiotherapist to teach the patient to cough effectively as this is a very important part of postoperative recovery, and she should make sure that the position chosen in which to do this is the most comfortable one for the patient. It could be half-lying, side-lying, or sitting over the edge of the bed, and this is for the patient to decide, in whichever position he feels balanced and well-supported. Extra support over the wound may be necessary. This can be achieved by the physiotherapist, or by her teaching the patient to place the hands *firmly* over the wound on expiration. If applying the support himself, the patient may choose to use a pillow, towel or 'cough-lock' (see Fig. 16.1*a–f*).

Prolonged immobility, whether as a result of surgery and/or pain, will result in contractures and eventually deformity. This is probably most apparent in cases of orthopaedic surgery, and therefore the physiotherapist encourages movement which can be either active or passive. There are situations where active movement cannot be achieved, or is not permitted, and in these situations, the physiotherapist will passively move the joint/s. For example, in internal fixation of the shaft of femur, active movement is initially discouraged, but if left in extension the knee then becomes fixed and flexion cannot be achieved easily at a later date. Thus a 90/90 regime is used where the leg is passively placed in flexion (90° at the hip and 90° at the knee) over a box, and extended alternately for fixed periods of time. This can only be done if excellent analgesia has been achieved. In some centres a continuous passive movement machine may be used to maintain joint range.

Thus it is important that the physiotherapist, having made sure that the patient is receiving the best possible analgesic regime, begins treatment as soon as possible. There is much that the physiotherapist can do that is vital to the patient's recovery: she has an in-depth knowledge of the musculo-skeletal system and can therefore recognise and correct deformity in the early stages of its development; she plays a vital role in restoring preoperative lung function to the patient by showing him the most effective way to deep-breathe and cough. She also supervises and helps the patient's general mobility, from passive or active exercises while the patient is on bed rest, to the patient's rehabilitation to full mobility.

Medication

In general, whatever the nature of the surgery, i.e. orthopaedic, cardiothoracic or abdominal, the most usual form of pain control employed is drug therapy. It is important, therefore, that the physiotherapist has an understanding of the drugs employed to control postoperative pain, their methods of action, their dosages and routes of administration, as well as any side-effects that may interfere with physiotherapeutic treatment. A great deal of investigation into the use of drugs to control postoperative pain has been made, and it would appear that it is as important to consider the method of administration as the type of drug and its dosage. It is vital that the medical staff look at the relative benefits of a drug and its method of administration in relation to each patient. There really is no room in modern medicine for a generalised regime. In some cases, there is a need for a mixture of drugs and methods of administration to be used. A comprehensive understanding of pain mechanisms when prescribing drugs is naturally important, as some drugs will, of course, be inappropriate (see Chapters 5, 6 and 7). For example, as postoperative pain is acute and intense there is no benefit in prescribing a drug which brings about its greatest relief from pain after a prolonged interval.

The most commonly prescribed drugs in the immediate postoperative period are the opiates, both natural and synthetic. Although these drugs are associated with severe side-effects, if they are prescribed well, and the patient is monitored closely, even the strongest can be used effectively without adverse reactions. It is worth mentioning the side-effects of opiates, because a physiotherapist may be responsible for recognising their existence should they occur, especially if these side-effects interfere with any planned treatment she may wish to give.

Side-effects of opiates

All opiates have side-effects regardless of the method used for administration. These side-effects are dependent upon the degree of agonist/antagonist activity (see Chapter 7, p. 50) each possesses.

All the drugs act on the central nervous system, the effects produced being due to the depression or excitation of the CNS. The effects due to the depression of the CNS are:

1. Respiratory depression due to a decrease in response to elevation of $P\text{co}_2$.
2. Depression of the cough reflex.
3. Decrease in tone and mobility of smooth muscle resulting in constipation.

Those effects due to stimulation of the CNS are:

1. Excitation of the emetic centre in the medulla resulting in nausea and/or vomiting. (The vestibular apparatus may also be disturbed exaggerating the problem of nausea and/or vomiting.)
2. Exaggeration of spinal cord reflexes resulting in convulsions. (This is *very* rare.)

All opiates are narcotic having a 'benumbing' effect resulting in mental tranquillity and euphoria, and thus a degree of tolerance might develop, which, however, does not generally seem to be a problem (Hull and Sibbald, 1981). Some of the side-effects, although unpleasant, are not dangerous to the patient and other drugs may be given prophylactically to negate this effect. However, the problem of respiratory depression is more sinister, and in view of this a tendency has developed for staff to administer the lowest

261

amount of drug available when a range has been prescribed; e.g. if a patient has been prescribed 15–20 mg morphine, 4–6 hourly then the patient will receive 15 mg every 6 h to 'see how it goes' (Cohen, 1980). This is not satisfactory, for in order to 'see how it goes' the patient will have to experience pain to be able to say 'it is not going well'.

Methods of opiate administration

Intramuscular

This is the most commonly used method of administering opiates postoperatively. In such cases, a dosage of an opiate is prescribed, e.g. morphine, pethidine, papaveretum to be given at regular intervals if the patient is in pain, via an intramuscular injection. As to whether the patient is actually in pain is left to the discretion of the nursing staff, and unless a patient complains he may well go many hours before receiving any analgesia.

The intermittent intramuscular method of opiate administration is considered to be the 'safest route' due to slow absorption. As a result of slow absorption, pain relief will not be instantaneous and any complications of a respiratory nature will therefore be delayed too.

Intrathecal

Morphine is the drug of choice in this case as it is a natural substance with no neurotoxic preservatives. The drug is injected via a fine gauge needle through the dura into the subdural space, so that it will act directly on the spinal cord. This is suitable for a once-only administration performed after induction of anaesthesia. A cannula is not left *in situ* because the puncture site has to be small thus eliminating the risk of leakage of cerebrospinal fluid.

Generally, good analgesia is achieved, which in some cases is total, lasting up to 24 h, with no need for the further administration of opiates in the postoperative period (Matthews and Abrams, 1980; Gjessing and Tomlin, 1981). Respiratory depression is only very occasionally a problem and it has been demonstrated that this can be reversed using an opiate antagonist, naloxone, without loss of analgesia.

Epidural

With this method damage to the spinal cord is very unlikely, thus a catheter can be left *in situ* to allow for 'topping up' or a continuous infusion. Again, the opiate is acting directly on the spinal cord so effects should be fast-acting. An epidural is usually sited below the level of L2 and thus the level of the spinal cord itself, but in cases of thoracic and upper abdominal surgery this is not satisfactory and the cannula will be sited in the thoracic region depending upon the level of the incision.

In the case of an epidural administration a number of drugs can be used both natural, e.g. morphine, papaveretum, or synthetic, e.g. fentanyl, alfentanyl and there is no conclusive evidence to suggest that any one drug is in all respects better than another as all relieve pain, with deleterious effects occurring only very rarely (Rutter *et al.*, 1981). As the effects are immediate any respiratory complications will be easily observed and can be reversed quickly. The epidural route is very flexible allowing not only intermittent administration but continuous infusion with the supplement of bolus doses if necessary (Bailey and Smith, 1980; Bowen-Wright and Goroszeniuk, 1980).

Intravenous

Administering opiates intravenously is not common practice, except perhaps in the intensive care situation or specialised units which have the facility for both central and peripheral lines and being able to monitor patients very closely. When this method is used a drug is delivered continuously by an electrically operated syringe pump, which usually gives 1–2 ml fluid/h. This method also allows for the administration of bolus doses if necessary.

Absorption is fast and hence analgesia is instant. The analgesia achieved is good and can easily be maintained, but respiratory depression seems to be more of a problem than in the aforementioned methods of administration. Even though tidal volume may increase as a result of a reduction in pain, the respiratory rate can fall dramatically resulting in periods of apnoea (Catling, *et al.*, 1980).

Although this method is not frequently used in the ward, it lends itself to allowing 'patient-control' with its rapid onset of analgesia. There are also electronically controlled devices available which have been specifically designed to allow the patient to manage his pain. One such device is the Cardiff Palliator which injects a solution of analgesic from a digitally controlled syringe pump. The quantity of drug is predetermined by the medical staff, and to lessen the risk of inadvertent operation (and hence overdose), the push-button has to be pressed twice in 1 s, or similarly should sedation occur it will not operate further until a set time has elapsed.

Opiates are obviously very good for maintaining analgesia in the postoperative period. Each method of administration is limiting in some respects, e.g. intrathecal and epidural injections requiring the skills of an experienced anaesthetist to establish. Monitoring of the patient in the ward is time-consuming, and knowledge of the action and side-effects of opiates is an essential part of management of postoperative pain. The intermittent intramuscular injection, however, is most unsatisfactory as the fears of opiate administration, coupled with poor communication with the patient, results in the time to effect satisfactory analgesia being prolonged (Editorial, 1980).

Opiates may well have adverse effects on the respiratory system and depress respiration, but then it is the experience of many physiotherapists that pain is also a severe respiratory depressant.

Oral

In the early stages following surgery this is not considered a satisfactory route for opiate administration, due to the delay in the passage of stomach contents. This delay may be caused by such problems as paralytic ileus, depressed smooth muscle activity and so on. This results in poor absorption of the drugs and thus poor analgesia (Editorial, 1980).

An opiate, buprenorphine, is available which can be taken sublingually and can be used to augment an existing analgesic regime which may not be giving good pain relief (Jørgensen *et al.*, 1985).

After about 48 h postoperatively gut action returns to normal, and as opiates are no longer required, other less potent drugs can be administered either in the tablet form by mouth or in the suppository form per rectum, e.g. oxycodone, codeine, paracetamol and indomethacin.

There are many other ways to use drugs to reduce postoperative pain; some are employed to inhibit nerve conduction. Surgical wounds irrigated with local anaesthetic can withstand very firm pressure without the patient complaining of pain, although an awareness of pressure exists (Goudie and Grant, 1985). Associated with this method is the lack of motor function of muscles around the wound, and in some cases this is not acceptable. This is also true of a local nerve block. In such cases, an anaesthetic agent is introduced by injection around the nerve root innervating the operation site; several nerve roots may be involved which may mean several applications of the anaesthetic.

Analgesia is achieved for several hours and if necessary can be augmented by drugs as appropriate. Although good analgesia is provided, mobility is reduced and pain, which could signal the onset of postoperative complications particularly in limb surgery, will not be apparent to the patient. Hence close observation of the patient for such complications is essential (Edmonds-Seal *et al.*, 1980).

Cryoanalgesia

This is another method of reducing nerve conduction, and involves the 'freezing' of peripheral nerves as near to the nerve root as possible. An instrument known as a *cryoprobe* is applied to the nerve which reduces the temperature of the nerve to $-60°C$. Easy access to the nerves innervating the incision site is necessary, so this procedure is not one that can be performed for all surgery. In cases of thoracotomy, it is particularly appropriate as the intercostal nerves are in close proximity to the incision site. All the intercostal nerves, from the one above the upper limit of the incision to the one below the lower limit of the incision or the chest drain site (whichever is the lower) are 'frozen'. There is a resultant anaesthetic and analgesic effect which is long-lasting (in some cases up to 3 months) and there is no detrimental effect on respiration. In only a few cases is additional analgesia required, and this is minimal and often of a non-narcotic nature (Keenan *et al.*, 1983).

In the author's experience, analgesia is well maintained in the postoperative period following thoracotomy. However, patients who have undergone surgery involving the diaphragm and oesophagus, which generally necessitate a larger thoracoabdominal incision, do not get such good pain relief from the use of the cryoprobe and require larger doses of opiates to effect a pain-free postoperative period. There is also evidence to suggest that after about 3 months chronic wound pain may become quite a severe problem.

Inhalation Therapy

In view of the respiratory problems associated with major surgery (see p. 253–4), patients frequently return to the ward receiving oxygen (2–4 l/min) via a face mask. Nitrous oxide, which is generally used as an anaesthetic, can be used in subanaesthetic doses (2–5 l/min) for its analgesic effect. This can be administered with the oxygen and titrated according to the patient's need, and although the action of nitrous oxide is central in such doses, there is no depressant effect on respiration, or the level of consciousness. Similarly, at such low concentrations, the known hazards of the gas, e.g. depression of white cell count, are not a problem and nitrous oxide can be administered continually for up to 48 h. Instead of continuous administration, nitrous oxide and oxygen can be given intermittently, particularly at times when the patient is expected to experience more discomfort than usual, e.g. during physiotherapy treatment, changing of dressings in the case of burns, removal of mediastinal drains. Thus it can be used in addition to other methods.

It is usual to administer the gases in a 50:50 ratio when they are then known as entonox. This is delivered to the patient from a cylinder via a face mask, the delivery being dependent on a 'demand' valve which requires respiratory effort on the part of the patient to operate. The patient must be fully awake to cooperate and the analgesia produced is short-lived.

It is appropriate to administer entonox to the patient while he is performing physiotherapy breathing exercises, as it should limit the pain on deep inspiration; however, the analgesia produced is not always sufficient because:

1. A very firm 'seal' is required around the mask which the patient may not be able to tolerate long enough to breathe sufficient entonox.
2. The patient may not be awake enough to cooperate fully.
3. Due to weakness or pain, the patient may be unable to make the

inspiratory effort required to operate the demand valve and thus allow gas flow. In such cases, only occasional breaths of gas or even none at all are delivered.

Insufficient delivery of the gas indicates to the patient that this technique is not satisfactory, and this is likely to worry him with a resultant increase in anxiety and muscle spasm and hence more pain.

The use of nitrous oxide is contraindicated in patients with an air-containing closed space, e.g. tension pneumothorax, surgical emphysema, for pressure will build up in the space as the nitrous oxide diffuses into it.

Transcutaneous Electrical Nerve Stimulation (TENS)

The rationale of TENS as a form of afferent stimulation is discussed in Chapter 10. TENS has been shown to be a valuable asset in the treatment of chronic pain and it is becoming more acceptable as a method of producing analgesia in the acute situation.

Following closure of an incision in the operating theatre, sterile electrodes are placed on either side of the wound and are kept in place with the usual strapping. The current is set to a comfortable level, which has been predetermined before the operation, and thus the patient will be familiar with the sensation. If necessary, the current can be altered once the patient is awake. Stimulus frequency and current intensity are critical in activating analgesic mechanisms, but when satisfactorily adjusted, analgesia is produced and can be maintained.

There is no detrimental effect on respiratory function (Tyler *et al.*, 1982). In fact, it has been shown that respiratory function improves following the application of TENS. Forced vital capacity (FVC), forced expiratory volume in 1 s (FEV_1) and peak expiratory flow rate (PEFR) have been shown to improve with a reduction in pain experienced following thoracotomy. After only 15 min TENS application, all three respiratory parameters improved indicating that patients are better able to generate a more effective cough.

Thus TENS can be used in conjunction with postoperative physiotherapy in order to improve lung function and assist in the early mobilisation of the patient (Ho *et al.*, 1987). This method allows for patient involvement in pain control. As the machinery is very simple to operate, all staff, as well as the patient, can be educated in its application and control.

Acupuncture

Acupuncture has been used in the Orient for many centuries, and in recent years it has become acceptable in the West as an alternative for achieving pain relief. Classical oriental acupuncturists claim that good analgesia may be achieved with no damaging respiratory side-effects or sedation. However, when being used postoperatively, it has been shown that acupuncture may take up to 3–4 h to have maximal effect after the end of stimulation (Facco *et al.*, 1981).

In the UK, acupuncture is not a commonly used method of producing effective analgesia postoperatively. The limitations are quite obvious: analgesic effect does not 'peak' for some hours following stimulation, and thus instant pain relief cannot be achieved. At present there are few centres equipped to provide this service, and so as a method of producing analgesia it cannot be considered as a practical option.

The role of acupuncture in pain relief has been discussed in Chapter 9.

It can be seen that there are many methods of achieving postoperative analgesia. There are methods whereby total analgesia may be produced with or without major or minor side-effects; some are rigid in their applications, whereas others allow a greater degree of flexibility in administration. Some methods are under the direct control of the medical staff, e.g. drug prescription and routes of administration, whereas other methods can be controlled by the patient, e.g. TENS.

The physiotherapist may well be involved in administering analgesia, e.g. entonox and TENS, but also plays an important role in monitoring the patient by communicating with him, making sure that he is pain-free postoperatively so that physiotherapy can begin as soon as possible. The physiotherapist can educate the patient to play an active part in the management of his own postoperative pain. The patient can be involved directly by controlling either his own drug infusions or his TENS application. The physiotherapist can actively involve and encourage the patient to monitor his own analgesia and to request analgesia as soon as it is necessary. This is particularly important in the case of the stoic patient who does not complain at the first perception of pain.

REFERENCES

Bailey P.W., Smith B.E. (1980). Continuous epidural infusion of fentanyl for postoperative analgesia. *Anaesthesia*; **35**: 1002–6.

Bowen-Wright R.M., Goroszeniuk T. (1980). Epidural fentanyl for pain of multiple fractures. *Lancet*; **2**: 1033.

Catling J.A., Pinto D.M., Jordan C., Jones J.G. (1980). Respiratory effects of analgesia after cholecystectomy: comparison of continuous and intermittent papaveretum. *Brit. Med. J*; **281**: 478–80.

Cohen F.L. (1980). Post-surgical pain relief: patients' status and nurses' medication choices. *Pain*; **9**: 265–74.

Editorial (1980). Patient-controlled analgesia. *Lancet*; **1**: 289–90.

Edmonds-Seal J., Patterson G.M.C., Loach A.B. (1980). Local nerve blocks for post-operative analgesia. *J. Roy. Soc. Med*; **73**: 111–14.

Facco E., *et al.* (1981). Comparison study between acupuncture and pentazocine analgesic and respiratory post-operative effects. *Amer. J. Chinese Med*; **IX(3)**: 225–35.

Gjessing J., Tomlin P.J. (1981). Postoperative pain control with intrathecal morphine. *Anaesthesia;* **36**: 268–76.

Goudie T.A., Grant I.S. (1985). Subcutaneous morphine infusion for post-operative pain. *Anaesthesia;* **40(3)**: 305.

Ho A., Hui P.W., Cheung J., Cheung C. (1987). Effectiveness of transcutaneous electrical nerve stimulation in relieving pain following thoracotomy. *Physiotherapy;* **73(1)**: 33–5.

Hull C.J., Sibbald A. (1981). Control of postoperative pain by interactive demand analgesia. *Brit. J. Anaesth;* **53**: 385–91.

Jørgensen B.C., Schmidt J.F., Risbo A., Pederson J., Kolby P. (1985). Regular interval preventive pain relief compared with on demand treatment after hysterectomy. *Pain;* **21**: 137–42.

Keenan D.J.M., Cave K., Langdon L., Lea R.E. (1983). Comparative trial of rectal indomethacin and cryoanalgesia for control of early post-thoracotomy pain. *Brit. Med. J;* **287**: 1335–7.

Matthews E.T., Abrams L.D. (1980). Intrathecal morphine in open heart surgery. *Lancet;* **2**: 543.

McQuay H.J., Moore R.A., Lloyd J.W., Bullingham R.E.S., Evans P.J.D. (1982). Some patients don't need analgesics after surgery. *J. Roy. Soc. Med;* **75**: 705–8.

Morgan J., Wells N., Robertson E. (1985). Effects of pre-operative teaching on post-operative pain: a replication and expansion. *J. Nursing Studies;* **22(3)**: 267–80.

Rutter D.V., Skewes D.G., Morgan M. (1981). Extra-dural opioids for post-operative analgesia. *Brit. J. Anaesth;* **53**: 915–20.

Tyler E., Caldwell C., Ghia J.N. (1982). Transcutaneous electrical nerve stimulation an alternative approach to the management of post-operative pain. *Anaesth. Anal;* **61(5)**: 449–55.

Wallace L.M. (1985). Surgical patients' expectations of pain and discomfort: does accuracy of expectations minimise post-surgical pain and distress? *Pain;* **22(4)**: 363–73.

FURTHER READING

Melzack R., Wall P. (1982). *The Challenge of Pain.* Bungay, Suffolk: The Chaucer Press Ltd. (Penguin Education).

Chapter 17

The Management of Cancer Pain in Terminal Care

BETTY O'GORMAN

INTRODUCTION

A dictionary definition of pain is 'a bodily or mental suffering, distress, ache, penalty or punishment, sensation of acute discomfort or emotional suffering or grief'. In caring for the terminally ill patient, it must be remembered that any combination of these factors may be present.

Pain is either acute or chronic, and this chapter is concerned with chronic pain. For example, in a hospice situation, in the year 1984–85 (Report, 1985), out of 805 patients admitted, 69% were complaining of chronic pain (68% male; 70% female). This was not necessarily their only symptom. Chronic pain is unrelenting and distressing for the patient, but it can sometimes be worse for the onlookers, the carers, family and friends; there is so little that they can do to help except be supportive. They feel useless. In these circumstances, where care extends for a family for 24 h, the resulting stress can be devastating. Similarly, the nurse who cares on a continuous 8 h shift can suffer in the same way as the family. The physiotherapist, who comes and goes, is likely to have a measure of relief and in turn can be supportive to the rest of the team.

A patient's attitude to pain is influenced by past memories of how that pain was dealt with, and bad experiences lead to apprehension and anxiety. It has been acknowledged for some time that anxiety and stress lead to an increase in pain felt. The problems caused by pain are the same whether the patient is cared for at home or in hospital.

THE MULTIDISCIPLINARY TEAM

The combined skill of the multidisciplinary team is much needed, with the appropriate disciplines being involved with the patient. In order to employ the correct member of the team in caring for the patient, a careful assessment of the patient must be made by the doctor, nurse and physiotherapist.

Physical pain is normally predominant and can be helped by medication and physiotherapy. Mental, emotional and spiritual factors can be present in varying degrees and will also need to be considered. Mental and emotional pain can be helped by counselling by the social worker or bereavement counsellor and spiritual pain by the appropriate minister's counsel.

CAUSES OF CANCER PAIN (Baines, 1985a)

Bone Pain

This is one of the more common causes of pain in advanced malignant disease. It is often severe and can be difficult to control. Patients' description of their pain is very variable. It may be termed 'a dull ache', 'red-hot' or even 'stabbing', and is frequently exacerbated by movement or by pressure.

It is thought that prostaglandins are liberated by tumour deposits in bone (Editorial, 1976) causing resorption of surrounding bone and sensitisation of nerve endings to painful stimuli. Bony metastases may therefore cause pain when they are relatively small, and as they enlarge they may cause stretching of the well-innervated periosteum, and eventually result in distortion of the bone under stress and pathological fracture.

Liver Pain

The pain is usually described as a constant dull ache in the right upper abdomen exacerbated by leaning forward, but some patients report a sudden stabbing pain over the liver coming in bouts and lasting for a few minutes once or twice a day. Tumours of the bronchus, pancreas, stomach, large bowel and breast are common causes of liver metastases.

Pelvic Pain

Pain, originating in the soft tissues of the pelvis, is usually felt in the rectum, even if this has been previously removed at operation. It is less commonly referred to the low back, hypogastrium, perineum and genitalia. It is often exacerbated by sitting down and sometimes by constipation. It may be described as rectal fullness 'like a tennis ball' or as a severe shooting pain 'like a red hot poker'. The great majority of patients with pelvic pain have primary tumours in the rectum, colon or (if female) in the reproductive tract. Such tumours may remain localised in the pelvis for long periods. In a survey of 40 patients with terminal disease, one-third had experienced pelvic pain for over a year (Baines and Kirkham, 1984).

Chest Pain

Pain from the thoracic viscera and true chest wall pain are both felt in the chest wall, but visceral pain is referred to the area supplied by the upper four thoracic nerve roots. Thus a complaint of pain in the lower chest usually indicates local disease, but upper chest pain may be caused by disease deeper in the chest. In a series of 78 patients with chest pain, it was usually described as 'an ache in the ribs' or a 'tightness'.

Intestinal Colic

This may occur in abdominal or pelvic malignancy where there is complete or partial (subacute) bowel obstruction. The most common primary tumour to cause obstruction is carcinoma of the ovary. Colic is felt centrally in the umbilical or hypogastric regions. The pain usually comes in paroxysms and can sometimes be relieved by local heat or pressure.

Nerve Compression Pain

Pain may be caused by compression or, less commonly, by infiltration of nerve roots, plexuses and peripheral nerves by tumour tissue. Such pain is experienced in the corresponding dermatome, i.e. the area of the body where pain is felt if the nerve is stimulated. Nerve compression pain is often described as 'aching' or 'burning', less often as 'shooting'. The pain is often associated with weakness, sometimes with paraesthesiae and numbness. As both cranial and peripheral nerves can be involved by tumour at any site along their lengths, there is a great variety of pain syndromes. Probably the most important are the painful arm due to metastases in the cervical spine or involvement of the brachial plexus, and the painful leg due to metastases in the lumbosacral spine or pelvis.

Headaches

These are due to raised intracranial pressure.

Non-malignant Causes of Pain

A considerable proportion of cancer patients report pains that are not directly related to the disease process. These may be caused in three ways:

1. *Related to treatment*. A thoracotomy scar may continue to be painful for months or years following surgery. Other surgical procedures also occasionally cause persistent pain. Bladder spasm is sometimes caused by a catheter. Constipation and dyspepsia can be due to medication.
2. *Associated with debilitating disease*. Patients with advanced cancer are often bed- or chair-bound and experience aches and pains as a result of being relatively immobile. Bedsores may develop and constipation be made worse by anorexia and lack of exercise.

3. *Due to other diseases*. Many elderly patients suffer with osteoarthritis, rheumatoid arthritis, haemorrhoids and other painful conditions.

SYMPTOM CONTROL

In order to be able to achieve the best care for the patient the physiotherapist must have an understanding of the appropriate drug regime and the principles of symptom control.

According to Baines (1985b), there are five basic principles of symptom control and these are as follows.

1. Analyse the Cause

An attempt should always be made to establish the cause of each symptom, but this should involve a clinical history and physical examination with the minimum of investigations. The cause should be sought under the following headings:

(a) Anatomy—*Where is the lesion causing this symptom?*
(b) Pathology—*What pathological process is at work?*
(c) Biochemistry—*Is the symptom caused by some biochemical disturbance?*
(d) Psychology—*Could the symptom be aggravated or even caused by some psychological problem?*

2. Modify the Disease Process

Modify the disease process that is causing the pain by radiotherapy, chemotherapy or hormonal manipulation. Palliative radiotherapy has an important part to play in the relief of pain from bone metastases. The relief usually begins within a few days of starting treatment and maximum effect is reached 2–4 weeks after completion.

3. Interrupt the Pain Pathways

Certain cancer pains are localised and are mediated by nerves which can be blocked without causing unacceptable side-effects. The most useful nerve blocks have proved to be the following:

(a) Coeliac plexus block for upper abdominal pain.
(b) Paravertebral block for chest wall pain.
(c) Lumbosacral intrathecal block for perineal pain.
(d) Lumbar sympathetic block for tenesmus.
(e) Brachial plexus nerve block for severe arm and shoulder pain.
(f) Hip block, injecting the nerve to quadratus femoris and the obturator nerve for painful metastases involving the hip joint.

4. Understand the Drugs

This involves an understanding of the site of action of the drugs used. Analgesics can be divided into those with a mainly peripheral action, the non-steroidal anti-inflammatory drugs, and those with a mainly central action, such as paracetamol and the narcotic analgesics. Pain from bony metastases is thought to be caused by the production of prostaglandins which sensitise free nerve endings. The non-steroidal anti-inflammatory drugs inhibit prostaglandin synthesis and their use may avoid the need for morphine, or allow the effective dose to be lower.

Symptom control also involves an understanding of the length of action of the drugs used. For example, oral morphine in solution has a plasma half-life of 2.5 h, so it needs to be given 4-hourly to maintain a constant plasma drug concentration in the therapeutic range. Other analgesics, with differing durations of action, require differing dose intervals. The dose given in every case should be the lowest compatible with pain control. It can be increased every 24 h and more frequently if pain is severe.

An understanding of drug side-effects is also needed so that concurrent laxatives and antiemetics can be given if necessary.

Oral medication is preferable to injection and tolerance is a minor problem which is usually self-limiting after a few weeks. Addiction to drugs does not occur in the cancer patient.

Analgesic drugs

Paracetamol

This is preferable to aspirin for the control of mild pain, unless the specific anti-inflammatory effect of aspirin is required, e.g. in pain from bone metastases. Paracetamol does not cause gastric disturbance, and up to 1 g 4-hourly may be given.

Morphine

If cancer pain is not controlled with non-narcotic and weak narcotic analgesics, and if appropriate adjuvants have already been introduced, a change should be made to a strong narcotic. Morphine remains the most useful strong narcotic. It is well absorbed by mouth, and has a plasma half-life of about 2.5 h. It should be given 4-hourly as this maintains an adequate blood level for analgesia and minimises toxic side-effects. Both morphine sulphate and morphine hydrochloride are widely available and are interchangeable.

Morphine is usually prescribed in chloroform water as this acts as an antimicrobial preservative. A typical prescription might read:
'morphine hydrochloride 20 mg; chloroform water to 10 ml; to take 10 ml 4-hourly'.

273

If pain has just escaped control by paracetamol and codeine/dextropropoxyphene, morphine 10 mg 4-hourly will probably be adequate. The dose can be increased every 24–48 h, or more frequently if pain is severe. Suggested doses are 10, 20, 30, 45 and 60 mg (90, 120 and 150 mg are only rarely needed). If changing from paracetamol alone, a 5 mg dose may suffice. MST-Continus is a controlled release preparation of morphine sulphate which can be given 12-hourly; 10, 30 and 100 mg tablets are available. Patients appreciate the simple twice-daily regime, but titration of dose is less easy. Severe pain is probably better controlled with 4-hourly morphine solution, at least initially.

Diamorphine

Diamorphine remains the drug of choice for injection because of its great solubility. Injections are required if the patient is vomiting, unable to swallow or semicomatose, but very rarely simply to control pain. A battery-operated syringe driver is manufactured by Graseby Medical and gives a continuous subcutaneous infusion. It is a convenient way of giving diamorphine, it can be reloaded every 24 h by the nurse and 4-hourly injections are avoided.

Phenazocine

A small number of patients have persistent nausea with morphine or dislike a liquid preparation. Phenazocine 5 mg is equivalent to morphine 25 mg and it can be given 6–8-hourly.

Dextromoramide

This has a short duration of action, about 2 h, and is sometimes useful to 'boost' analgesics, e.g. before a painful procedure such as wound dressing.

Adjuvant medication

This includes the non-steroidal anti-inflammatory drugs. Tumours in bone (and possibly elsewhere) liberate prostaglandins which sensitise nerve endings to painful stimuli. Anti-inflammatory drugs inhibit prostaglandin synthesis and are therefore effective at the site of the pain, whereas narcotic analgesics act centrally. They are the treatment of choice in bone pain and are occasionally used with benefit in other types of pain. There is no general consensus as to the most effective drug, probably a first-line treatment should be aspirin or a propionic acid derivative such as flurbiprofen or ketoprofen. Indomethacin is equally effective but causes more gastrointestinal side-effects.

Glucocorticosteroids

These are widely used in the control of many types of pain in the cancer patient. The common factor in 'steroid responsive' pain is that it is caused by pressure from tumour plus peritumour inflammatory oedema. Corticosteroids reduce the inflammatory response and thus diminish pain. The following are examples of steroid use:

(a) Headaches due to raised intracranial pressure. Dexamethasone 16 mg/day is given.
(b) Nerve compression pain. Most patients will require narcotic analgesics but adjuvant steroids using dexamethasone 4–6 mg/day may help in intractable pain.
(c) Visceral pain, especially hepatomegaly and pelvic pain.
(d) Lymphoedema, caused by pelvic tumour.
(e) Bone pain. Corticosteroids are less effective than non-steroidal anti-inflammatory drugs but are occasionally of value if the latter are not tolerated or are not giving relief.

In all these situations, there is no guaranteed response and a week's trial of a corticosteroid is recommended. The drug can be discontinued if ineffective or reduced to an acceptable maintenance dose if pain control is achieved.

Muscle relaxants

(a) Diazepam or baclofen are used for muscle spasm secondary to anxiety, bone metastases or in spastic paraplegia.
(b) Smooth muscle relaxants such as hyoscine and the antidiarrhoeal loperamide are used to control intestinal colic in patients with inoperable bowel obstruction. Emepronium is of value in bladder or urethral spasm secondary to tumour, infection or catheter.

Antibiotics

(a) Pleural pain is often caused by secondary infection rather than malignant involvement of the pleura.
(b) Deep infections, especially in the pelvis increase pain as well as causing an offensive discharge. Metronidazole is used, often in combination with a broad spectrum antibiotic.
(c) Superficial infections, such as fungating breast tumours rarely benefit from antibiotics unless there is considerable surrounding cellulitis. Local applications, such as povidone–iodine with liquid paraffin are more effective.

There is much discussion about the use of psychotropic drugs in the management of cancer pain. It is generally recognised, however, that anxiety and depression increase the experience of pain. It is preferable to treat these

275

with non-drug methods: emotional support from staff, diversional therapy, physiotherapy and relaxation. If such methods are inadequate then psychotropic drugs should be prescribed, usually diazepam for anxiety and amitriptyline for depression.

5. Emotional, Social and Spiritual Factors

Symptom control in terminal illness is not just a technique of using drugs correctly. It involves attention to the whole personality of the patient, his hopes, his fears, his family, his philosophy of life. Unless these are taken into account, the likelihood of good symptom control is small.

PHYSICAL MANAGEMENT

It is only because of good pain control that physiotherapy can be practised in terminal care. Primary pain relief is due to medication and not to physiotherapy. Total cooperation between the medical, nursing and physiotherapy staff is needed to achieve this. This cooperation and effort must not be undermined by inefficient physiotherapy that could cause pain. There are no pain barriers to be pushed through in this field.

General Principles of Physiotherapy

In all treatments the following essential guidelines should apply:

1. Commence treatment as soon as possible and on a daily basis.
2. Consider the patient totally.
3. Consider the safety of the patient.
4. Do not make false promises.
5. Take care at all times. Inappropriate, vigorous physiotherapy could cause distress, an increase in pain or even a pathological fracture.
6. Listen to the patient's own observations of his symptoms, they could indicate a pathological fracture or an incipient paraplegia as pain-relieving drugs may mask a new pain.
7. Do not make a patient's deterioration obvious to them by their physiotherapy. Do not take the patient off treatment while they are aware. Scale the treatment down to their capabilities.
8. Be prepared to counsel the patient.
9. Consider the relatives, involve them in the patient's treatment and goals and share their achievements.

Rehabilitation programmes cannot be set, but treatment must be given on a day to day basis.

Physiotherapeutic Measures to Alleviate Pain

Exercise

Preventive treatment

Regular exercise, either active, active-assisted, self-assisted active or passive, is needed to prevent joint and muscle stiffness possibly leading to contractures. All paralysed or partially paralysed limbs must be exercised and instruction given to the patient, nursing staff and relatives on how to perform them. Deformities must be prevented as they lead to unnecessary discomfort and distress making even simple nursing procedures difficult.

Similarly appropriate exercise is needed for any non-malignant condition that the patient has, e.g. osteoarthritic joints or spine, rheumatoid arthritis, neurological conditions—multiple sclerosis or previous polio, amputations, etc. If the patient has sustained a pathological fracture with or without operative repair appropriate exercise will be needed.

Mobilisation of stiff joints

Regular exercises are needed to attempt to mobilise stiff joints. Occasionally, radiant heat pads, ice, or (if there are no metastases present) ultrasound may be used on the affected joint plus appropriate manual therapy techniques, e.g. the gentler 'mobilisation' procedures.

General mobilisation of patient

Many patients lose their ability to be mobile as a result of various factors. Uncontrolled symptoms, pain, loss of appetite, nausea, vomiting, diarrhoea or constipation can all lead to immobility and therefore weakness. The physiotherapist is not necessarily treating the condition from which the patient is suffering, merely the consequence. If the patient is allowed to remain inactive he is quite likely to suffer general aches and pain.

Almost inevitably the patient will have weakened legs and so an active scheme of leg exercises is taught. These are kept simple and the patient is encouraged to repeat them 2–3 times in the day. When the quadriceps will contract against gravity, standing with assistance (if necessary) will be attempted followed by walking. When the patient is mobile, attention can be paid to any other weak areas and they can then be exercised accordingly. Rollator walking frames are particularly useful for the generally weak patient (Fig. 17.1) or those with pathology in the arms, thorax or upper spine as they allow the normal walking pattern to continue without the need to lift a walking frame. Those patients who remain only just mobile need encouragement from a physiotherapist, sometimes a scheme of active leg exercises and possibly assessment for a walking aid.

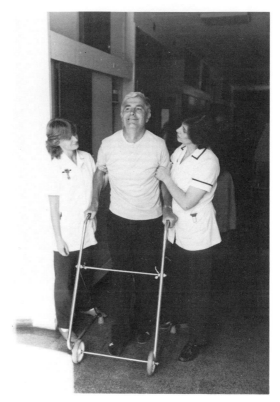

Fig. 17.1   Rollator walking frame.

Positioning

The physiotherapist needs to advise the nursing team on the positioning of patients in bed, reclining armchairs and wheelchairs. The use of small pillows and cushions, often custom-made, are far more effective than large conventional pillows for supporting limbs and head (Fig. 17.2). Bed cradles are necessary to relieve the pressure on the legs and also allow the patient some freedom of movement.

Limbs that are paralysed, grossly oedematous, fractured, affected by osteoarthritis or rheumatoid arthritis, etc. will need maximum support in a good anatomical position. Particular attention needs to be paid to keeping the ankle joint at a right angle and abducting the arm away from the trunk at approximately a 15°–20° angle.

When there are primary or secondary lesions in the spine, collars and/or spinal supports may be needed. The position of the trunk and head in relation to gravity needs to be considered.

In order to minimise the effect of gravity on the body the patient should be inclined back from the vertical (Figs. 17.3 *a* and *b*). By doing this, either in bed or in a reclining armchair or wheelchair, the line of gravity will then pass in front of the head and neck through the thorax. A further advantage to the

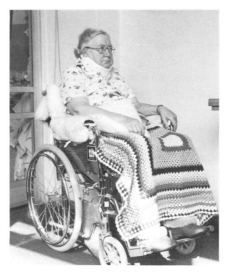

Fig. 17.2 Small, custom-made pillows used to support the patient's arm.

patient of being placed in the semi-reclining position is the relief of pressure of the thorax on the abdomen. This allows the diaphragm to work more efficiently and so aid breathing. This is relevant when the spine is collapsing due to pathological changes.

Special mattresses and cushions such as Spenco, Roho and Ripple, or sheepskin will all aid comfort by minimising pressure on the body and the pain that comes from constant pressure. Radiant heat pads can be used for the relief of breakthrough pain or pain associated with attempting to mobilise.

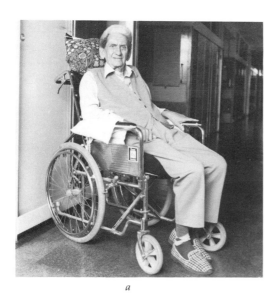
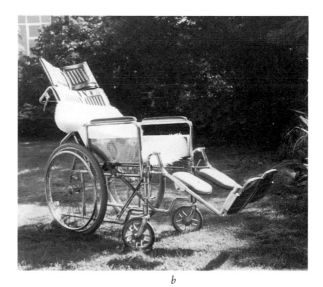

a   *b*

Fig. 17.3a and **b**   The semi-reclining wheelchair.   279

Splints and supports

Lively or rigid splints and lightweight orthoses may be needed, but careful assessment of their value is constantly needed so that the patient is not inconvenienced by them more than can be helped.

A sling, especially a gutter sling (Fig. 17.4), is useful for supporting a fractured or oedematous arm. Soft collars from sheet foam, or lightweight rigid ones sometimes help pain in the cervical region, although positioning plus the use of small neck pillows as mentioned before (p. 278) are often of more help.

Fig. 17.4 A gutter sling, especially useful for supporting a fractured or oedematous arm.

General relaxation

The teaching of general relaxation is particularly valuable in the patient suffering from emotional pain or anxiety. If relaxation is taught in conjunction with a tape recording the patient can practise while alone and, when proficient, use the tape during times of acute anxiety or attacks of pain. Occasionally, several patients will benefit from relaxation therapy in a group.

Positive pressure machines

The Jobst or Flowtron intermittent compression pump (Fig. 17.5) will often aid the reduction of oedema in a lymphoedematous limb. Gentle, active, active-assisted or passive exercises should also be given plus support from small pillows and possibly a gutter sling.

Massage

This can play a small part in helping to reduce oedema in limbs. It can also

Fig. 17.5   The Flowtron intermittent compression pump.

help in the treatment of acute stiff necks and low back pain in conjunction with gentle mobilisation of the affected area. Sometimes massage is used when a patient has local pain but also has the need for a one-to-one contact treatment (see Chapter 13).

Breathing exercises

Pain in the chest is not necessarily relieved by physiotherapy, but discomfort can be helped by the use of breathing exercises, light clapping and shaking or expiration and the teaching of efficient coughing. Similarly, correct positioning and support of the patient in conjunction with teaching local relaxation of the head, neck, shoulder girdle and thorax will all help patients with chest pain and discomfort.

Assessment of Pain Control

It is the physiotherapist who must assess whether a patient is pain-controlled or not. Many patients are judged quite accurately to have no pain at rest. However, on mobilisation this may not be so. It is here that the physiotherapist must use her skills of assessment and report back to the team.

Counselling

It is often during the course of treatment that the patient will seek more knowledge or advice about his condition from the physiotherapist. As part of a team, the physiotherapist must feel able to seek help from whichever discipline is best suited to deal with the patient's needs. Should it be the

281

physiotherapist herself who provides the relevant information, she must ensure that not only does the family and patient receive it, but that the rest of the team know also.

ACKNOWLEDGEMENTS

The author wishes to thank Dr Mary Baines for her help in allowing her work on drug control of common symptoms and cancer pain to be used in this chapter, Mrs Christine Kearney for typing it, Miss Margaret Stewart for her constructive advice, and Mr L. Hodgson for taking the photographs.

REFERENCES

Baines M.J. (1985a). Cancer pain. *Postgrad. Med. J*; 60(710): 852–7.

Baines M.J. (1985b). *Introduction to Symptom Control.* St Christopher's Hospice, Sydenham, London.

Baines M.J., Kirkham S. (1984). Clinical aspects of diseases in which pain predominates—carcinoma. In *Textbook of Pain* (Wall P.D., ed.). London: Churchill Livingstone.

Editorial. (1976). Ostolytic metastases. *Lancet*; **2**: 1063.

Report. (1985). *St Christopher's Hospice Annual Report 1984–1985.* St Christopher's Hospice, Sydenham, London.

Chapter 18

Pain Relief in Obstetrics and Gynaecology

MARGARET POLDEN

INTRODUCTION

Pregnancy and labour are natural physiological events most commonly experienced by normal young women who are fit and healthy. In spite of this, and because of the magnitude of their bodily changes, many women suffer discomfort and pain (sometimes acute) during pregnancy; while the pain of labour is said to range from 10 (mild) to over 60 (intense) on the McGill pain questionnaire (see Chapter 2, p. 14). In the postpartum period, perineal, back, or breast pain can mar the early days of motherhood, while women who have undergone caesarean section have to cope with the pain of major abdominal surgery while they are learning to be mothers. Although the hormones of pregnancy affect the cardiovascular, respiratory, alimentary and renal systems of the body, the major changes likely to involve the obstetric physiotherapist will be those affecting the musculoskeletal system and the genital tract.

ANTENATAL PAIN

As long ago as 1934, relaxation of the symphysis pubis, beginning in the first half of pregnancy and increasing during the last months, was noted (Abramson et al., 1934). This is due to softening of the body's ligaments by the hormones progesterone and relexin, and is not restricted to the pelvic region (Calguneri et al., 1982). The reason for this increased ligamentous elasticity is to allow movement in normally immobile pelvic joints during labour and delivery with consequent increase in the size of the pelvic outlet.

A highly significant increase in joint laxity occurs in women having their second baby compared to those who are pregnant for the first time, although further increase in elasticity does not develop in subsequent pregnancies. These ligamentous changes reach their maximum at 38 weeks and full recovery is only achieved 4–5 months after the birth.

The most dramatic effect of hormonal stimulation during pregnancy is on the size of the uterus, which is normally a small pear-shaped pelvic organ weighing approximately 50–60 g. At term, it will have grown and stretched into a large muscular sac, reaching the xiphisternum at 36 weeks, and weighing about 1000 g. As the uterus grows, it forces the abdominal wall to stretch pulling on its spinal attachments, and eventually the two recti abdominis muscles will separate.

The main pain problems likely to be encountered in the antenatal period and that are responsive to physiotherapy are:

1. Backache.
2. Pubic diastasis.
3. Costal margin pain.
4. Carpal tunnel syndrome.
5. Pain from relaxed stretched uterine ligaments.
6. Pelvic floor discomfort.
7. Cramp.

Backache

Backache is probably the most common 'pain' of pregnancy. Some women experience backache as early as the 1st or 2nd month; the peak of the problem is reached between the 5th and 7th month. In a survey at the London Hospital (Mantle *et al.*, 1977), 48% of women mentioned significant back pain.

Back pain in pregnant women tends to be experienced at a slightly lower level in the spine than that in non-pregnant women (Mantle *et al.*, 1981) the sacroiliac joints being frequently involved. Due to the physiological changes previously mentioned, these joints and their ligaments are more vulnerable to everyday stresses during pregnancy and the puerperium. The lumbosacral junction is another common site for backache in pregnancy. This is probably due to the increase in lumbar lordosis resulting from postural changes as the uterus grows and the abdomen distends. Pressure from the uterus on pain sensitive structures within the pelvis may be an additional cause of this troublesome problem.

Pregnancy back problems can be mild or acute and incapacitating. Age and the number of pregnancies appear to increase the likelihood of backache, and aggravating and relieving factors vary enormously. Unfortunately, many women still struggle unnecessarily through painful months of pregnancy, often with little children, and are frequently told by their doctors and midwives *'your back hurts because you're pregnant—the pain will go when you've had the baby'*! In later years, however, many women receiving physiotherapy for long-standing chronic back pain will say that it began during a pregnancy.

Treatment

Preventive measures

It has been shown that early pregnancy back care advice offered to women reduces the incidence of subsequent backache (Mantle *et al.*, 1981). Most hospitals offer an early 'introductory' evening class as part of their antenatal programme. This is the obvious and logical time for the obstetric physiotherapist to present back care advice, and back pain should be discussed and simple methods of relieving it (if it occurs) can be suggested. Ergonomic advice, adapted to pregnancy, favourable working positions and lifting techniques should be included. A short illustrated leaflet could be valuable as a reminder until the physiotherapist meets the mothers-to-be again during the antenatal course which will begin at about 28–30 weeks into the pregnancy. A telephone number, where the obstetric physiotherapist can be quickly contacted should problems arise, is essential.

Pain-relieving techniques

All women with back problems should be thoroughly assessed. An exact pattern of their problem will emerge from a detailed subjective and objective examination of the lumbo–pelvo–hip complex. Most should receive some relief from the following suggestions for positions and exercises.

1. Pelvic tilting in prone kneeling with careful 'humping and hollowing' (Fig. 18.1).
2. Head rest kneel position with a hollowed back (Fig. 18.2).
3. Sitting astride a chair (Fig. 18.3).
4. Placing a cushion or lumbar roll behind the waist (Fig. 18.4).
5. Back extension in the standing position (Fig. 18.5).
6. Pelvic rotation exercise (Fig. 18.6).
7. Lying on her back, the mother draws her knee up towards the shoulder and the heel towards the opposite groin, this position should be held for a few moments (Fig. 18.7).
8. Lying on the back with one leg hanging over the edge of the bed (Fig. 18.8).
9. Postural correction (Fig. 18.9).

Additional suggestions:

1. A sacroiliac support designed to be used in pregnancy, e.g. 'Fembrace' made by Seton Limited. This comes in small, medium, large and extra large sizes and can be fitted at any stage of pregnancy.
2. Spinal 'mobilisations' directed to the appropriate area can give relief.
3. A longitudinal leg stretching technique has been suggested (see Golightly, 1982).

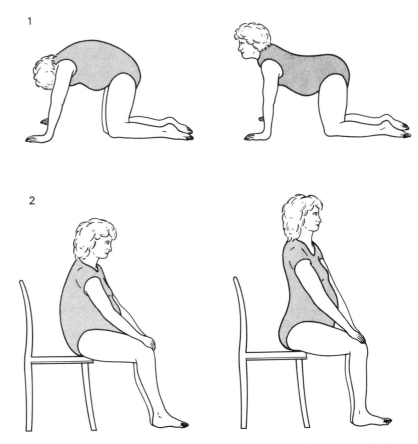

Fig. 18.1 Pelvic tilting in prone kneeling and sitting with careful and controlled 'humping and hollowing'.

Fig. 18.2 Resting in this position can relieve backache.

Fig. 18.3 Sitting astride a chair is less likely to lead to a stiff, aching back.

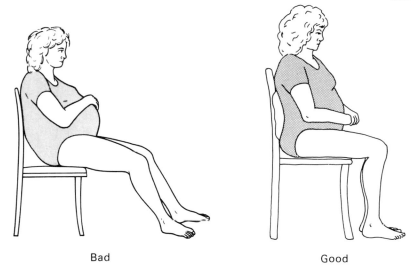

Bad   Good

Fig. 18.4 Using a pillow or lumbar roll to support the back when sitting is more comfortable.

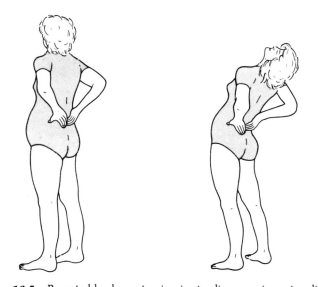

Fig. 18.5 Repeated lumbar extension in standing can give pain relief.

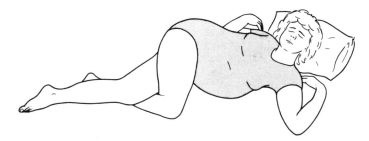

Fig. 18.6 Lying flat, rotate the pelvis away from the pain. Rock gently in this position.

287

Fig. 18.7 Draw the knee up towards the shoulder and the heel towards the opposite groin, then hold the position for a few moments.

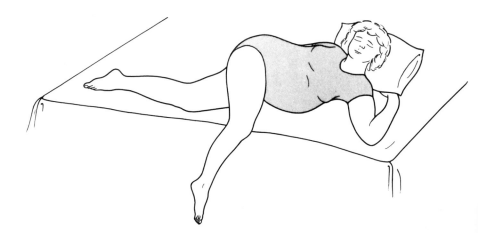

Fig. 18.8 Allow the leg to hang comfortably over the edge of the bed.

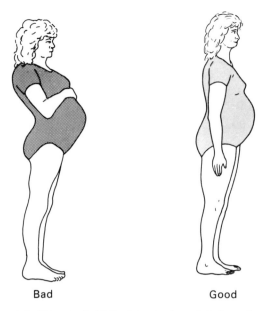

Bad   Good

Fig. 18.9   Use pelvic tilting to hold the fetus in the pelvis for as long as possible and to maintain good posture.

Pubic Diastasis

This distressing condition, separation of the symphysis pubis, can occur as early as 22 weeks gestation and is often associated with sacroiliac discomfort. When severe, and accompanied by pain as it often is, the mother may be unable to walk. The old remedy of binding the hips with a roller towel may be necessary; a firm pantie girdle could also give relief. The use of a walking frame or sticks may be indicated and advice regarding transfers and turning in bed should be given. The mother is advised to keep her knees bent and pressed together when rolling from side to side.

Costal Margin Pain

As the uterus rises in the abdomen, the rib cage 'flares' out sideways, and the circumference of the chest wall may increase by as much as 10–15 cm. It is often associated with pain or 'bruising' along the costal margin.

Side flexion *away* from the pain, with the arm of the affected side raised over the head or stretching with both arms raised above the head and with the hands clasped, may give relief.

Carpal Tunnel Syndrome

As the pregnancy advances, as much as 5.25 l (7 pints) of fluid can be retained in the tissue spaces of the body.

Oedematous compression of the median nerve in the carpal tunnel may give rise to 'pins and needles' in the median nerve distribution of the hand, resulting in numbness and clumsiness in the hands and night pain. Wrist splints preventing palmar flexion, hand exercises in elevation, ice and ultrasound are helpful in reducing these symptoms. Frequently the condition will persist until after delivery and the subsequent diuresis. A similar condition, the so-called T4 syndrome (McGuckin, 1986), may arise from the thoracic spine. Where this is present passive mobilisation techniques directed to the appropriate thoracic level may give great relief.

Pain From Stretched Uterine Ligaments

The woman who is pregnant for the first time is often alarmed by sharp 'shooting pains' or a dull aching low in the abdomen. Reassurance may be all that is needed. An explanation that the pain is caused by the 'guy-ropes' of the uterus softening and stretching or the tissue holding muscles together 'giving' will convince her that she is not in labour and will give her confidence. Warmth (a comfortable bath or a hot water bottle) is useful.

Pelvic Floor Discomfort

At the end of the pregnancy women frequently complain of 'pressure' or a 'dropping out' sensation. Pelvic floor contractions or resting with the hips raised on pillows can be helpful. Adopting the position shown in Fig. 18.2 (p. 286) temporarily takes the weight of the pelvic contents off the pelvic floor and can give relief.

Cramp

Calf cramp frequently disturbs sleep, and it is a common pregnancy 'pain' the exact cause of which is not known (lack of calcium, vitamin D or salt have all been suggested), but it is triggered by stretching in bed with the feet plantar-flexed. Prevention is often possible if the woman remembers to stretch with the feet in dorsiflexion. A spasm may be relieved by active or passive dorsiflexion of the foot and extending the knee. Calf massage immediately will ease the severe bruised feeling which often remains.

LABOUR

Since biblical times it has been recognised that labour is a painful experience for women of all races and cultures, women in primitive societies showing the same pain behaviour as those in the USA and UK (Freedman and Ferguson, 1950).

The pregnant uterus is a hollow muscular bag composed of smooth muscle fibres set in a connective tissue matrix (*myometrium*). The proportion of muscle fibres to connective tissue is greater in the uppermost part (the *fundus*), becoming less in the lower segment, and even less in the *cervix* which is mainly composed of collagen.

During labour the cervix, which is softened and 'ripened' by hormonal action, is gradually drawn up over the fetal head by rhythmical contraction of the myometrium. Most research shows that the pain of the first stage of labour is due to the progressive dilatation of the cervix and the lower uterine segment and may be ischaemic due to strong muscle contraction, and that of the second stage to pressure on pain sensitive structures in the pelvis, stretching of the pelvic outlet, and distension and damage to the soft tissues of the pelvic floor and perineum. In 1981, Melzack *et al.* (Fig. 18.10) showed that labour pain recorded on the McGill pain questionnaire ranged from 2 to 62. It was greater for women having their first babies (primigravidae) than those having second or subsequent babies (multigravidae), labour pain scored higher than pain syndromes such as back, cancer, or phantom limb pain, or post-herpetic neuralgia.

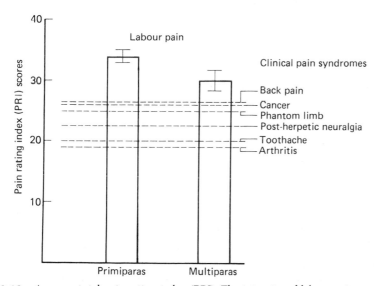

Fig. 18.10   Average total pain rating index (PRI). The intensity of labour pain compared with other clinical pain syndromes (from Melzack *et al.*, 1981, with permission).

In common with other visceral pain, labour pain is referred to the dermatomes supplied by nerve roots which innervate the uterus and cervix: T10–L1 and S2–4. The physiological reactions to labour pain are the same as for other acutely painful conditions, i.e. increased tension of skeletal muscle and an increase in blood pressure, ventilation, cardiac output and oxygen consumption. Preparation for childbirth has always been based on the fact that knowledge will remove fear and instil confidence in the mother, both in her own body and its ability to give birth, and in those caring for her. Many women are apprehensive at the thought of losing control in labour, but at the same time express the hope that they will achieve the birth of their baby 'on their own' without active intervention or analgesia. Melzack *et al.* (1981) showed that primiparae who elected to have prepared childbirth training had significantly lower pain scores than those who did not attend antenatal classes.

The obstetric physiotherapist has much to offer women, both in the relief of their labour pain and the control of their pain behaviour, by teaching techniques that are free of side-effects to mother or baby.

Relaxation

Relaxation was first suggested for use in labour by Minnie Randall (a physiotherapist at St Thomas's Hospital) and Dr Grantley Dick-Read in the 1920s. There are many techniques for achieving relaxation: the *contrast* method (in which the muscles are tensed and then relaxed) and *disassociation* (where one part of the body is relaxed while tightening another). These are two techniques which were frequently taught in antenatal classes together with *imaging* (imagining pleasant and relaxing experiences) and *touch relaxation* (relaxing a part of the body in response to touch). Most obstetric physiotherapists now use the Mitchell method of relaxation for easing tension (Mitchell, 1977). It is suggested that woman greet each uterine contraction by relaxing through it in whatever position they find comfortable. In this way, the natural physiological pain responses will be modified, the mother will feel calmer and more in control of her body, will require less oxygen, and her metabolic rate will be lower thus decreasing the need for glycogen (which is essential for good uterine activity).

Breathing

Unprepared women frequently hyperventilate during uterine contractions and even those who have attended antenatal classes will find it difficult to maintain normal respiration. Hypocapnia (a drop in the carbon dioxide concentration in the blood) could result and can be followed by a period of hypoventilation between contractions as a response to the hypocapnia. This could decrease the Pao_2 in the fetus with consequent distress. Breathing into cupped hands or a paper bag can help to prevent and alleviate the effects of hyperventilation.

The breathing techniques in the psychoprophylactic method of preparation for childbirth (Buxton and Buxton, 1966) actually increase the risk of maternal hyperventilation.

The most calming and a safer way for the mother to breathe during contractions is slowly, easily, and as normally as possible—starting a contraction with a breath out (and relaxing); pausing momentarily between expiration and inspiration, and quietly allowing as much air into her lungs as she needs. Emphasis is always on the outward breath and thus the instruction *'breathe in'* is never given. Concentrating on breathing and relaxation, 'riding the waves' of labour contractions, greeting each pain as a positive experience bringing her closer to her unborn baby, helps the mother cope with the intensity of her experience and gives her a feeling of control and increased confidence.

As labour progresses the contractions will become stronger, more frequent, and will last longer. It is then helpful to allow the breathing to become shallower and slightly faster (but still calm and quiet); air passing in and out through the nose or through relaxed, slightly parted lips. At the end of the first stage of labour the contractions will be very fierce and powerful, and may seem to the mother almost continuous. Occasionally the urge to push is felt before the cervix is fully dilatated and while the baby's head is still high in the pelvis. It is then helpful to use breathing techniques which prevent breath holding and bearing down. Sighing *'hoo hoo hah hah'* breaths or saying *'I won't push'* with expiration can help at this difficult time.

Some women find the second stage of labour painful and others find that the urge to push overwhelming but pain free. Careful preparation antenatally can prevent panic as the pelvic floor stretches around the baby's head. Pushing with the breath held, or while breathing out should both be taught so that the mother can use whichever technique her midwife thinks best at the time.

Massage

When experiencing discomfort or pain, the instinctive response is to 'rub it better'. Labour pain can be relieved by massaging the back or abdomen during contractions. It has been suggested that this stimulates the afferent nerves and gives pain relief by the pain gate control mechanism (see p. 30); massage may also stimulate the production of endorphins.

Back massage

This should be deep, slow and painless (enthusiastic partners can inflict more pain than they relieve if not taught properly during antenatal classes!). Double handed kneading over the sacrum, or deep slow effleurage over the sacral and lumbar regions with the mother sitting astride a chair and leaning forward can successfully increase her pain tolerance level.

Abdominal massage

This is very light, the fingers just brushing the skin over the pain. It can be carried out with one hand stroking from side to side over the pain, or by a double-handed effleurage. It can be done by the woman herself during a contraction in conjunction with relaxation and controlled breathing. Alternatively, it can be performed by her partner or labour companion.

293

Transcutaneous Electrical Nerve Stimulation (TENS)

In common with other acute pain syndromes the pain of childbirth may be relieved by the use of TENS (Bundsen *et al.*, 1981; Bundsen and Erickson, 1982; Bundsen *et al.*, 1982; Harrison *et al.*, 1986). Units for use in labour, most of which are adaptations of existing TENS stimulators, are available from several companies. The Obstetric Pulsar (made by Spembly Medical), has been specially designed to meet the demands of labour and is easily operated by the parturient. It has two channels and both burst and continuous modes. There is a patient control switch so that the stimulation can be changed from the burst, low frequency mode (which is used in-between contractions), to the continuous, high frequency mode (which has an automatic 10% boost in amplitude) for use during uterine contractions.

Electrodes are placed paravertebrally (Fig. 18.11) preferably in early labour, over nerve roots T10–L1 and S2–4 (the innervation of the uterus, cervix, vagina, vulva and perineum). Intense back pain, often a feature of the first stage of labour, is felt in the sacral region; the lower electrodes are actually over the site of pain (Chapter 10, p. 97, Fig. 10.4, 11*a* and *b*). Lower abdominal pain may also be experienced during the first stage of labour. Some women find that abdominal massage used in conjunction with dorsally placed electrodes is sufficient to help them cope with contractions. Robson (1979) found that suprapubic abdominal electrodes in addition to the electrodes on the back were helpful. Brundsen and Erickson (1982) describe a specially made abdominal electrode which gives shallow stimulation and some pain relief. They also mention a theoretical possibility that high intensity stimulation with conventional electrodes over the parturient's lower abdomen could, in unfavourable cases, induce irregularities in fetal heart function, although this did not occur during their trials. Occasionally, TENS causes interference on the cardiotocograph (fetal heart monitor) trace, when a scalp electrode is attached to the baby's head. A filter can eliminate this. This problem does not arise with external monitoring. The major

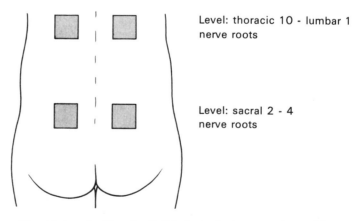

Level: thoracic 10 - lumbar 1
nerve roots

Level: sacral 2 - 4
nerve roots

Fig. 18.11 Positions for TENS electrode placement during labour.

benefit of TENS in labour is that it allows the mother to remain mobile. It has been shown (Medez-Bauer *et al.*, 1976) that the woman who is able to walk, move freely and change her position at will during the first stage of labour has fewer, stronger, more efficient contractions and requires less analgesic medication. Traditional obstetric analgesia (pethidine, entonox or epidural anaesthesia) is invasive, prevents mobility and affects the baby as well as the mother. TENS may not give sufficient relief for those women experiencing high levels of pain, but it is undoubtedly useful in many cases; the relief it gives is said to be equivalent to 100 mg of pethidine (Tawik *et al.*, 1982).

In 1984, Clifford Woolf wrote in *The Textbook of Pain*:

'The ability of a clinician to reduce pain in a patient by exploiting the patient's own in-built neurophysiological control mechanisms must surely rank as one of the great achievements of contemporary medical science'.

The analgesic effect of TENS is said to be based on this premise. Its use in labour is comparatively new and much remains to be learnt. The position of the electrodes, the mode of stimulation, the frequency and wave form are all important factors which could usefully be altered so that the woman in labour receives better analgesia.

POSTNATAL PAIN

In spite of the joy most women feel following the safe delivery of their baby the immediate postnatal period (puerperium) is frequently uncomfortable to say the least! Perineal, back, or breast pain are physical discomforts widely experienced; and fatigue, anxiety and uncertainty about handling and feeding her baby may lower the woman's pain tolerance level. The obstetric physiotherapist, who has hopefully built up a caring relationship with the new mother during antenatal classes, is the ideal person to treat and relieve pain, and to reassure and support the mother as part of the team on the postnatal ward.

Many women refuse to resort to analgesics such as paracetamol or Distalgesic while breast feeding, because of the possibility that small amounts may reach their baby in their milk. Physiotherapy techniques can relieve pain without affecting the baby.

Perineal Pain

Many mothers recall the perineal pain they felt following the pain of their babies as the worst part of their childbirth experience. Episiotomy (the cut in the vaginal and perineal tissue to enlarge the opening as the baby's head is being delivered) can give rise to intense post-partum pain especially when it is complicated by post-forceps bruising and oedema. Haemorrhoids can also be a postnatal problem. Physiotherapy techniques normally used for the treatment of soft tissue injury can often give speedy relief and in this way facilitate the development of a happy mother/baby relationship.

Ice

Ice 'massage', using an ice cube, performed by the woman herself, is often successful in relieving pain. Nerve conduction drops with decreasing temperature and this reduces nociceptive impulses from the damaged area (Lehmann and de Lateur, 1984). A crushed ice 'compress' in a disposable polythene bag warpped in a wet towel, or a sanitary pad dipped into ice cold water applied to the painful area several times a day reduces pain and swelling.

Ultrasound

The traumatic oedema and bruising which often develops after a difficult vaginal delivery can be treated with ultrasound in the same way as other acute soft tissue injuries. It is not essential for the site of the affected area to be sterile as the post-partum lochia (bleeding) makes this impossible to achieve, however cleanliness *is* important. The treatment head is washed before treatment with Hibisol and then wiped with an Alcowipe (or its equivalent). The damaged area is gently swabbed clean and the coupling medium applied. Using a pulsed beam a low intensity (0.5 W/cm^2) is applied for 3–5 min depending on the size of the bruise. If the improvement does not occur the intensity of the ultrasound and the length of treatment time can be increased at the next session.

The analgesia produced by the ultrasound and the removal of the traumatic exudate enables the mother to gently contract and relax the pelvic floor which further improves her condition. Treatment is continued on a daily basis until the woman feels better.

Infrared radiation

Many women find that infrared radiation is both soothing and relaxing when mild heating is applied to their painful perineum. The mother lies on her side, with her knees drawn up, or on her back, legs apart and supported on pillows. If possible, 10–20 min exposure twice a day is adequate. Where there is a shortage of infrared lamps, time, or obstetric physiotherapists, a hand held hairdrier is often successful in relieving the pain and promoting healing.

Infrared is particularly useful where the wound has broken down or is infected and is an inexpensive method of helping a new mother cope with this unaccustomed discomfort.

Pulsed High Frequency Energy (Pulsed Electromagnetic Energy, PEME)

An, as yet, unpublished trial from Bristol Maternity Hospital (see letter in Bewley, 1985), showed that megapulse treatment of the damaged perineum resulted in rapid healing; thrombosed haemorrhoids responding particularly well. Pulse widths of 40–65 µs used in conjunction with low pulse repetition rates were used for 15 min initially. Bruising and oedema resolved and pain was reduced over the 3 day trial period. This form of treatment could beneficially be used for broken down episiotomy wounds.

Exercise

Women are often scared of moving their legs or using their pelvic floor muscles after delivery if they have had an episiotomy or tear which has been stitched. However, actively contracting and relaxing their muscles improves perineal circulation and promotes absorption of exudate thus relieving pain. Four contractions every 15 min is recommended in the beginning. It is advisable to inspect the perineum to check that the mother is able to use her muscles; it has been found that neurapraxia and faecal incontinence can follow a forceps delivery (Snooks *et al.*, 1984). Many women complain of vaginal 'numbness' and 'sluggish muscles' in the immediate post-partum period, and find it difficult to contract the pelvic floor during the first few days following delivery.

Backache

Postnatal back pain is different from that experienced during pregnancy. Most women find that the problems they had in the lumbosacral region vanish (or become less severe) with the birth of their baby. Some, though, who may have been pain-free antenatally will complain of pain in this area postnatally. This can sometimes be caused by their legs being lifted into the lithotomy position one at a time instead of simultaneously for forceps delivery or perineal suturing. The enlargement of the pelvic outlet during labour and delivery may also be a contributory factor. Specific sacroiliac pain can be treated by 'mobilisations', with the mother in prone lying, or some other suitable position. A diffuse low back pain can also be helped by suggesting that the mother lies on her front (a very welcome position after such a long time!) and rhythmically contracts and relaxes her buttocks. Severe discomfort can be helped by supplying a double Tubigrip support (sizes K and L make a good 'roll-on'). Women who have had an epidural anaesthetic often complain of pain around the site where the catheter was inserted. This may be due to the pressure of a small blood clot in the epidural space and can be relieved with a hot pack and support, often with rapid improvement.

A very common cause of back pain in the thoracolumbar region is a poor position adopted when feeding the baby (Fig. 18.12). It is imperative that the back is well supported if the mother sits on her bed or in a chair while she feeds her baby. Probably the worst and most uncomfortable position is the most commonly seen, i.e. sitting on the edge of the bed, legs dangling, body slumped and sagging forward, back rounded! The mother must be shown how to make herself comfortable by placing a pillow in the small of her back, another on her lap to raise the baby and by using a footstool for her feet. This can change an ordeal into a restful pleasure. Elbow circling and arm swinging exercises also give rapid relief, but prevention is as important as cure.

One of the ways in which the obstetric physiotherapist can prevent backache in the months and years following childbirth is by discussing ways in which babycare and household chores can be done without stooping and misusing the back. Particularly, back pain school advice should be taught and reinforced by practice during the daily postnatal exercise class, and suggestions for nappy changing positions which do not strain the back should be shown (Fig. 18.13). Pram and buggy handle height are also important points to consider in the prevention of back pain. It is most important that the woman with unresolving postnatal low back pain is examined and treated by a physiotherapist with the necessary training and expertise.

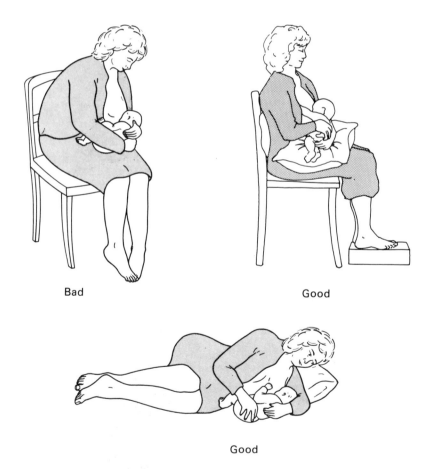

Bad   Good

Good

Fig. 18.12 Feeding positions which can cause backache must be avoided. Unless the mother chooses to feed lying down, the back must be well supported.

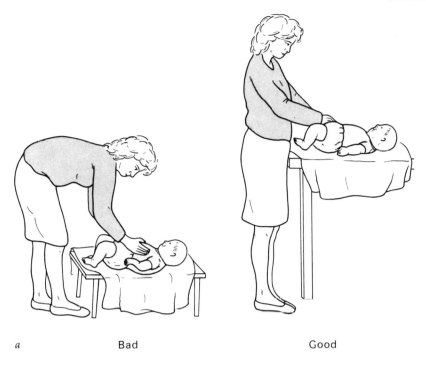

a   Bad   Good

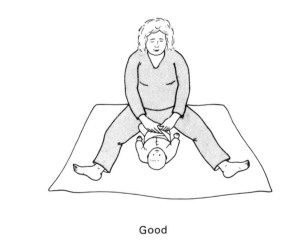

b   Good

Fig. 18.13a and b   Nappies can be changed on the mother's lap, if she is sitting on a low
surface of the correct height, or on the floor with the back straight.

Sore Breasts

Although not strictly the province of the obstetric physiotherapist, suggestions for the relief of pain from hard engorged breasts are often welcome.

Contrast bathing (alternate hot and cold compresses) and gentle elbow circling can alleviate this transitory condition. The experienced obstetric physiotherapist will become knowledgeable about the problems encountered during the early days of breast feeding and may be asked to help treat them. Gentle massage from the periphery of the breast towards the nipple (Heardman, 1954) has been used to relieve engorgement. Ultrasound can be given with good effect if the condition is severe. Interferential therapy is said to be beneficial for mastitis-severe inflammation and possible infection in the breast (Maslem, 1982; Collinson, 1986).

Sore nipples are said to be caused by poor positioning and fixing of the baby on the breast. The obstetric physiotherapist may see this and can correct the way the baby is being held to the breast when in the postnatal ward.

Caesarean Section

During the past 20 years the caesarean section rate in the Western world has increased tremendously, in some centres it is as high as 20%. The woman whose baby is delivered in this way has more than her fair share of discomfort to cope with; she has to learn her new role as a mother while incapacitated by the pain of major abdominal surgery. Apart from the pain of the incision itself, postoperative uterine contractions and abdominal 'wind' are two frequent problems. TENS can play an important role as an analgesic. Electrodes can be placed one above and one below the Pfannenstiel's ('Bikini') incision in common with other postsurgery TENS techniques. However, because of the low position of the incision and the lochia, this may not be comfortable. Alternative sites for the electrodes are above the wound or on the back, over the dermatomes of the site. The Obstetric Pulsar can be used. Burst, low frequency mode should be in operation all the time; with a switch to continuous high frequency when the mother experiences a contraction, a wind spasm or needs to cough or move. It is most important that comprehensive advice is given concerning moving, getting in and out of bed, picking up the baby and feeding positions so that extra pain from carrying out these activities incorrectly is avoided.

Relaxation and breathing techniques as used in labour can be most helpful in the early postcaesarean days. Postoperative wind can give rise to severe pain and can be helped by a deep breathing exercise with the emphasis on expiration together with abdominal muscle contractions. Pelvic tilting in crook lying is also useful. The postoperative complications of wound infection or haematoma can be treated with infrared, ultrasound or PEME.

Fatigue, Anxiety and Tension

Although not strictly speaking 'painful', tiredness and worry are normal postnatal problems. Encouragement to rest and relax while the baby is sleeping are positive suggestions which should be made to new mothers during the daily postnatal exercise class. The 'blues' and depression are both exacerbated by fatigue. It is useful to teach relaxation in positions other than lying (Fig. 18.14) so that the woman can make best use of 'cat naps'. A reminder about slow, calm breathing emphasising expiration with relaxation could prove beneficial.

Fig. 18.14   A very useful position for a quick 'cat nap'.

GYNAECOLOGICAL PAIN

There is usually no role for physiotherapy in the direct treatment of acute gynaecological pain. However, there are some conditions of gynaecological origin which produce chronic pain and physiotherapeutic techniques may be requested for these. Gynaecological pain is referred to a ventral lower abdominal zone or to a dorsal upper sacrogluteal zone, or to both sites simultaneously (Fig. 18.15).

Gynaecological Backache

It has been estimated that one-third of the women on general practitioners' lists who are over the age of 35 will, when questioned specifically, admit to suffering from backache; in only 10% of these will it be directly attributable to a gynaecological cause (Chamberlain and Dewhurst, 1984).

   If the backache can be reproduced when the doctor performs a bimanual (vaginal and abdominal) examination of the adnexa, uterus and cervix, it is almost certainly of gynaecological origin. Lumbar and lumbosacral back pain are generally caused by orthopaedic problems (Renaer, 1984).

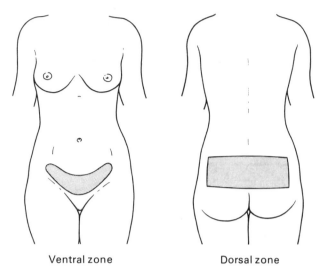

Ventral zone   Dorsal zone

Fig. 18.15   Usual localisation of chronic pain of gynaecological origin (adapted from Renaer, 1981).

Gynaecological causes of backache
(See also Chamberlain and Dewhurst, 1984.)

1. Dysmenorrhoea.
2. Malposition of the uterus.
3. Pelvic infection.
4. Endometriosis and ovarian blood cysts.
5. Pelvic masses.
6. Pregnancy and its after-effects.

These conditions, and others, can also give rise to chronic lower abdominal pain. Physiotherapy will usually only be requested for the after-effects of acute pelvic infection (pelvic inflammatory disease), when pain will most probably be due to adhesions preventing the normal mobility of the pelvic viscera, and dysmenorrhoea. The pain arising from pregnancy and its aftermath has been dealt with in the previous section.

Pelvic inflammatory disease (PID)

In the acute phase of this illness, antibiotics and, possibly, bed rest will be prescribed. The patient may be left with pelvic adhesions and chronic inflammation of the fallopian tubes (salpingitis or salpingo-oophoritis). The symptoms may include persistent lower abdominal and sacrogluteal pain with premenstrual or menstrual exacerbation, deep dyspareunia (pain on intercourse), heavy periods and menstrual irregularities. Sometimes there is a chronic vaginal discharge.

    Shortwave diathermy (continuous or pulsed) is sometimes requested although there is no documented evidence as to its success. High thermal doses are contraindicated and treatment should be mild or 'athermal' and a cross-fire technique is often used. Increase in pain with a flare-up of symptoms could indicate a too vigorous heat application. If it continues the patient should be referred back to the gynaecologist.

Some women receive pain relief from superficial heat such as a hot pack, a hot water bottle can be used at home.

Dysmenorrhoea

Between 5% and 10% of young women suffer from severe dysmenorrhoea. Although the pathophysiological mechanism is not certain, and many theories have been suggested, poor uterine vascularity is one theory that has been put forward. Gynaecologists may occasionally refer women for pelvic shortwave diathermy in an effort to improve the uterine circulation. Superficial heat application to the back or abdomen (hot packs or a hot water bottle) can also relieve menstrual cramps. TENS is another possible analgesic technique.

Dyspareunia

Pain from an episiotomy scar sometimes occurs during intercourse following childbirth and this can given rise to longstanding problems for the couple. Ultrasound is used by some physiotherapists (Dyson, 1985) to soften the scar and relieve pain. The experienced obstetric physiotherapist can also, beneficially, use the treatment time to enable the patient to voice her anxieties about her sexual relationship and can frequently give helpful practical advice or suggest that she asks her doctor to refer her for psychosexual counselling if this is indicated.

Although the aches and pains of pregnancy labour and the puerperium, and the conditions giving rise to gynaecological pain are normally not life threatening, they can affect the quality of life of thousands of women and should not be ignored. Physiotherapists involved in obstetric and gynaecological care are in a unique position. Their specialised knowledge and access to women during the childbearing years and later enables them to prevent, by education, as well as treat and relieve some of the physical problems experienced by women of every age.

Obstetric physiotherapy was one of the first special interest groups of the Chartered Society of Physiotherapists (CSP). The Obstetric Association of Chartered Physiotherapists was set up in the 1940s. Later, logically, gynaecology was included and the group is now known as the Association of Chartered Physiotherapists in Obstetrics and Gynaecology (ACPOG). Fully qualified members of ACPOG will have completed the postqualification training (now validated by the CSP) which consists of Part I and Part II.

The role of the physiotherapist specialising in obstetrics and gynaecology as part of the team caring for women during the adventure of pregnancy and childbirth and its aftermath, and those experiencing gynaecological life changes consists of much more than the relief of pain. Because many physiotherapists take up this specialty when they have already had their own families, they can bring to their work a depth of knowledge and understanding, sympathy and empathy, which can help patients in a way which pure knowledge and technique cannot. The experienced member of ACPOG may be forced to work part-time because of family commitments but women of all ages can benefit from her training and should be able to have access to her expertise both in hospital and in the community.

REFERENCES

Abramson D., Roberts S.M., Wilson P.D. (1934). Relaxation of the pelvic joints in pregnancy. *Surg. Gynecol. Obstet;* **58**: 595–613.

Bewley E. (1985). Letter: pulsed high frequency energy. *Physiotherapy;* **71(4)**: 191.

Bundsen P., Petersen L.E., Selstam U. (1981). Pain relief in labour by transcutaneous electrical nerve stimulation. A prospective matched study. *Acta Obstet. Gynecol. Scand;* **60**: 459–68.

Bundsen P. Erickson K. (1982). Pain relief in labour by transcutaneous electrical nerve stimulation. Safety aspects. *Acta Obstet. Gynecol. Scand;* **61**: 1–5.

Bundsen P., Erickson K., Petersen L.E., Thiringer K. (1982). Pain relief in labour by transcutaneous electrical nerve stimulation. Testing of a modified stimulation technique and evaluation of the neurological and biochemical condition of the infant. *Acta Obstet. Gynecol. Scand;* **61**: 129–36.

Buxton R.S., Buxton J. (1966). Maternal respiration in labour. Newsletter of Obstetric Association of Chartered Physiotherapists, London.

Calguneri M., Bird H.A., Wright V. (1982). Changes in joint laxity occurring during pregnancy. *Ann. Rheumat. Dis;* **41**: 126–8.

Chamberlain G., Dewhurst J. (1984). *A Practice of Obstetrics and Gynaecology*, p. 176. London: Pitman.

Collinson T. (1986). *Relative Merits of the use of Interferential Therapy and Ultrasound in the Treatment of Mastitis.* Lecture at the Australian Physiotherapy Association Conference.

Dyson M. (1985). Therapeutic applications of ultrasound. In *Clinics in Diagnostic Ultrasound*, Vol 16. (Nyberg W.L., Ziskin M.C., eds). Edinburgh: Churchill Livingstone.

Freedman L.Z., Ferguson V.S. (1950). The question of 'painless childbirth' in primitive cultures. *Amer. J. Orthopsychiatr;* **20**: 363–79.

Golightly R. (1982). Pelvic arthropathy in pregnancy and the puerperium. *Physiotherapy;* **68**: 216–20.

Harrison R., Woods T., Shore M., Matthews A.U. (1986). Pain relief in labour using transcutaneous electrical nerve stimulation (TENS). A TENS/TENS placebo controlled study in two parity groups. *Brit. J. Obstet. Gynaecol;* **93**: 739–46.

Heardman H. (1954). *A Way to Natural Childbirth.* London: Churchill Livingstone.

Lehmann J.F., de Lateur B.J. (1984). Ultrasound, shortwave diathermy, microwave superficial heat and cold in the treatment of pain. In *Textbook of Pain* (Wall P.D., Melzack R., eds) pp. 717–24. Edinburgh: Churchill Livingstone.

Mantle M.J., Greenwood R.M., Currey H.L.F. (1977). Backache in pregnancy. *Rheumatol. Rehabil;* **16**: 95–101.

Mantle M.J., Holmes J., Currey H.L.F. (1981). Backache in pregnancy II: prophylactic influence of back care classes. *Rheumatol. Rehabil;* **20**: 227–32.

Maslem J. (1982). Interferential therapy in the treatment of a blocked duct in a lactating breast. *Nat. Obstet. Gynaecol. J. Aust. Physio. Assoc;* **April**.

McGuckin N. (1986). The T4 syndrome. In *Modern Manual Therapy of the Vertebral Column.* (Grieve G., ed.) p. 370. Edinburgh: Churchill Livingstone.

Melzack R., Taenzer P., Feldman P., Kinch R.A. (1981). Labour is still painful after prepared childbirth training. *Can. Med. Assoc. J;* **125**: 357–63.

Mendez-Bauer C., *et al.* (1976). Effects of different maternal positions during labour. In *5th European Congress of Perinatal Medicine, Uppsala, Sweden:* 9–12: 233–37. Stockholm: Almqvist and Wiksell.

Mitchell L. (1977). *Simple Relaxation.* London: John Murray.

Renaer M. (1984). Gynaecological pain. In *Textbook of Pain* (Wall P.D., Melzack R., eds) pp. 359–76. Edinburgh: Churchill Livingstone.

Robson J.E. (1979). Transcutaneous nerve stimulation for relief of pain in labour. *Anaesthesia;* **34**: 357–61.

Snooks S.J., Setchell M., Swash M., Henry M.M. (1984). Injury to innervation of pelvic floor sphincter musculature in childbirth. *Lancet;* **Sept. 8**: 546–50.

Tawfik O., Badraqui M.H.H., El-Ridi F.S. (1982). The value of transcutaneous nerve stimulation (TNS) during labour in Egyptian mothers. *Schmerz;* **2**: 98–105.

Woolf C.J. (1984). Transcutaneous and implanted nerve stimulation. In *Textbook of Pain.* (Wall P.D., Melzack R., eds) p. 679. Edinburgh: Churchill Livingstone.

FURTHER READING

Mitchell L. (1977). *Simple Relaxation.* London: John Murray.

Polden M., Whiteford B. (1984). *Postnatal Exercises: A Sixth Month Fitness Programme for Mother and Baby.* London: Century Publishing.

Semmler D.M. (1982). The use of ultrasound therapy in the treatment of breast engorgement. *Nat. Obstet. Gynaecol. J. Aust. Physio. Assoc;* **July**.

Index